First World War
and Army of Occupation
War Diary
France, Belgium and Germany

16 DIVISION
Divisional Troops
155 Field Company Royal Engineers
4 August 1915 - 31 May 1919

WO95/1965/1

The Naval & Military Press Ltd
www.nmarchive.com
Published in association with The National Archives

Published by

The Naval & Military Press Ltd

Unit 10 Ridgewood Industrial Park,

Uckfield, East Sussex,

TN22 5QE England

Tel: +44 (0) 1825 749494

www.naval-military-press.com

www.nmarchive.com

This diary has been reprinted in facsimile from the original. Any imperfections are inevitably reproduced and the quality may fall short of modern type and cartographic standards.

Contents

Document type	Place/Title	Date From	Date To
Heading	WO95/1965 16 Division Headquarters Branches & Services Dec 1915-May 1919 155 Field Company Royal Engineers		
Heading	16th Division 155th Field Coy R.E. Dec 1915-May 1919		
Heading	16th Div B.E.F. 19.12.15 155th F.C.R.E. Vol I		
War Diary		04/08/1915	18/12/1915
War Diary	Le Havre	19/12/1915	31/12/1915
Heading	Attached Dismounted Division 155 Field Coy Res 1916 Jan-1916 Feb		
Heading	155th F.C.R.E. Vol. 2 Jan		
War Diary		01/01/1916	31/01/1916
War Diary	Philosophe	01/02/1916	10/02/1916
War Diary	Houchin	11/02/1916	11/02/1916
War Diary	Nedon	12/02/1916	12/02/1916
War Diary	Ranneville	13/02/1916	28/02/1916
War Diary	Bourecq	29/02/1916	29/02/1916
Heading	Cover for Documents. Nature of Enclosures. War Diaries of 155th Field Coy R.E. Period. Jan. of Feb. 1916		
War Diary		01/01/1916	31/01/1916
War Diary	Philosophe	01/02/1916	10/02/1916
War Diary	Houchin	11/02/1916	11/02/1916
War Diary	Nedon	12/02/1916	12/02/1916
War Diary	Ranneville	13/02/1916	28/02/1916
War Diary	Bourecq	29/02/1916	29/02/1916
Heading	155 F C R E Vol 4		
War Diary	Bourecq	01/03/1916	07/03/1916
War Diary	Le Reveillon	08/03/1916	24/03/1916
War Diary	Mazingarbe	25/03/1916	30/06/1916
Miscellaneous	47th Infantry Brigade Raid Scheme. Appendix A	26/06/1916	26/06/1916
Miscellaneous	Consolidating Of New Craters. App I		
Map			
Miscellaneous	Report of Occurrences on Night of 26/27 June 1916 Appendix B	28/06/1916	28/06/1916
Heading	War Diary 155th Field Coy Royal Engineers 1st July To 31st July 1916 Volume No. 8		
War Diary	Mazingarbe	01/07/1916	31/07/1916
Miscellaneous	Appendix F Report on Consolidation of live new craters at old Seaforth crater carried out at the same time as 49th Infantry Bde Scheme at 11 pm on 15th July 1916.	16/07/1916	16/07/1916
Diagram etc			
Heading	War Diary 155th Field Co RE Month Of August, 1916 Volume 9		
War Diary	Mazingarbe	01/08/1916	23/08/1916
War Diary	Verquin	24/08/1916	24/08/1916
War Diary	Cauchy-A-La-Tour	25/08/1916	29/08/1916
War Diary	Corbie	30/08/1916	30/08/1916
War Diary	Sandpit Camp E.24.b.1.1	31/08/1916	31/08/1916
Miscellaneous	16th Divn No. 7371 Appendix K	25/08/1916	25/08/1916

Miscellaneous	Programme Of Move Of 16th Division From First To Fourth Army.	06/08/1916	06/08/1916
Miscellaneous	No. 7371	27/08/1916	27/08/1916
Miscellaneous	16th Divn No. 7371	27/08/1916	27/08/1916
Heading	War Diary 155th Field Company R.E. For Month Of September, 1916 Volume 10		
War Diary	Sandpit Camp E.24.B.1.1.	01/09/1916	02/09/1916
War Diary	Nr Billon Farm	03/09/1916	03/09/1916
War Diary	Minden Post	04/09/1916	05/09/1916
War Diary	Carnoy	06/09/1916	08/09/1916
War Diary	Guillemont	08/09/1916	08/09/1916
War Diary	Bernafay Wood	09/09/1916	09/09/1916
War Diary	Morlancourt	10/09/1916	10/09/1916
War Diary	Corbie	11/09/1916	17/09/1916
War Diary	Limeux	18/09/1916	21/09/1916
War Diary	Kemmel	22/09/1916	30/09/1916
Heading	War Diary Month Of October, 1916 Volume 11 155th Field Co. R.E.		
War Diary	Kemmel	01/10/1916	31/10/1916
Heading	War Diary For Month Of November, 1916 Volume 12 155th Field Coy. R.E.		
War Diary	Kemmel	01/11/1916	30/11/1916
Heading	War Diary For Month Of December, 1916 Volume 13 155th Field Coy. R.E.		
War Diary	Near Kemmel	01/12/1916	31/12/1916
Heading	War Diary For Month Of January, 1917 Volume 14 Royal Engineers 155th Field Compy.		
War Diary	Nr Kemmel	01/01/1917	06/01/1917
War Diary	Kemmel	06/01/1917	31/01/1917
Heading	War Diary For Month Of February, 1917 Volume 15 Unit 155th Field Coy R.E.		
War Diary	Kemmel	01/02/1917	28/02/1917
Heading	War Diary For Month Of March. 1917 Volume 16 Unit 155th Field Company R.E.		
War Diary	Kemmel	01/03/1917	30/03/1917
War Diary	Fletre	31/03/1917	31/03/1917
Heading	War Diary For Month Of April, 1917 Volume 17 Unit 155th Field Coy R.E.		
War Diary	Fletre	01/04/1917	06/04/1917
War Diary	Mont Rouge	07/04/1917	20/04/1917
War Diary	Kemmel	21/04/1917	30/04/1917
Heading	War Diary Volume 18 For Month Of May, 1917 Unit 155th Fd Coy Royal Engineers		
War Diary	Kemmel	01/05/1917	02/05/1917
War Diary	La Clytte	03/05/1917	10/05/1917
War Diary	Locre	11/05/1917	31/05/1917
Heading	War Diary For Month Of June, 1917 Volume 19 Unit 155 Field Company R.E.		
War Diary	Locre	01/06/1917	06/06/1917
War Diary	Kemmel	07/06/1917	07/06/1917
War Diary	Near Kemmel In Action	07/06/1917	07/06/1917
War Diary	In Action	07/06/1917	08/06/1917
War Diary	In The Field	08/06/1917	09/06/1917
War Diary	Mont Rouge	10/06/1917	13/06/1917
War Diary	Kemmel	14/06/1917	17/06/1917
War Diary	Strazeele	18/06/1917	19/06/1917

War Diary	Steenvoorde	20/06/1917	20/06/1917
War Diary	Arneke	21/06/1917	21/06/1917
War Diary	Merckeghem	22/06/1917	30/06/1917
Heading	War Diary For Month Of July, 1917 Volume 20 Unit 155th Field Coy RE		
War Diary	Merckeghem	01/07/1917	27/07/1917
War Diary	Poperinghe	28/07/1917	30/07/1917
Heading	War Diary For Month Of August, 1917 Volume 21 Unit 155th Field Company R.E.		
War Diary	Brandhoek	31/07/1917	15/08/1917
War Diary	Ypres	16/08/1917	18/08/1917
War Diary	Poperinghe	19/08/1917	20/08/1917
War Diary	Wormhoudt	21/08/1917	21/08/1917
War Diary	Courcelles Le-Comte	22/08/1917	27/08/1917
War Diary	Boiry-Becquerelle	28/08/1917	31/08/1917
Heading	War Diary For Month Of September, 1917 Volume 22 Unit 155th Fa Co RE		
War Diary	Boiry-Becquerelles	01/09/1917	30/09/1917
Heading	War Diary For Month Of October, 1917 Unit 155th Field Coy RE Volume Number 23		
War Diary	Boiry-Becquerelles	01/10/1917	31/10/1917
Heading	War Diary For Month Of November, 1917 Volume 24 Unit 155th Field Coy R.E.		
War Diary	Boiry-Becquerelle	01/11/1917	30/11/1917
Heading	War Diary For Month Of December, 1917 Volume 25 Unit 155th Field Coy R.E.		
War Diary	Boiry-Becquerelle	01/12/1917	03/12/1917
War Diary	Rocquigny	04/12/1917	04/12/1917
War Diary	Courcelles	05/12/1917	05/12/1917
War Diary	Ronssoy	06/12/1917	09/12/1917
War Diary	Villers Faucon	10/12/1917	31/12/1917
Heading	War Diary For Month Of January, 1918 Volume 26 Unit 155th Fld. Coy. R.E.		
War Diary	Villers Faucon	01/01/1918	31/01/1918
Heading	War Diary For Month Of February, 1918 Volume 27 Unit 155th Field Compy R.E.		
War Diary	Villers Faucon	01/02/1918	28/02/1918
Heading	16th Divisional Engineers 155th Field Company R.E. March 1918		
War Diary	Villers Faucon	01/03/1918	21/03/1918
War Diary	Tincourt Green Line	22/03/1918	22/03/1918
War Diary	Tincourt-Bussu Rd	22/03/1918	22/03/1918
War Diary	Courcelles	23/03/1918	23/03/1918
War Diary	Birches	23/03/1918	23/03/1918
War Diary	Herbecourt	23/03/1918	23/03/1918
War Diary	Cappy	24/03/1918	24/03/1918
War Diary	Froissy	25/03/1918	25/03/1918
War Diary	Bray	25/03/1918	25/03/1918
War Diary	Proyart	25/03/1918	26/03/1918
War Diary	Mericourt	26/03/1918	26/03/1918
War Diary	Morcourt	26/03/1918	26/03/1918
War Diary	Morcourt Line	27/03/1918	27/03/1918
War Diary	Lamotte	27/03/1918	27/03/1918
War Diary	Trenches behind Lamotte	27/03/1918	27/03/1918
War Diary	Hamel	28/03/1918	31/03/1918
War Diary	Aubigny	31/03/1918	31/03/1918

Heading	Original War Diary Of 155 Field Coy RE From 1-4-18 To 30-4-18 (Volume XXIX)		
War Diary	Aubigny	01/04/1918	03/04/1918
War Diary	Saleux	03/04/1918	04/04/1918
War Diary	Grebault	05/04/1918	05/04/1918
War Diary	Mesnil	05/04/1918	08/04/1918
War Diary	Dargnies	09/04/1918	10/04/1918
War Diary	Bout De La Ville	11/04/1918	14/04/1918
War Diary	La Roupie	15/04/1918	15/04/1918
War Diary	Thiennes	16/04/1918	20/04/1918
War Diary	Steenbecque	21/04/1918	30/04/1918
Heading	Original War Diary Of 155 Field Com RE From 1-5-18 To 31-5-18 (Volume XXX)		
War Diary	Steenbecque	01/05/1918	15/05/1918
War Diary	Desvres	16/05/1918	31/05/1918
Heading	Original War Diary Of 155 Field Co RE From 1-6-18 To 30-6-18 (Volume XXXI)		
War Diary	Desvres	01/06/1918	30/06/1918
Heading	Original War Diary Of 155th Field Company. R.E. From 1st July. 1918 To 31st July. 1918 (Volume XXXII)		
War Diary	Desvres	01/07/1918	23/07/1918
War Diary	Hardelot	24/07/1918	31/07/1918
Heading	Original War Diary Of 155th Field Company. R.E. From 1-8-18 To 31-8-18 (Volume XXXIII)		
War Diary	Desvres	01/08/1918	22/08/1918
War Diary	Sailly La Bourse	22/08/1918	31/08/1918
Heading	Original War Diary Of 155th Field Company. R.E. From 1-9-18 To 30-9-18 (Volume XXXIV)		
War Diary	Annequin North & Hohenzollern Sector	01/09/1918	17/09/1918
War Diary	Annequin North	18/09/1918	29/09/1918
War Diary	Annequin	29/09/1918	30/09/1918
Heading	Original War Diary Of 155th Field Company. R.E. From 1-10-18 To 31-10-18 (Volume XXXIV)		
War Diary	Annequin	01/10/1918	05/10/1918
War Diary	Auchy	05/10/1918	07/10/1918
War Diary	Annequin	07/10/1918	16/10/1918
War Diary	Auchy	17/10/1918	18/10/1918
War Diary	Berclaw	19/10/1918	19/10/1918
War Diary	Camphin	19/10/1918	20/10/1918
War Diary	Camphin Pont-A-Marcq	21/10/1918	21/10/1918
War Diary	Pont-A-Marcq Florent	22/10/1918	22/10/1918
War Diary	Florent	23/10/1918	31/10/1918
Heading	War Diary Of 155th Field Company. R.E. From 1-11-18 To 30-11-18 (Volume XXXVI)		
War Diary	Taintignies Ferme Florent	01/11/1918	10/11/1918
War Diary	Billets Antoing	10/11/1918	12/11/1918
War Diary	Antoing	13/11/1918	16/11/1918
War Diary	Plage Comte	17/11/1918	17/11/1918
War Diary	Moncheaux	17/11/1918	22/11/1918
War Diary	Moncheaux Billets Huts	23/11/1918	25/11/1918
War Diary	Billets In Factory At X28 B 5-9 Near Fretin 2 Sections Pont-A-Marcq	26/11/1918	30/11/1918
War Diary	Billets In Factory At X 28b 5-9 S Of Fretin 1 Sections At Pont-A-Marcq & Section At Attiches	30/11/1918	30/11/1918

Heading	War Diary Of 155th Field Co RE From 1-12-18 To 31-12-18		
War Diary	Company Headquarters & N Of 2+4 Sections In Factory At X 28b 5-9 No 3 Section Pont-A-Marcq No 1 Section Attiches	01/12/1918	06/12/1918
War Diary	Coy. H.Q. Nos 2-3+4 Sections In Factory At X28b 5-9 No 1 Section Attiches	07/12/1918	23/12/1918
War Diary	Factory X28b 5.9	24/12/1918	27/12/1918
War Diary	Coy. HQ With Nos 1-2 & 3 Sections Factory X28b 5-9 No 4 Section In Billets At Attiches	27/12/1918	31/12/1918
Heading	War Diary Confidential War Diary Of 155th Field Company, R.E. From 1-1-19 To 31-1-19 Volume 1 1919 Vol 38		
War Diary	Coy. HQ. & Nos 1-2 + 3 Sections + Transport In Factory X28.b 5-9 No 4 Section Billets At Attiches	01/01/1919	11/01/1919
War Diary	Coy. HQ & 3-2 + 3 Sects At X28 b 5-9 in Factory No 4 Sect. On Detachment Attiches	12/01/1919	15/01/1919
War Diary	Coy. HQ No 4 Section	16/01/1919	18/01/1919
War Diary	Coy. HQ 1-2-3+4 Sections & Transport In Factory Billets X28b-5-9	19/01/1919	26/01/1919
War Diary	Coy HQ And Transport In Billets At Factory X28b 5-9 Fretin	27/01/1919	31/01/1919
Heading	War Diary Of 155th Field Coy RE From 1-2-19 To 28-2-19 (Volume II)		
War Diary	HQ Sections & Transport In Billets At Factory X28.b. 5-9 Near Pretin	01/02/1919	10/02/1919
War Diary	Factory Near Fretin X.28.b 5.9	11/02/1919	28/02/1919
Heading	War Diary Of 155 Field Co RE From 1-3-19 To 31-3-19 (Volume 3.)		
War Diary	Company In Billets At X 28b 5.9 Factory Nr Fretin	01/03/1919	09/03/1919
War Diary	Company In Billets At Factory X 28b 5.9 Fretin	10/03/1919	23/03/1919
War Diary	H.Q + Coy. In Billets At Factory X 28b 5-9 Fretin Transport Parked At Templeuve	24/03/1919	31/03/1919
Heading	War Diary Of 155 Field Co RE From 1-4-19 To 30-4-19 (Volume 4)		
War Diary	Coy. H.Q. In Billets Factory X28b 5-9 Fretin Transport Parked At Templeuve	01/04/1919	13/04/1919
War Diary	Coy. H.Q. In Billets At Factory X28b 5-9 Fretin Transport Less Animals Parked At Templeuve	14/04/1919	25/04/1919
War Diary	Coy. HQ In Billets At Factory X 28b 5-9 Fretin Transport Parked At Templeuve	26/04/1919	30/04/1919
Heading	War Diary 155th Field Coy. R.E. May. 1919		
War Diary	Fretin Billets In Factory X 28b 5-9 Transport Parked At Templeuve	01/05/1919	13/05/1919
War Diary	Factory Fretin Coy. HQ + Billets Cadre X 28b 5-9 Transport At Templeuve	14/05/1919	26/05/1919
War Diary	Coy. H.Q. In Factory X28b 5-9 Fretin Transport Parked At Templeuve	27/05/1919	31/05/1919

(1) WO95/1965

16 Division

Headquarters Branches &

Services

Dec 1915 - May 1919

155 FIELD COMPANY ROYAL ENGINEERS

16TH DIVISION

155TH FIELD COY R.E.

DEC 1915-MAY 1919

16th Div

155th F.C.R.E.
Vol I

Dec '15
May '19

B.E.F 19.12.15

121
7935.

Instructions regarding War Diaries and Intelligence Summaries are contained in F. S. Regs., Part II. and the Staff Manual respectively. Title Pages will be prepared in manuscript.

WAR DIARY
or
~~INTELLIGENCE SUMMARY~~
(Erase heading not required.)

Army Form C. 2118

155th Fd Coy RE

Place	Date	Hour	Summary of Events and Information	Remarks and references to Appendices
	1915 Aug 4		CAPT A.D. StG BREMNER R.E. arrived at CHATHAM from DOVER to assume command. (authority W.O.L/O.B/154(A.G.7) d/27/7/15.	
	7		First parade of N.C.O.s + men from Billeting Bn R.E. and separated into Coys.	
			2/Lt. J. O'SULLIVAN (T.C.) joined Coy.	
	9		Coy. formed + men interviewed by O.C. Men mostly enlisted since May 11th 1915 + had done drills + a little Military Engineering.	
			Carried on training, drills, etc under Coy. instructor	
			Coy under canvas.	
	17		Advance party left under 2/Lt C.W. GAGE (T.C.)	
	23/24		Coy left CHATHAM + arrived MOORE PARK, KILWORTH with O.C + 2/Lts E. HARPER + J. O'SULLIVAN. Accommodated in huts.	
			Coy divided into Sections + training in trench work commenced.	
			Two cooks sent to DUBLIN for training.	
			Further drafts of Sappers + drivers arrived.	

F.A. Clifford Capt R.E.
for O.C. 155th Fd Coy R.E.

1875 Wt. W593/826 1,000,000 4/15 J.B.C. & A. A.D.S.S./Forms/C. 2118.

Army Form C. 2118

Instructions regarding War Diaries and Intelligence Summaries are contained in F. S. Regs., Part II. and the Staff Manual respectively. Title Pages will be prepared in manuscript.

WAR DIARY
or
~~INTELLIGENCE SUMMARY~~
(Erase heading not required.)

155th Fd Coy R.E.

Place	Date	Hour	Summary of Events and Information	Remarks and references to Appendices
	1915 Sept 2		2/Lt. R.B. JENNINGS (T.C.) joined coy and left with advance party.	
	3		Coy. left KILWORTH + arrived at BLACKDOWN.	
	6/7		Trench-work training continued. Further drafts of sappers and drivers arrived. Horses + mobilisation equipment began to be issued.	
			F. A. Clifford Capt RE for O.C. 155th Fd Coy RE	

1875 Wt. W593/826 1,000,000 4/15 J.B.C. & A. A.D.S.S./Forms/C. 2118.

Instructions regarding War Diaries and Intelligence Summaries are contained in F. S. Regs., Part II. and the Staff Manual respectively. Title Pages will be prepared in manuscript.

WAR DIARY
or
~~INTELLIGENCE SUMMARY~~
(Erase heading not required.)

Army Form C. 2118

155th Fd Coy R.E.

Place	Date	Hour	Summary of Events and Information	Remarks and references to Appendices
	1915 Oct. 5		Coy out for first time on Divisional Route March.	
			2/Lts A. E. HUGHES (T.C.) + J. C. MOAKES (T.C.) joined Coy	
			Mining + Lashed trestle work.	
	31		Coy proceeded to HENLEY-ON-THAMES for pontooning + preliminary musketry.	
			2/Lt. GAGE left behind i/c Details + animals.	
			F. A. Clifford Capt RE for O.C. 155th Fd Coy R.E.	

1875 Wt. W593/826 1,000,000 4/15 J.B.C. & A. A.D.S.S./Forms/C. 2118.

Instructions regarding War Diaries and Intelligence Summaries are contained in F. S. Regs., Part II. and the Staff Manual respectively. Title Pages will be prepared in manuscript.

WAR DIARY

or

~~INTELLIGENCE SUMMARY~~

(Erase heading not required.)

Army Form C. 2118

155th Fd Coy R.E.

Place	Date	Hour	Summary of Events and Information	Remarks and references to Appendices
	1915 Nov 6.		2/Lt E. HARPER promoted to LIEUT.	
	20		Coy returned to BLACKDOWN.	
			2/Lts HUGHES, MOAKES, & GAGE promoted to LIEUT.	
	23.		LIEUT & TEMPY. CAPT. F.A. CLIFFORD (S.R.) joined Coy (Dates of promotion 26.6.14 & 23.9.15)	
	24–27		Musketry.	
	27		Coy, less reserves proceeded on final overseas leave.	
			F.A. Clifford Capt R.E. for O.C. 155th Fd Coy R.E.	

1875 Wt. W593/826 1,000,000 4/15 J.B.C. & A. A.D.S.S./Forms/C. 2118.

Instructions regarding War Diaries and Intelligence Summaries are contained in F. S. Regs., Part II. and the Staff Manual respectively. Title Pages will be prepared in manuscript.

WAR DIARY
or
~~INTELLIGENCE SUMMARY~~

(Erase heading not required.)

Army Form C. 2118

155th Fd Coy RE

Place	Date	Hour	Summary of Events and Information	Remarks and references to Appendices
	1915 Dec. 2		Queen's inspection of Divn. Coy not on parade.	
	6		Packing wagons + getting sections together complete.	
	8		Complete Coy inspected by I.G. R.E.	
	9+10		Filling in trenches + adjusting saddlery. Deficiencies drawn from A.O.D.	
	13		Inspection by Maj-Gen HICKIE new G.O.C 16th Divn during Divl route march.	
	14-17		Fitting clothing, instruction in explosives, bombs + gas helmets.	
	18		Parades 12·30 a.m + 1·30 a.m marching out for overseas via FARNBOROUGH (L+S.W.R) + SOUTHAMPTON DOCKS in two trains. MARCHING OUT STATE CAPT. A.D. StG. BREMNER R.E, LIEUT + TEMPY CAPT. F.A. CLIFFORD. (S.R) LIEUT A.E. HUGHES (T.C.), LIEUT J.C. MOAKES (T.C.), 2/Lt J. O'SULLIVAN (T.C), 2/Lt R.B. JENNINGS (T.C) W.O. Class II 1, Sergts 7, Corpls 8, 2/Cpls 9. L/cpls + Sappers 151, Drivers (including 1 ASC) 49. Total 231 Riding horses 18, L.D. 10, H.D. 2, Pack-horses 4, mules 47, Total 81. 4-wheel vehicles (including 1 supply wagons) 11, 2 wheeled vehicles 9, Bicycles 33. F.A. Clifford Capt RE for O.C 155th Fd Coy RE	

1875 Wt. W593/826 1,000,000 4/15 J.B.C. & A. A.D.S.S./Forms/C. 2118.

Instructions regarding War Diaries and Intelligence Summaries are contained in F. S. Regs., Part II. and the Staff Manual respectively. Title Pages will be prepared in manuscript.

WAR DIARY
or
~~INTELLIGENCE SUMMARY~~
(Erase heading not required.)

Army Form C. 2118

155th Fd Coy RE

Place	Date	Hour	Summary of Events and Information	Remarks and references to Appendices
	Dec 1915.			
LE. HAVRE	19th	7.a.m	Docked. 4 Offrs, HdQrs section, drivers, animals + vehicles on S.S. ARCHIMEDES	
			2. Offrs, Nos, 1, 2, 3. 4 sections (dismounted) on ~~SS~~ P.S. PRINCESS HENRIETTA	
			Disembarked by 1.30 p.m + marched to No 5 Rest Camp.	
	20th		Entrained at GARE DES MARCHANDISES in one train and left at 11.59 a.m	
			Travelled via ROUEN	
	21st		In accordance with orders received at ST. OMER, detrained at FOUQUEREUIL arriving at 8. a. m. Marched via BETHUNE, BEUVRY, and SAILLY-LA-BOURSE to PHILOSOPHE (8 miles), and billetted.	
	22nd		making billets inhabitable with stores from 1/3 LONDON Fd Coy RE.	
			Attached to 47th Divl. Engineers (T) for work + instruction.	
			no 2 section attached to 1/3 Lond Fd Coy	
			No 3 " " " 2/3 " "	
			Nos 1+4 " repairing O.B.1, North + South of HULLUCH ALLEY.	
	23rd		Capt BREMNER, Lts HUGHES + MOAKES with Capt LOVE (2/3 Lond Fd Coy) visited Old British 1st line from 10 a.m to 2 p.m.	
			FAC	

1875 Wt. W593/826 1,000,000 4/15 J.B.C. & A. A.D.S.S./Forms/C. 2118.

Instructions regarding War Diaries and Intelligence Summaries are contained in F. S. Regs., Part II. and the Staff Manual respectively. Title Pages will be prepared in manuscript.

WAR DIARY
or
~~INTELLIGENCE SUMMARY~~
(Erase heading not required.)

Army Form C. 2118

155th Fd Coy RE

Place	Date	Hour	Summary of Events and Information	Remarks and references to Appendices
	Dec 1915 24th		Morning O.C + Section Officers arranging night work with 1/3 Ln + 2/3 Ln RET	
			Evening 500 8th R. MUNSTER FUSILIERS arrived at 6 pm for work on O.B.1. Mix up at O.B.1. Deep mud. Difficulty in extending inexperienced R.E. and Infantry. Very little work done. One officer RMF. wounded in thigh and stomach & taken home with party to VERMELLES ambulance.	
	25th		400 6th CONNAUGHT RANGERS arrived at 6.30 pm.	
			Lt HUGHES with 150 C.R. worked at clearing mud from O.B.1.	
			Capt BREMNER with 125 C.R. blocked by out-going reliefs, changed to GORDON ALLEY by RAILWAY, party lost touch, then got mixed up with in-coming reliefs, reached O.B.4 at 10.15 pm & returned home. No work done.	
			Lt MOAKES wasted 1½ hours clearing garrison out of O.B1, did good work & returned by 12.45 a.m.	
	26th		400 7th LEINSTERS. work as before, arrived 7.pm.	
			Capt BREMNERS party started out at 8 pm, reached O.B1. at 11.pm + worked 1 hour.	
			Lt HUGHES party brought up trench ~~[illegible]~~ boards.	
			F.A.C	

1875 Wt. W593/826 1,000,000 4/15 J.B.C. & A. A.D.S.S./Forms/C. 2118.

Instructions regarding War Diaries and Intelligence Summaries are contained in F. S. Regs., Part II. and the Staff Manual respectively. Title Pages will be prepared in manuscript.

WAR DIARY
or
~~INTELLIGENCE SUMMARY~~
(Erase heading not required.)

155th Fd Coy RE

Army Form C. 2118

Place	Date	Hour	Summary of Events and Information	Remarks and references to Appendices
	Dec 1915 27		No 491 Cpl G.V. Smith 4th Ln Fd Coy arrived for imparting instruction & attached to Coy.	
			6. R. IRISH REGT working party (300 men), working in O.B.1 & laying trench-boards.	
	28		C.R.E. 47th DIVN ordered a new trench in front of VERMELLES round HULLUCH ROAD. Trench laid out during day.	
			Working party 250 men 8th MUNSTERS. 200 laying out new trench, 50 carrying trench-boards to O.B.1	
	29.		~~May~~ Orders received from CRE 47th DIVN that working parties from 47th Bde no longer available & nos 1+4 sections to report for work with 1/3 + 2/3 Ln Fd Coys respectively.	
			Lt. HUGHES at HOGS BACK from 8 p.m, relieved 4. a. m.	
			Lt O'SULLIVAN at St. ELIE ALLEY, revetting.	
	30.		CAPT. BREMNER visited sector D with MAJ. BIRCH (1/3 Ln Fd Coy) + Lt GRIMSLEY 1st Fd Sqn. Witnessed several mines blown up by enemy at HAIRPIN, at 4.15 pm heavy rifle & shell fire followed.	
			F.A.C.	

1875 Wt. W593/826 1,000,000 4/15 J.B.C. & A. A.D.S.S./Forms/C. 2118.

Instructions regarding War Diaries and Intelligence Summaries are contained in F. S. Regs., Part II. and the Staff Manual respectively. Title Pages will be prepared in manuscript.

WAR DIARY

or

~~INTELLIGENCE SUMMARY~~

(Erase heading not required.)

Army Form C. 2118

155th Fd Coy RE

Place	Date	Hour	Summary of Events and Information	Remarks and references to Appendices
	1915 Dec 31		Orders received from C.R.E to take over Section D, & duly took over in morning. ~~Working~~	
			Received orders to report to 140th Inf Bde HQ 4.p.m 1st.	
			Received orders from Lt Col Williams Director of Mines 1st Army to start 4 mines & listening galleries each side of QUARRIES until 173rd Mining Coy takes over in a week. Nos 3 & 4 Sections detailed & withdrawn from 2/3 London Fd Coy.	
			Lt. HUGHES 8.30 p.m for SAP 7.	
			Lt JENNING " " " KINK	
			F. A. Clifford Capt R.E. for O.C. 155th Fd Coy RE	

1875 Wt. W593/826 1,000,000 4/15 J.B.C. & A. A.D.S.S./Forms/C. 2118.

ATTACHED DISMOUNTED DIVISION

155 Field Coy RE's

1916 JAN – 1916 FEB

155th F.C.R.E.
Vol: 2

TAW

16

Instructions regarding War Diaries and Intelligence Summaries are contained in F. S. Regs., Part II. and the Staff Manual respectively. Title Pages will be prepared in manuscript.

(1)

WAR DIARY
or
~~INTELLIGENCE SUMMARY~~
(Erase heading not required.)

Volume II

Army Form C. 2118

155th Fd Coy R.E.

Place	Date	Hour	Summary of Events and Information	Remarks and references to Appendices
	1916 Jan 1		Sites for mines selected 2 opposite QUARRIES at head of CHAPEL ALLEY and GRIMWOOD TRENCH, one in each branch of HAIRPIN.	
			Road-gangs ~~prad~~ paraded at 9. a. m & detailed to work.	
			Work detailed for Permanent Working Parties.	
			1 Troop 1st Fd. Sqn arrived.	
			Received orders transferring 155th Coy to 1st Corps on 4th at 2.p.m. also orders re relief of 47th Divn by Dismounted Divn in Sectors C&D	
	2.		Permanent Working Parties & Road Gangs confused owing to misunderstandings.	
			Maj JOHNSON A/C.R.E. Cav Dismounted Div Engrs visited billets with 3 officers & took over Sector D; arranged that 155th Coy should concentrate on 4 mines at HAIRPIN, ~~and~~ GRIMWOOD ALLEY & CHAPEL ALLEY.	
			Mining actually commenced night of 1st/2nd with preparing timber & entrance to shaft. ZAC	

1875 Wt. W593/826 1,000,000 4/15 J.B.C. & A. A.D.S.S./Forms/C. 2118.

Instructions regarding War Diaries and Intelligence Summaries are contained in F. S. Regs., Part II. and the Staff Manual respectively. Title Pages will be prepared in manuscript.

(2)

WAR DIARY
or
~~INTELLIGENCE SUMMARY~~
(Erase heading not required.)

Volume II
155th Fd Coy RE

Army Form C. 2118

Place	Date	Hour	Summary of Events and Information	Remarks and references to Appendices
	1916 Jan 3		47th Divn relieved by Dismounted Cavalry on 2nd, 3rd + 4th.	
			3 Officers 253rd (Tunnelling) Coy RE visited billets re mining	
			Mines at HAIRPIN, GRIMWOOD + CHAPEL ALLEYS continued, visited by section officers every 12 hours	
			Enemy sent 3 shells at 9 a.m into Bomb Store 200 yds from billets + fired house, exploding all the bombs + ammunition	
			Weather, sunny, clear + fine.	
	4		3 officers 253rd Coy visited mines with Section Officers.	
			Two shells from new German gun hit two houses adjoining billets between noon + 1 pm. No Casualties.	
			One of the houses is the stable for our two mules but they were out at work. Fuse of shell recovered.	
			Line of fire from direction of ~~over~~ VERMELLES.	
			Weather sunny with misty rain in morning, misty + cloudy in afternoon. Fae	

1875 Wt. W593/826 1,000,000 4/15 J.B.C. & A. A.D.S.S./Forms/C. 2118.

Instructions regarding War Diaries and Intelligence Summaries are contained in F. S. Regs., Part II. and the Staff Manual respectively. Title Pages will be prepared in manuscript.

(3)

WAR DIARY
or
~~INTELLIGENCE SUMMARY~~
(Erase heading not required.)

Volume II
155th 7d Coy R.E.

Army Form C. 2118

Place	Date	Hour	Summary of Events and Information	Remarks and references to Appendices
	1916 Jan 5		A/C.R.E. ordered that, after mines had been handed over & dug-outs completed for Mining Coy, 155th Coy is to repair Reserve line (OB5) at head of QUARRY, BARTS & GORDON ALLEYS.	
			Lt. O'SULLIVAN with Lt. CURRIE (253rd Coy) chose at CHAPEL KEEP dug-outs which require repair for Mining Coy.	
	6.		O.C. visited OB5 between GORDON & BARTS ALLEYS, where work is shortly to proceed.	
			Lt. O'SULLIVAN found dug-outs in OB1 for personnel of 253rd Coy and arranged for timber supply & carriers.	
			Handed over both HAIRPIN mines to 253rd Coy; work proceeding on GRIMWOOD and CHAPEL ALLEY mines	
			A/CRE arranged for a working party of 50 Cavalry daily at PHILOSOPHE cross-roads to return by 1.30 p.m.	
			112397 Sapr GRIFFITHS. D. sent to 7d. Amb. for innoculation (tetanus) after being slightly wounded in jaw & leg by live cartridges put in the fire	
			7ae.	

1875 Wt. W593/826 1,000,000 4/15 J.B.C. & A. A.D.S.S./Forms/C. 2118.

Instructions regarding War Diaries and Intelligence Summaries are contained in F. S. Regs., Part II. and the Staff Manual respectively. Title Pages will be prepared in manuscript.

(4)

WAR DIARY
or
~~INTELLIGENCE SUMMARY~~
(Erase heading not required.)

Volume II
155th Fd Coy RE

Army Form C. 2118

Place	Date	Hour	Summary of Events and Information	Remarks and references to Appendices
	1916 Jan 7		O.C. visited QUARRY ALLEY & Reserve line to BARTS ALLEY.	
			O.C. 253rd Coy arranged re dug-outs	
			Work on CHAPEL & GRIMWOOD ALLEY mines proceeding shortage of candles at mines & dug-outs.	
			50 men, Cavalry working party carried timber & sandbags to CHAPEL ALLEY mines	
			Weather drizzly but sunny at times	
	8		O.C visited CHAPEL KEEP dug-outs & CURLY magazines	
			Work on dug-outs ceased through shortage of candles.	
			GRIMWOOD & CHAPEL ALLEY mines handed over to 253rd Coy at midnight 8/9	
			50 men cavalry working party carrying & cleaning CHAPEL ALLEY.	
			Weather, dull, dry, cold-windy.	
			JAC	

1875 Wt. W593/826 1,000,000 4/15 J.B.C. & A. A.D.S.S./Forms/C. 2118.

Instructions regarding War Diaries and Intelligence Summaries are contained in F. S. Regs., Part II. and the Staff Manual respectively. Title Pages will be prepared in manuscript.

(5)

WAR DIARY
or
~~INTELLIGENCE SUMMARY~~
(Erase heading not required.)

Army Form C. 2118

Volume II
155th Fd Coy R E

Place	Date	Hour	Summary of Events and Information	Remarks and references to Appendices
	1916 Jan 9		Nos 2+3 Sections continued work on magazines in CURLY CRESCENT but short of timber & Candles.	
			No 1 section clearing mud out of Reserve line from QUARRY ALLEY Southwards.	
			No 4 section clearing mud out of Reserve line from GORDON ALLEY Northwards, good progress made, work safe by daylight.	
			Weather cold & Sunny.	
	10		see next page	
	11		Nos 1+4 sections, each with working party of 50 Cavalry working on Reserve line. No 1 section cleared 300 yds of bottom of trench, + another 300 yds to do between QUARRY and BARTS ALLEYS.	
			No 4 deepening trench to North of head of GORDON ALLEY.	
			Nos 2+3 sections on dug-outs + magazines for 253rd Coy. Started temporary magazine in O.B.4. Employed working parties of 50 men carrying timber to dug-outs.	
			Weather cold & Sunny.	
			½ No 1 Section wiring Reserve line from QUARRY ALLEY by night	

7ae

1875 Wt. W593/826 1,000,000 4/15 J.B.C. & A. A.D.S.S./Forms/C. 2118.

Instructions regarding War Diaries and Intelligence Summaries are contained in F. S. Regs., Part II. and the Staff Manual respectively. Title Pages will be prepared in manuscript.

(6)

WAR DIARY
or
~~INTELLIGENCE SUMMARY~~
(Erase heading not required.)

Army Form C. 2118

Volume II 155th Fd Coy R.E

Place	Date	Hour	Summary of Events and Information	Remarks and references to Appendices
	1916 Jan 10		No 1 Section between QUARRY & BARTS ALLEYS in Reserve line Nos 2+3 sections sawing timber for 253rd Coy mines & making magazines. No 4 Section between BARTS & GORDON ALLEYS in Reserve line. Nos 1 & 4 each had 50 men working parties. No 1 had in addition 50 men carrying wire. Weather sunny but cold.	
	12		Nos 2+3 sections making 4 dug-outs at CHAPEL KEEP, 2 magazines in CURLY CRESCENT, + 1 temporary magazine in OB4, in reliefs, also carpenters sawing timber VERMELLES CHURCH stores, all for 253rd Coy. No 1 section, QUARRY ALLEY – Reserve line. No 4 Section, GORDON ALLEY – Reserve line, no working party turned up. Warned of Bombardment of HAIRPIN for 1.p.m. Withdrew No 4 Section at 12.30 p.m. & stopped afternoon relief of Nos 2+3 sections till after dark. Weather clear & sunny morning, later dull to fine rain. FAC	

1875 Wt. W593/826 1.000,000 4/15 J.B.C. & A. A.D.S.S./Forms/C. 2118.

Instructions regarding War Diaries and Intelligence Summaries are contained in F. S. Regs., Part II. and the Staff Manual respectively. Title Pages will be prepared in manuscript.

(7)

WAR DIARY

or

~~INTELLIGENCE SUMMARY~~

(Erase heading not required.)

Army Form C. 2118

Volume II
155th Fd Coy RE

Place	Date	Hour	Summary of Events and Information	Remarks and references to Appendices
	1916 Jan 13		Weather cold, sunny, changing to rain, high wind. a/CRE Inism Div ordered 100 yds right & left at head of main alleys on reserve line to be made habitable. O.C 253rd Tunnelling Coy arranged for work to cease on WEST CURLY magazine ~~bu~~ and to be concentrated on EAST CURLY + O.B.4 Magazines, also finish timbering two men's dug-outs in CHAPEL KEEP. & abandon two dug-outs under HULLUCH ROAD. 7 men of No 1 section walking up main road near Railway Crossing, Fosse 3, at noon, off duty going to Estaminet, caught by Enemy shell, burst 15 yds away just off pavé + 30 yds from Railway Crossing. KILLED 97846 Spr HEATON. H. WOUNDED 97810 L/cpl SHORT W. very seriously 98244 Spr HARRIS A } seriously 97841 " WOODS H } 98050 " FEAST C slightly ~~97781~~ 98283 Spr PERRYMAN J.F at duty Pack-horse No R18 destroyed, suffering from kidney disease + paralysis FAC	

1875 Wt. W593/826 1,000,000 4/15 J.B.C. & A. A.D.S.S./Forms/C. 2118.

Instructions regarding War Diaries and Intelligence Summaries are contained in F. S. Regs., Part II. and the Staff Manual respectively. Title Pages will be prepared in manuscript.

(8)

WAR DIARY
or
~~INTELLIGENCE SUMMARY~~
(Erase heading not required.)

Army Form C. 2118

Volume II
155th Fd Coy RE

Place	Date	Hour	Summary of Events and Information	Remarks and references to Appendices
	1916 Jan 14		Weather sunny but cold, light S.W wind.	
			15th Divn relieving 1st Divn, next sector to South.	
			Sections carrying on as before.	
			Nos 1 & 4 sections wiring Reserve line by night.	
	15.		Weather dull	
			Nos 1 & 4 sections on O.B.5, no working party for No 4 section, 100 men for No 1 section.	
			Nos 2 & 3 sections carried on with dug-outs & magazines	
			O.C. 253rd Coy decided that the dug-out in O.B.4 is not suitable for a magazine as it has only 6 feet of cover, decided to finish it off and use for stores only.	
			EAST CURLY CRESCENT magazine to have at least 15 feet of cover.	
			F.a.C.	

Instructions regarding War Diaries and Intelligence Summaries are contained in F. S. Regs., Part II. and the Staff Manual respectively. Title Pages will be prepared in manuscript.

(9)

WAR DIARY
or
~~INTELLIGENCE SUMMARY~~
(Erase heading not required.)

Army Form C. 2118

Volume II
155th Fd Coy RE.

Place	Date	Hour	Summary of Events and Information	Remarks and references to Appendices
	1916 Jan 16		Weather dull. Work as before	
	17		Magazine in OB4 compleeted 5' high, 6' wide, 10' long. Door being fitted. CURLY MAGAZINE 19 frames in shaft. No 1 section 50 men working party. Nos 2 & 3 sections had to carry timber for themselves. No 4 section had no carrying party or working party. Work as before	
	18.		O.C visited Reserve line with a/CRE Dismtd Divn & selected sites for M.G. emplacements. (1) between BARTS & GORDON ALLEYS. (2) Head of GORDON ALLEY at O.B.1. (3) Head of HULLUCH ALLEY, O.B.1 (4) (to be selected later) Head of QUARRY ALLEY Reserve line. Work as before. Weather drizzly. F.A.C	

1875 Wt. W593/826 1,000,000 4/15 J.B.C. & A. A.D.S.S./Forms/C. 2118.

Instructions regarding War Diaries and Intelligence Summaries are contained in F. S. Regs., Part II. and the Staff Manual respectively. Title Pages will be prepared in manuscript.

(10)

WAR DIARY
or
~~INTELLIGENCE SUMMARY~~
(Erase heading not required.)

Volume II
155th Fd Coy RE

Army Form C. 2118

Place	Date	Hour	Summary of Events and Information	Remarks and references to Appendices
	1916 Jan 19		Weather, sunny & cold, Full moon & very clear.	
			No 2 section only on CURLY MAGAZINE in reliefs	
			No 1 section work as before working party 50 men, No 4 sect working party 60 men	
			No 3 section nightwork on OB1 GORDON ALLEY, 30 working party	
			No 4 section nightwork on M.G emplacements & T heads, 30 working party	
	20		Weather sunny, turning to rain	
			No 1 section, 78 working party, clearing both ends of RESERVE LINE between QUARRY and BARTS ALLEYS. Making firesteps, revetting & 1 M.G emplacement. About 250 yds out of 700 yds nearly completed	
			No 2 Section magazine for 253rd Coy (miners) at CURLY CRESCENT. Shaft complete. Chamber about half done, timbered close with 9"x3" + pitprops at 4' intervals. Section in reliefs	
			No 3 section Two M.G emplacements in O.B 1 at HULLUCH + GORDON ALLEYS. Clearing O.B 1 + repairing firestep. 30 working party by day also by night	
			No 4 Section one M.G Emplacement S of BARTS ALLEY, clearing + fire steps between BARTS + GORDON ALLEYS, 30 working party by day also by night	
			Part of Company bathed & changed underclothing at Divnl Div Baths at MINE LA BOURSE	
			FAE	

1875 Wt. W593/826 1,000,000 4/15 J.B.C. & A. A.D.S.S./Forms/C. 2118.

Instructions regarding War Diaries and Intelligence Summaries are contained in F. S. Regs., Part II. and the Staff Manual respectively. Title Pages will be prepared in manuscript.

(11)

WAR DIARY
or
~~INTELLIGENCE SUMMARY~~
(Erase heading not required.)

Volume II
155th Fd Coy R.E.

Army Form C. 2118

Place	Date	Hour	Summary of Events and Information	Remarks and references to Appendices
	1916 Jan 21		Weather dull, strong SW wind	
			Work as before.	
			No 1 section had no working party owing to reliefs.	
			No 4 section had 60 men working party (30 from No 3 section).	
			Fixed up. Coy bath house next to No 1 section Billet	
	22		Weather, fine rain.	
			Work as before.	
			Working parties, No 1 section very late & only half strength	
			No 3 section 30 men day & night.	
			No 4 section 30 men day & night.	
			No 97592 Spr TODD L slightly wounded in back of neck by spent bullet at entrance to GORDON ALLEY.	
			Cpl MAHER & Spr LEE ~~did~~ would not bath & remanded for F.G.C.M	
			Remainder of Company bathed at LABOURSE	
			F.A.C.	

Instructions regarding War Diaries and Intelligence Summaries are contained in F. S. Regs., Part II. and the Staff Manual respectively. Title Pages will be prepared in manuscript.

(12)

WAR DIARY
or
~~INTELLIGENCE~~ SUMMARY
(Erase heading not required.)

Volume II
155th Fd Coy RE

Army Form C. 2118

Place	Date	Hour	Summary of Events and Information	Remarks and references to Appendices
	1916 Jan 23		Weather fine & Sunny	
			No 1 section 70 working party, 50 carriers. 4 RE nightwork.	
			Remaining sections as usual.	
	24		O C met G.O.C Dismtd Divn & a/CRE at 7 a.m. on HULLUCH Road & visited Reserve line, returning at noon. Various details of M.G emplacements, their dug-outs & defence of heads of alleys were settled.	
			No 1 section 50 carriers with trench-boards, 75 making fire steps, 40 cleaning N of QUARRY ALLEY	
			No 2 section – magazine	
			No 3 section Part M.G emplacements & T-heads, part at night working party 24 on T-heads	
			No 4 section on M.G emplacements, 10 carriers with brick-bats	
			F.A.C.	

1875 Wt. W593/826 1,000,000 4/15 J.B.C. & A. A.D.S.S./Forms/C. 2118.

Instructions regarding War Diaries and Intelligence Summaries are contained in F. S. Regs., Part II. and the Staff Manual respectively. Title Pages will be prepared in manuscript.

(13)

WAR DIARY
or
~~INTELLIGENCE SUMMARY~~
(Erase heading not required.)

Volume II
155th Fd Coy RE

Army Form C. 2118

Place	Date	Hour	Summary of Events and Information	Remarks and references to Appendices
	1916 Jan 25		No 1 section M G Emplacements + completing half-finished fire-steps. Working party 10 (+30 called away after one hours work) No 2 section, 3/4 on magazine, 10, 9" frames completed in chamber + centre struts (2 sets) fixed. 1/4 night shift No 3 section, 14 RE, no working party arrived, work held up till timber arrived with 20 carriers, work on M.G Emplacements + marked out "dogs legs" + dug-out for M.G in GORDON ALLEY. 10 RE on night work. No 4 Section 1/2 RE + 1 Off + 20 men working party on M.G. Emplacements + completing fire-steps, cleaning dug-outs. CRE visited section + ordered splinterproof shelters to be provided before dug-outs are begun + approved loophole for M.G. All M.G. Emplacements held up for roof-girders Weather fine + sunny. No 97836 Spr STEEL J. wounded slightly in left arm by shell-burst outside magazine about 3 p m. F.A.C.	

1875 Wt. W593/826 1,000,000 4/15 J.B.C. & A. A.D.S.S./Forms/C. 2118.

Instructions regarding War Diaries and Intelligence Summaries are contained in F. S. Regs., Part II. and the Staff Manual respectively. Title Pages will be prepared in manuscript.

(14)

WAR DIARY
or
~~INTELLIGENCE SUMMARY~~
(Erase heading not required.)

Volume II
155th Fd Coy R.E.

Army Form C. 2118

Place	Date	Hour	Summary of Events and Information	Remarks and references to Appendices
	1916 Jan 26		Weather dull, sunny at times. no 1 Section 20 working party, on 2 M.G Emplacements + Completing half-done fire steps. No 2 Section 14 frames in Magazine Chamber No 3 Section 20 Carriers, 20 working party, on 2 M.G Emplacements dug-outs + fire-steps. No 4 Section 25 Carriers, 20 working party. Carried 16 girders roofed M.G emplacement complete, filled in front with bricks & stayed roof. Fire steps in ~~B~~ BARTS ALLEY and shelters. O.C. sent for ~~by~~ by CRE Decmtd Divn at 7.15 pm to Sqn Mess. Information received ~~that~~ of an attack by enemy ~~on~~ at 6 p m on KINK & KAISERIN TRENCH. (evening ~~of the~~ before KAISER'S birthday). Sections, 1, 3 + 4 sent minimum numbers of RE to finish of 5 M G emplacements + make them occupyable by morning tomorrow 1/2 RE to completely finish emplacements + 1/2 in Reserve. J.A.C.	

1875 Wt. W593/826 1,000,000 4/15 J.B.C. & A. A.D.S.S./Forms/C. 2118.

Instructions regarding War Diaries and Intelligence Summaries are contained in F. S. Regs., Part II. and the Staff Manual respectively. Title Pages will be prepared in manuscript.

(15)

WAR DIARY
or
~~INTELLIGENCE SUMMARY~~

(Erase heading not required.)

Army Form C. 2118

Volume II
155th Fd Coy RE

Place	Date	Hour	Summary of Events and Information	Remarks and references to Appendices
	1916 Jan 27		C.R.E (D Div) visited billets at 7 p.m & further work ordered as situation had quieted down.	
			M.G emplacements in progress to proceed normally with ½ sections	
			½ sections in Reserve. Day work.	
			No 1 STANSFIELD ROAD; No 2 STAFFORD LANE; No 3 HULLUCH ALLEY; No 4 FOSSEWAY } about 6 men each to dig loop-holed (2) traverses just behind short "dogs-leg" cut from RESERVE line. Picketed out "dogs legs". Materials provided for blocking way round traverses	
			½ sections at work. Day work	
			No 1 M G Empl QUARRY ALLEY + 6 Carriers from No 2 Sect	
			No 2 Carrying. Work on Magazine postponed.	
			No 3 2 M.G. Empts GORDON + HULLUCH ALLEYS + 6 carriers from No 2	
			No 4 1 M.G. Empt nearly finished & loop holed (2) traverse at BARTS ALLEY & picketed out "dogs-legs".	
			Remainder of ½ sections in Reserve night-work	
			20 dig dogs legs with 20 Car on long leg & 10 on short leg	
		3 pm	CRE ordered no heavy work on dogs-legs & to confine work to M.G empts & loop-holed traverses. Dogs legs only possible on STAFFORD LANE & HULLUCH ALLEY needs shaving.	
			No 1 section secured 34 girders for M.G. empts.	
			FGC	

1875 Wt. W593/826 1,000,000 4/15 J.B.C. & A. A.D.S.S./Forms/C. 2118.

Instructions regarding War Diaries and Intelligence Summaries are contained in F. S. Regs., Part II. and the Staff Manual respectively. Title Pages will be prepared in manuscript.

(76)

WAR DIARY
or
INTELLIGENCE SUMMARY
(Erase heading not required.)

Volume II
155th Fd Coy R.E

Army Form C. 2118

Place	Date	Hour	Summary of Events and Information	Remarks and references to Appendices
	1916 Jan 28		Weather Foggy morning, then sunny, light SW wind. Had to cease work, ~~temporarily~~ on M.G Empt. N of QUARRY ALLEY owing to shelling. No 1 section ½ RE QUARRY Reserve line, ½ RE STANSFIELD Reserve line 50 carriers brought up 40 I girders Preparing for traverse in STANSFIELD ROAD No 2 section ½ RE Magazine 16 frames in chamber, nearly finished ½ RE STAFFORD LANE, Reserve line, dogs-legs (2) No 3 section RE night work dogs-legging HULLUCH ALLEY 50 Cav carried up 22 I girders No 4 section RE on M.G. empt + BARTS fire steps + Reserve line fire steps. Preparing for traverse in BARTS 25 working-party M.G. Emplacement nearly finished. FAE	

1875 Wt. W593/826 1,000,000 4/15 J.B.C. & A. A.D.S.S./Forms/C. 2118.

Instructions regarding War Diaries and Intelligence Summaries are contained in F. S. Regs., Part II. and the Staff Manual respectively. Title Pages will be prepared in manuscript.

(17)

WAR DIARY
or
~~INTELLIGENCE SUMMARY~~
(Erase heading not required.)

Army Form C. 2118

Volume II
155th Fd Coy R.E.

Place	Date	Hour	Summary of Events and Information	Remarks and references to Appendices
	1916 Jan 29		Weather, foggy to Sunshine. Very mild, no wind. O.C. went round 1st Dismtd Bde M.G. Empts with Bde M.G officer planting guns in the loop-holes. CRE, Dismtd Divn ordered all loop-holes to be cased in timber No 1 Section ½ RE M.G Empts (2), ½ RE loopholed traverse STANSFIELD 25 Carriers carrying timber frames for M.G Empts 25 working party fire-stepping QUARRY ALLEY allday work No 2 Section ⅓ RE finishing magazine, ⅓ RE loopholed traverse STAFFORD LANE, ⅓ RE on dogs legs. No evening working party arrived. No 3 Section 5 RE on M.G Empt, 5 preparing HULLUCH ALLEY for dogs legs, 2 as guides 25 carriers + 20 working party carrying girders. night work 15 RE on M.G Empts (2) + dogs legs. 50 working party carrying bricks for bursters + digging not arrived. No 4 Section ½ RE firestepping BARTS + GORDON ALLEYS + M.G Empts. ½ RE on traverses in BARTS ALLEY + FOSSEWAY. 25 working party on whole all day work No 98299 Spr GRAY A wounded slightly in back of legs by bullet. ZAC	

1875 Wt. W593/826 1,000,000 4/15 J.B.C. & A. A.D.S.S./Forms/C. 2118.

Instructions regarding War Diaries and Intelligence Summaries are contained in F. S. Regs., Part II. and the Staff Manual respectively. Title Pages will be prepared in manuscript.

(18)

WAR DIARY
or
~~INTELLIGENCE SUMMARY~~
(Erase heading not required.)

Army Form C. 2118

Volume II
155th Fd Coy RE

Place	Date	Hour	Summary of Events and Information	Remarks and references to Appendices
	1916 Jan 30.		No 1 section 33 working party + 25 Carriers day + 25 working party night.	
			No 2 Section 33 working party day + 25 working party night	
			No 3 Section 25 working party night	
			No 4 Section 33 working party + 25 carriers day + 25 working party night.	
			all work as on 29th.	
			O.C. attended F.G.C.M on Cpl MAHER + Spr LEE at SAILLY-LA-BOORSE, Capt CLIFFORD Prosecutor.	
			~~The~~ New Coy Recreation room opened today + also used as medical Inspection Room.	
			Weather, dense fog, cold, damp.	
	31.		No 1 Section ½ RE on M.G. Empts. ½ RE on STANSFIELD. 25 working party by day + 25 by night	
			No 2 Section ¼ RE + 25 working party loopholed traverse by day	
			¾ RE + 25 working party, loop holing + wiring by night	
			No 3 section ½ RE + 25 Carriers with girders + frames for GORDON MG Empt + HULLUCH ~~traverse~~ ALLEY traverse by day + night	
			No 4 Section BARTS M.G. Empt + traverse etc. 25 working party day + night 25 Carriers day only	
			Weather, foggy, turning to Sunshine	
			A.D. G. Bremner Capt RE O.C. 155th Fd Coy RE.	

Instructions regarding War Diaries and Intelligence Summaries are contained in F. S. Regs., Part II. and the Staff Manual respectively. Title Pages will be prepared in manuscript.

(1)

WAR DIARY
or
~~INTELLIGENCE SUMMARY~~
(Erase heading not required.)

Volume III
155th Fd Coy RE.

Army Form C. 2118

Place	Date	Hour	Summary of Events and Information	Remarks and references to Appendices
PHILOSOPHE	1916 Feb 1		Fighting strength of Coy 6 Offrs 216 O.R. Weather, foggy, cold, to sunshine. No 3 section 10 RE HULLUCH ALLEY traverse & dogs leg by day. 100 Cav. Carriers with bricks 12 RE on M.G & traverses ~~BARTS ALLEY~~ by day. No 4 sect ½ RE, 25 working party, firesteps, M.G. & traverses BARTS ALLEY by day.	
"	2.		No 1 sect ½ RE by day on M.G's & fire steps of M.G's ½ RE. by night, roofing M.G's. No 2 section ⅓ RE revetting, firesteps, loopholes by day, STAFFORD LANE ⅔ RE wiring & dogs legs by night No 3 section 10 RE dogs leg HULLUCH & firestep O.B.1 by day. No 4 section ½ RE. firesteps & traverses BARTS & FOSSEWAY by day ½ RE M.G trench by night No workers, day or night, or carriers ~~available~~ arrived Weather sunny but cold, slight frost at night. German anti-aircraft shell burst inside roof of Officers' mess, Capt Bremner & Spr Berry hit by pieces but merely bruised & clothes not cut. F.A.C.	
"				

1875 Wt. W593/826 1,000,000 4/15 J.B.C. & A. A.D.S.S./Forms/C. 2118.

Instructions regarding War Diaries and Intelligence Summaries are contained in F. S. Regs., Part II. and the Staff Manual respectively. Title Pages will be prepared in manuscript.

(2)

WAR DIARY
or
~~INTELLIGENCE SUMMARY~~
(Erase heading not required.)

Army Form C. 2118

Volume III
155th Fd Coy R.E

Place	Date	Hour	Summary of Events and Information	Remarks and references to Appendices
PHILOSOPHE	1916 Feb 3		No 1 section ½ RE, 25 working party + 50 carriers, M.G's, firesteps, + carrying stores by day 1 RE + 15 working party M.G's, + remainder RE + 10 working party STANSFIELD by night No 2 section ⅔ RE firesteps by day, no working party or carriers by day ⅓ R.E. Cutting away traverses by night No 3 section ½ R.E + 20 working party, loopeholed traverses, firesteps O.B.1 clearing + 25 carriers. by day ½ RE + 25 working party, M.G. dog's leg + carrying bricks by night No 4 section 4 carpenters CLARKE'S KEEP on frames for traverse + shelters. ⅓ RE + 20 working party, traverse, firesteps, shelters in BARTS Reserve line 4 RE + 5 working party FOSSEWAY by day ½ RE + 25 working party, carrying stores, levelling BARTS parapet, digging shelters, filling in disused trenches by night Weather, fine, cold + sunny. Strong S.W wind	
"	4		No 1 sect ½ RE + 25 working party by day + night on M.G's. Firesteps by day. No 2 sect ⅔ RE + 20 working party sapping shelters, revetting + loopholes STAFFORD LANE by day ⅓ RE + 25 working party traversing STANSFIELD in addition, by night No 3 sect ½ RE + 25 working party + 25 carriers on M.G's firesteps + traverse in GORDON ALLEY by day + by night (except no 25 cavalry) No 4 sect 4 RE FOSSEWAY, ⅓ RE + 6 working party traverses, fire bays + shelters by day ½ RE + 6 working party shelters reserve line by night. Weather, strong S.W wind + fine rain. 7 a.e.	

1875 Wt. W593/826 1,000,000 4/15 J.B.C. & A. A.D.S.S./Forms/C. 2118.

Instructions regarding War Diaries and Intelligence Summaries are contained in F. S. Regs., Part II. and the Staff Manual respectively. Title Pages will be prepared in manuscript.

(3)

WAR DIARY
or
~~INTELLIGENCE SUMMARY~~
(Erase heading not required.)

Army Form C. 2118

Volume III
155th Fd Coy RE.

Place	Date	Hour	Summary of Events and Information	Remarks and references to Appendices
PHILOSOPHE	1916 Feb 5		No 1 sect 3 RE + 25 working party on M.G.s QUARRY by day. 3 RE on MG by night. Remainder RE + 30 working party carrying wire by night.	
			No 2 sect 1/3 RE revetting, 25 working party, 25 carriers, carrying wire by day. 2/3 RE + 25 work party carried pickets + digging shelters STAFFORD LANE by night	
			No 3 sect. 1/2 RE on M.G.s + 25 working party + 25 carriers with wire by day. Night 1/2 RE lowering M.G.s + 30 working party with wire + doing dog's legs, traverses.	
			No 4 sect. 1/2 RE FOSSEWAY & BARTS traverses, firesteps, shelters + 25 working party by day 1/2 RE & 35 working party wiring GORDON – CENTRAL BOYAU by night.	
			Weather, fine, sunny + warm.	
"	6		No 1 sect 6 RE MGs + 25 working party + firesteps QUARRY by day, Remainder + 30 working party wiring STANSFIELD by night	
			No 2 sect 1/3 RE revetting traverses + fire-steps + 25 working party + 25 carrying timber + wire 2/3 RE (working party sent home, no pickets) on low wire CHAPEL ALLEY.	
			No 3 sect 1/2 RE + 20 working party, firesteps O.B.1, traverse by day. M.Gs almost finished, no night work. Working party sent home. No pickets.	
			No 4 sect same as on 5th	
			Weather cold, strong SW wind, fine rain at night.	
			FAC	

1875 Wt. W593/826 1,000,000 4/15 J.B.C. & A. A.D.S.S./Forms/C. 2118.

Army Form C. 2118

Instructions regarding War Diaries and Intelligence Summaries are contained in F. S. Regs., Part II. and the Staff Manual respectively. Title Pages will be prepared in manuscript.

(4)

WAR DIARY
or
~~INTELLIGENCE SUMMARY~~
(Erase heading not required.)

Volume III
155th Fd Coy RE

Place	Date	Hour	Summary of Events and Information	Remarks and references to Appendices
PHILOSOPHE	1916 Feb 7		Nos 1 + 4 sects same as 6th except that no night workers arrived.	
			No 2 sect 1/3 RE + 25 working party + 25 carriers with pickets, revetting by day 2/3 RE wiring by night	
			No 3 sect 1/2 RE firesteps + shelters + 20 working party with timber by day. No night work as no party	
			Practice Gas alarm at 7.0 a.m, Coy gas helmets inspected by CRE Dis Div + his M.O	
			Weather wet S.W. wind	
"	8		No 1 sect 6 RE (no working party) on M.Gs 25 carriers with barbed wire by day.	
			Remainder RE + 20 working party wiring 3 rows of wire about 100x by night.	
			No 2 sect 1/3 RE (no working party) revetting OB1 firesteps by day. 2/3 RE + 22 working party wiring 3 rows of pickets about 150x by night	
			No 3 sect 10 RE (no working party) (25 carriers with pickets) firesteps + shelters by day. 16 RE + 22 working party wiring HULLUCH — GORDON by night. Wiring finished.	
			No 4 sect 1/2 RE (no working party) shelters, firesteps etc by day 1/2 RE + 22 working-party wiring by night	
			CRE 16th Divn visited QUARRY — CHAPEL with O.C	
			Weather alternately wet + sunny. Cold S.W. wind	
			F.A.C.	

1875 Wt. W593/826 1,000,000 4/15 J.B.C. & A. A.D.S.S./Forms/C. 2118.

Instructions regarding War Diaries and Intelligence Summaries are contained in F. S. Regs., Part II. and the Staff Manual respectively. Title Pages will be prepared in manuscript.

(5)

WAR DIARY
or
~~INTELLIGENCE SUMMARY~~
(Erase heading not required.)

Army Form C. 2118

Volume III
155th Fd Coy RE

Place	Date	Hour	Summary of Events and Information	Remarks and references to Appendices
PHILOSOPHE	1916 Feb 9		No 1 sect 2 RE + 25 working party on M.G's ~~by day~~ + shelters by day	
			Remainder RE + 30 working party wiring by night, Completed.	
			No 2 sect 1/3 RE + 5 working party revetting O.B.1., 20 working party carried wire by day.	
			2/3 RE + 21 working party finished wiring + lowered STAFFORD LANE parapet by night.	
			No 3 sect 9 RE + 20 carriers clearing out dug-out + framing by day	
			14 RE + 30 working party on dug-out + shelter + repairs to parapet by night	
			No 4 sect 5 RE + 25 ~~carriers~~ working party + 25 carriers, shelters, traverses, short cut, by day	
			Remainder RE + 25 working party finished wiring by night	
			Weather fine + sunny	
			3 officers 12th Divl Engrs (70th Fd Coy RE) arrived with the news that 155th Coy is to move on 11th.	
"	10.		section officers reporting on state of completion of Reserve line.	
			Working parties as usual, finishing off programme of work by day only.	
			O.C. handed over QUARRY – HULLUCH + Lt. JENNINGS STANSFIELD – DEVON LANE to 12th Divl Engrs.	
			Orders Received from 16th Divn for Coy to move to HOUCHIN on 11th, NEDON on 12th + BOURECQ on 13th	
			Weather cold + sunny	
HOUCHIN	11		Orders received to proceed to Area E under direction of 47th Inf Bde on 13th instead of to BOURECQ.	
			Coy left PHILOSOPHE at 9.30 a.m (pontoons from LABOURSE) + marched to HOUCHIN CAMP (6 miles) + accommodated under canvas for the night; no cooking arrangements.	
			Motor lorry did two trips with extra baggage.	
			Weather very wet.	
			F.a.C.	

Instructions regarding War Diaries and Intelligence Summaries are contained in F. S. Regs., Part II. and the Staff Manual respectively. Title Pages will be prepared in manuscript.

(6)

WAR DIARY
or
~~INTELLIGENCE SUMMARY~~
(Erase heading not required.)

Army Form C. 2118

Volume III
155th Fd Coy RE.

Place	Date	Hour	Summary of Events and Information	Remarks and references to Appendices
NEDON	1916 Feb. 12		Coy left 9.0 a m & marched to NEDON (15 miles). Two motor lorries with extra baggage. CRE + adjt 16th Divl Engrs met Coy at AMETTES. Coy arrived 4 p m. Capt CLIFFORD arrived 11 p m with pontoons after unloading extra stores into two motor lorries at AUCHEL. An officer of R. DUBLIN FUSILIERS had arranged billets. Orders received to proceed to MONT CORNET & RANNEVILLE. Weather fine, a few showers	
RANNEVILLE	13		O.C & interpreter went ahead at 9.0 a m to inspect the two billets, Coy following as far as HURTUBISE. Decided to put whole Coy in RANNEVILLE + Coy brought there 12.30 p m (5 miles) Weather very wet. Telephone line laid by 47th Bde Signal Section from Bde H.Q.	
"	14		Rest day for all ranks to improve billets + clean up. G.O.C. 47th Inf Bde, CRE + Adjt 16th Divl Engrs visited billets, informally in aft. Weather wet morning, fine afternoon.	
"	15.		Cleaning, harness & wagons & improving roads etc round billets. Received orders to be ready to move at 2 hrs notice as division is reserve to G.H.Q. Weather fine, strong S.W. wind.	
"	16.		Moving animals from paddock into farm yards etc. Preparing men, harness, vehicles & animals for G.O.C. 16th Div's inspection. Lts HUGHES + MOAKES reconnoitred road to BOURECQ (starting point for emergency move. Received March table from 47th Bde in case of emergency move. Weather. Heavy rain & high S.W. ~~wind~~ gale in morning fine in afternoon.	

Fac

1875 Wt. W593/826 1,000,000 4/15 J.B.C. & A. A.D.S.S./Forms/C. 2118.

Instructions regarding War Diaries and Intelligence Summaries are contained in F. S. Regs., Part II. and the Staff Manual respectively. Title Pages will be prepared in manuscript.

(7)

WAR DIARY
or
INTELLIGENCE SUMMARY
(Erase heading not required.)

Volume III
155th Fd Coy RE

Army Form C. 2118

Place	Date	Hour	Summary of Events and Information	Remarks and references to Appendices
RANNEVILLE	1916 Feb 17		Coy paraded for inspection by G.O.C. 16th Divn at 11. a.m. G.O.C. very pleased with turnout of Coy & congratulated them, also on their work in the trenches. & ordered a whole holiday for next day. afternoon, making horse lines & cleaning ~~[illegible]~~ roads etc. Weather fine & Sunny.	
"	18		Holiday for Coy by order of G.O.C. Interpreter POTEL proceeded on leave Weather very wet & windy.	
"	19		Nos 1 & 2 secs Pontooning across pond near billets Nos 3 & 4 secs Brushwood work. Weather fine to fine rain.	
"	20		Weather fine & sunny Coy drill 9.30 a.m – 11.0 a.m Officers' riding school in afternoon	
"	21		G.O.C 1st corps inspected Coy with 47th Inf Bde in line on HURTUBISE road at 11. a.m & afterwards troops marched past in column of route. No vehicles 2. p.m Coy drill. 2 N.C.O.S sent to LAIRES to assist Lt MOAKES. Weather fine & frosty, sunny.	
	20		Lt MOAKES proceeded to Divl Grenade School LAIRES as instructor in M.E. 2 N.C.O.S proceeded to LAIRES for 1 weeks instruction in grenades. F.A.C.	

1875 Wt. W593/826 1,000,000 4/15 J.B.C. & A. A.D.S.S./Forms/C. 2118.

Instructions regarding War Diaries and Intelligence Summaries are contained in F. S. Regs., Part II. and the Staff Manual respectively. Title Pages will be prepared in manuscript.

(8)

WAR DIARY
or
~~INTELLIGENCE SUMMARY~~
(Erase heading not required.)

Army Form C. 2118

Volume III
155th Fd Coy RE

Place	Date	Hour	Summary of Events and Information	Remarks and references to Appendices
RANNEVILLE	1916 Feb 22		Weather, snowing all day. 9.a.m Sections doubling up & down road, then knotting & splicing. N.C.O.s & cyclists map-reading classes under Lts. HUGHES & JENNINGS. Lt. O'SULLIVAN ill in bed with headache.	
"	23		Weather snowing all day. no 1 section firing on 30x picture range No 2 section Brushwood hurdles. No 3 " unloading pontoons No 4 " various Coy drill 9 a.m - 10 a.m except No 1 sect O.C. Capt. CLIFFORD & Sergt MEREDITH re-inocculated by Lt BOYD.	
"	24		Weather, ~~snowing~~ on ground & hard frost Nos 2 & 3 sections firing on 30x picture range & afternoon packing No 1 Pontoon wagon. No 1 & 4 Section, squad drill, N.C.O.s & cyclists map-reading in morning & finding way on maps in afternoon. Remainder Brushwood hurdling on H.Q mule stables. 1 new riding horse received from remounts.	
"	25		Weather hard frost, snowing hard & strong N.E. wind Nos 1 & 4 sections shooting on 30x range. No 2 & 3 squad drill, gas helmet drill & march, then packing trestle wagon & brushwood N.C.O.s & cyclists map reading class. Afternoon Whole Coy marched past Gen Sir CHAS. MUNRO Comdg 1st ARMY, at HURTUBISE cross-roads in blinding snowstorm. Cyclist orderly returning to 47th Bde HQ had to return to Coy HQ owing to snow knee deep on roads. Rations sent out by motor lorry snowed up at LIVOSSART, No 2 sect with cook's cart & light spring wagon sent out to bring in rations. Capt CLIFFORD unable to attend Trench mortar conference in BETHUNE owing to after-effects of inocculation. FAC	

1875 Wt. W593/826 1,000,000 4/15 J.B.C. & A. A.D.S.S./Forms/C. 2118.

Instructions regarding War Diaries and Intelligence Summaries are contained in F. S. Regs., Part II. and the Staff Manual respectively. Title Pages will be prepared in manuscript.

(9)

WAR DIARY
or
~~INTELLIGENCE SUMMARY~~
(Erase heading not required.)

Volume III
155th Fd Coy RE

Army Form C. 2118

Place	Date	Hour	Summary of Events and Information	Remarks and references to Appendices
RANNEVILLE	1916 Feb 26		Weather, slight thaw + slight snow showers. Morning Nos 2+3 secs firing on 30x range. Nos 1+4 secs cleaning snow off HURTEBISE – MONT CORNET road. N.C.Os + Cyclists, map reading with Lt. HUGHES afternoon: Coy clearing snow from vehicles, cleaning + oiling, 3 Signallers under Cpl BUXTON. Lt. O'SULLIVAN ill in bed all day with eye-headache Interpreter POTEL returned from leave 3 p.m. Orders received from 47th Inf Bde + 16th Divl Engrs to move to BOURECQ on 29th.	
"	27		Weather same as 26th, cold. Coy drill, then cleaning of vehicles. Parade of animals harnessed up on vehicles. Orders received re supply + transport arrangements for day of move, 29th; also re advance billetting party. Lt. HUGHES proceeded to 6th CONNOUGHT RANGERS at FEBVIN PALFART + blew up 12 defective detonators.	
"	28		Weather, slushy thaw, occasional snow Coy repairing damages to billets, cleaning up generally, preparatory to move. 6. G.S. Wagons (Divl Trn) arrived 1.30 p.m. + orders received these were instead of 3 motor lorries. Orders by wire received from 47th Inf Bde re being in G.H.Q. reserve from today. 7 O.C.	

Instructions regarding War Diaries and Intelligence Summaries are contained in F. S. Regs., Part II. and the Staff Manual respectively. Title Pages will be prepared in manuscript.

(10)

WAR DIARY
or
~~INTELLIGENCE SUMMARY~~
(Erase heading not required.)

Army Form C. 2118

Volume III
155th Fd Coy RE

Place	Date	Hour	Summary of Events and Information	Remarks and references to Appendices
BOURECQ	1916 Feb 29		Coy left RANNEVILLE 9.a.m + marched 2½ miles to starting point, where joined by H.Q 47th Inf Bde, 6th CONNAUGHT RANGERS + 7th LEINSTERS. Marched as Bde to COTTES, then Coy turned off + arrived BOURECQ at 12.15 p.m + settled into billets spread out along the town. Weather fine & sunny, light wind. Capt. CLIFFORD reported arrival of Coy personally to Divl HQ at BUSNES [illegible signature] Capt RE O.C. 155th Fd Coy RE	

1875 Wt. W593/826 1,000,000 4/15 J.B.C. & A. A.D.S.S./Forms/C. 2118.

Army Form W.3091.

Cover for Documents.

152

Nature of Enclosures.

War Diaries

of

[illegible] Field Coy R.E.

[illegible] Jan. & Feb. 1916

Notes, or Letters written.

Army Form C. 2118

Instructions regarding War Diaries and Intelligence Summaries are contained in F. S. Regs., Part II. and the Staff Manual respectively. Title Pages will be prepared in manuscript.

WAR DIARY
or
~~INTELLIGENCE SUMMARY~~
(Erase heading not required.)

Volume II

155th Fd Coy R.E.

163

Place	Date	Hour	Summary of Events and Information	Remarks and references to Appendices
	1916 Jan		Sites for mines selected 2 opposite QUARRIES at head of CHAPEL ALLEY and GRIMWOOD TRENCH, one in each branch of HAIRPIN.	
			Road-gangs ~~[illegible]~~ paraded at 9. a m & detailed to work	
			Work detailed for Permanent Working Parties	
			1 troop 1st Fd Sqn arrived	
			Received orders transferring 155th Coy to 1st Corps on 4th at 2 p m.	
			Also orders re relief of 47th Divn by Dismounted Divn in Sector C & D	
	2		Permanent Working Parties & Road Gangs confused owing to misunderstandings.	
			Maj JOHNSON A/CRE Cav Dismounted Div Engrs visited billets with 3 officers & took over Sector D, arranged that 155th Coy should concentrate on 4 mines at HAIRPIN, ~~and~~ GRIMWOOD ALLEY & CHAPEL ALLEY	
			Mining actually commenced night of 1/2nd with preparing timber & entrance to shaft.	
			JAC	

Instructions regarding War Diaries and Intelligence Summaries are contained in F. S. Regs., Part II and the Staff Manual respectively. Title Pages will be prepared in manuscript.

WAR DIARY

or

~~INTELLIGENCE SUMMARY~~

(Erase heading not required.)

Volume II

155th Fd Coy RE

Army Form C. 2118.

Place	Date	Hour	Summary of Events and Information	Remarks and references to Appendices
	1916 Jan 3		47th Divn relieved by Dismounted Cavalry on 2nd 3rd & 4th.	
			3 Officers 253rd (Tunnelling) Coy RE visited billets re mining	
			mines at HAIRPIN, GRIMWOOD & CHAPEL ALLEYS continued, visits	
			by section officers every 12 hours.	
			Enemy sent 3 shells at 9 a.m. into Bomb Store 200 yds from	
			billets & fired house, exploding all the bombs & ammunition	
			Weather sunny, clear & fine.	
	4		3 Officers 253rd Coy visited mines with Section Officers	
			Two shells from new German gun hit two houses	
			adjoining billets between noon & 1 p.m. No casualties.	
			One of the houses is the stable for our two mules	
			but they were out at work. Fuse of shell recovered	
			Line of fire from ~~east~~ direction VERMELLES	
			Weather sunny with misty rain in morning, misty &	
			cloudy in afternoon. FGC	

1875 Wt. W593/826 1,000,000 4/15 J.B.C. & A. A.D.S.S./Forms/C. 2118.

Instructions regarding War Diaries and Intelligence Summaries are contained in F.S. Regs., Part II and the Staff Manual respectively. Title Pages will be prepared in manuscript.

Duplicate

(3)

WAR DIARY
or
~~INTELLIGENCE SUMMARY~~
(Erase heading not required.)

Volume II
155th Fd Coy RE

Army Form C.

Place	Date	Hour	Summary of Events and Information 165
	1916 Jan 5		A/CRE ordered that, after mines had been handed over & dug-outs completed for Mining Coy, 155th Coy is to repair Reserve line (OB5) at head of QUARRY, BARTS + GORDON ALLEYS.
			Lt O'SULLIVAN with Lt CURRIE (253rd Coy) chose at CHAPEL KEEP dug-outs which require repair for Mining Coy.
	6		O.C. visited OB5 between GORDON + BARTS ALLEYS where work is shortly to proceed.
			Lt O'SULLIVAN found dug-outs in OB1 for personnel of 253rd Coy and arranged for timber supply & carriers.
			Handed over both HAIRPIN mines to 253rd Coy, work proceeding on GRIMWOOD and CHAPEL ALLEY mines.
			A/CRE arranged for a working party of 50 Cavalry daily at PHILOSOPHE cross roads to return by 1.30 pm.
			112397 Sapr GRIFFITHS D sent to Fd Amb for inoculation (tetanus) after being slightly wounded in jaw & leg by live cartridges put in the fire.
			FAC

Instructions regarding War Diaries and Intelligence Summaries are contained in F. S. Regs., Part II and the Staff Manual respectively. Title Pages will be prepared in manuscript.

(4)

WAR DIARY
or
~~INTELLIGENCE SUMMARY~~
(Erase heading not required.)

Volume II
155th Fd Coy R.E

Army Form C. 2118.

166

Place	Date	Hour	Summary of Events and Information	Remarks and references to Appendices
	1916 Jan 7		O.C. visited QUARRY ALLEY & Reserve line to BARTS ALLEY	
			O.C. 253rd Coy arranged re dug outs.	
			Work on CHAPEL & GRIMWOOD ALLEY mines proceeding	
			shortage of candles at mines & dug outs	
			50 men, Cavalry working party carried timber & sandbags	
			to CHAPEL ALLEY mines	
			Weather drizzly but sunny at times	
	8		O.C. visited CHAPEL KEEP dug outs & CURLY magazines	
			Work on dug outs ceased through shortage of candles	
			GRIMWOOD & CHAPEL ALLEY mines handed over to 253rd Coy	
			at midnight 8/9	
			50 men, cavalry working party carrying & cleaning CHAPEL	
			ALLEY.	
			Weather, dull, dry, cold windy	
			F.O.C.	

1875 Wt. W593/826 1,000,000 4/15 J.B.C. & A. A.D.S.S./Forms/C. 2118.

Instructions regarding War Diaries and Intelligence Summaries are contained in F. S. Regs., Part II. and the Staff Manual respectively. Title Pages will be prepared in manuscript.

Duplicate

(5)

WAR DIARY
or
~~INTELLIGENCE SUMMARY~~
(Erase heading not required.)

Volume II
155th Fd Coy R.E.

Army Form C. 2118.

167

Place	Date	Hour	Summary of Events and Information	Remarks and references to Appendices
	1916 Jan 9		Nos 2 + 3 Sections Continued work on Magazines in CURLY CRESCENT but short of timber & Candles	
			No 1 Section clearing mud out of Reserve line from QUARRY ALLEY Southwards.	
			No 4 section clearing mud out of Reserve line from GORDON ALLEY Northwards, good progress made, work safe by daylight	
			Weather cold + Sunny.	
	10		see next page	
	11		Nos 1 + 4 sections each with working party of 50 Cavalry working on Reserve line. No 1 section cleared 300 yds of bottom of trench, + another 300 yds to do between QUARRY and BARTS ALLEYS.	
			No 4 deepening trench to North of head of GORDON ALLEY.	
			Nos 2 + 3 sections on dug-outs + magazines for 253rd Coy. Started temporary magazine in O.B.4. Employed working parties of 50 men carrying timber to dug-outs.	
			Weather cold + Sunny	
			½ No 1 Section wiring Reserve line from QUARRY ALLEY by night	

7 a e

1875 Wt. W593/826 1,000,000 4/15 J.B.C. & A. A.D.S.S./Forms/C. 2118.

Army Form C. 2118.

Instructions regarding War Diaries and Intelligence Summaries are contained in F. S. Regs., Part II. and the Staff Manual respectively. Title Pages will be prepared in manuscript.

Duplicate (6)

WAR DIARY
or
~~INTELLIGENCE SUMMARY~~
(Erase heading not required.)

Volume II 155th Fd Coy R.E.

(68)

Place	Date	Hour	Summary of Events and Information	Remarks and references to Appendices
	1916 Jan 11		No 1 section between QUARRY + BARTS ALLEYS in Reserve line Nos 2+3 sections sawing timber for 253rd Coy mines + making magazines. No 4 section between BARTS + GORDON ALLEYS in Reserve line. Nos 1+4 each had 50 men working parties No 1 had in addition 50 men carrying wire. Weather sunny but cold.	
	12/1		Nos 2+3 sections making 4 dugouts at CHAPEL KEEP, 2 magazines in CURLY CRESCENT, + 1 temporary magazine in OB4 in relief, also carpenters sawing timber VERMELLES CHURCH stores, all for 253rd Coy. No 1 section, QUARRY ALLEY – Reserve line. No 4 section, GORDON ALLEY – Reserve line, no working party turned up. Warned of Bombardment of HAIRPIN for 1 p.m. Withdrew No 4 section at 12.30 pm + stopped afternoon relief of Nos 2 + 3 sections till after dark. Weather clear + sunny morning, later dull to fine rain.	
			FAC	

1875 Wt. W593/826 1,000,000 4/15 J.B.C. & A. A.D.S.S./Forms/C. 2118.

Instructions regarding War Diaries and Intelligence Summaries are contained in F. S. Regs., Part II. and the Staff Manual respectively. Title Pages will be prepared in manuscript.

Duplicate

(7)

WAR DIARY
or
~~INTELLIGENCE SUMMARY~~
(Erase heading not required.)

Army Form C. 2118.

Volume II
155th Fd Coy R E

Place	Date	Hour	Summary of Events and Information	Remarks and references to Appendices
	1916 Jan 13		169 Weather cold, sunny, changing to rain, high wind. a/CRE [illegible] Div ordered 100 yds rights & left at head of main alleys on reserve line to be made habitable. O.C 253rd Tunnelling Coy arranged for work to cease on WEST CURLY magazine ~~[illegible]~~ and to be concentrated on EAST CURLY + O.B.4 Magazines, also finish timbering two man's dug-outs in CHAPEL KEEP + abandon two dug-outs under HULLUCH ROAD. 7 men of No 1 section walking up main road near Railway Crossing, Fosse 3, at noon, off duty going to Estaminet, caught by Enemy shell, burst 15 yds away just off pavé + 30 yds from Railway Crossing. KILLED 97946 Spr HEATON H WOUNDED 97810 L/Cpl SHORT W very seriously 98444 Spr HARRIS A } seriously 97841 " WOODS H } 98050 " FEAST C slightly ~~[illegible]~~ 98233 Spr PERRYMAN J F at duty Pack horse No R18 destroyed suffering from kidney disease + paralysis FAC	

Instructions regarding War Diaries and Intelligence Summaries are contained in F. S. Regs. Part II and the Staff Manual respectively. Title Pages will be prepared in manuscript.

(8)

WAR DIARY
or
~~INTELLIGENCE SUMMARY~~
(Erase heading not required.)

Army Form C. 2118.

Volume II
155th Fd Coy RE

Place	Date	Hour	Summary of Events and Information	Remarks and references to Appendices
	1916 Jan 14		Weather sunny but cold light S.W wind.	179
			15th Divn relieving 1st Divn next section to South.	
			Sections carrying on as before.	
			Nos 1 & 4 sections wiring Reserve line by night.	
	15		Weather dull	
			Nos 1 & 4 sections on O.B.5, no working party for No 4 section, some for No 1 section.	
			Nos 2 & 3 sections carried on with dug-outs & magazines	
			O.C. 253rd Coy decided that the dug-out in O.B.4 is not suitable for a magazine as it has only 6 feet of cover, decided to finish it off and use for stores only	
			EAST CURLY CRESCENT magazine to have at least 15 feet of cover.	
			F.A.C.	

Instructions regarding War Diaries and Intelligence Summaries are contained in F. S. Regs., Part II. and the Staff Manual respectively. Title Pages will be prepared in manuscript.

[illegible] (9)

WAR DIARY
or
~~INTELLIGENCE SUMMARY~~
(Erase heading not required.)

Army Form C. 2118

Volume II
155th Fd Coy R.E.

171

Place	Date	Hour	Summary of Events and Information	Remarks and references to Appendices
	1916 Jan 16		Weather dull Work as before	
	17		Magazine in O.B.4 completed 5' high, 6' wide, 10' long. Door being fitted CURLY MAGAZINE 19 frames in shaft No 1 section 50 men working party Nos 2 & 3 sections had to carry timber for themselves No 4 section had no carrying party or working party Work as before	
	18		O.C. visited Reserve line with a/CRE [illegible] Divn & selected sites for M.G. emplacements (1) between WATS & GORDON ALLEYS (2) head of GORDON ALLEY at O.B.1 (3) head of HULLUCH ALLEY, O.B.1 (4) (to be selected later) head of QUARRY ALLEY Reserve line Work as before Weather drizzly.	

F.A.C.

Instructions regarding War Diaries and Intelligence Summaries are contained in F. S. Regs., Part II. and the Staff Manual respectively. Title Pages will be prepared in manuscript.

(10)

WAR DIARY
or
~~INTELLIGENCE SUMMARY~~
(Erase heading not required.)

Volume II
155th Fd Coy R.E.

Army Form C. 2118.

Place	Date	Hour	Summary of Events and Information	Remarks and references to Appendices
	1916 Jan 19		Weather, sunny & cold, full moon & very clear.	172
			No 2 section only on CURLY MAGAZINE in reliefs.	
			No 1 section work as before working party 50 men, No 4 [illegible] working party 60 men	
			No 3 section nightwork on OB1 GORDON ALLEY, 30 working party	
			No 4 section nightwork on M.G. emplacements & T heads, 30 working party	
	20		Weather sunny turning to rain	
			No 1 section 78 working party clearing both ends of RESERVE LINE between QUARRY and BARTS ALLEYS making firesteps, revetting & 1 M G emplacement about 250 yds out of 700 yds [illegible] completed	
			No 2 Section magazine for 253rd Coy (miners) at CURLY CRESCENT shaft complete chamber almost half done, timbered close with 9"x3" pit props at 4' intervals. Section in reliefs.	
			No 3 section two M.G. emplacements in OB1 at HULLUCH & GORDON ALLEYS clearing OB1 & repairing firestep. 30 working party by day, also by night	
			No 4 Section one M G Emplacement S of BARTS ALLEY clearing & firesteps between BARTS & GORDON ALLEYS. 30 working party by day also by night	
			Part of Company bathed & changed underclothing at [illegible] Div Baths at MINE LA BOURSE	
			FAC	

1875 Wt. W593/826 1,000,000 4/15 J.B.C. & A. A.D.S.S./Forms/C. 2118.

Instructions regarding War Diaries and Intelligence Summaries are contained in F.S. Regs., Part II and the Staff Manual respectively. Title Pages will be prepared in manuscript.

(11)

WAR DIARY
or
~~INTELLIGENCE SUMMARY~~
(Erase heading not required.)

Army Form C. 2118

Volume II
155th Fd Coy RE

173

Place	Date	Hour	Summary of Events and Information	Remarks and references to Appendices
	1916 Jan 21		Weather dull, strong SW wind	
			Work as before	
			No 1 section had no working party owing to reliefs	
			No 4 section had 60 men working party (30 from No 3 section)	
			Fixed up Coy bath house next to No 1 section Billet	
	22		Weather fine rain	
			Work as before	
			Working parties No 1 section very late & only half strength	
			No 3 section 30 men day & night	
			No 4 section 30 men day & night	
			No 97572 Spr TODD L slightly wounded in back of neck by stray bullet at entrance to [illegible] ALLEY	
			Cpl MAHER & Spr LEE ~~did~~ would not bath & remanded for FGCM	
			Remainder of Company bathed at LABOURSE	
			F.G.C.	

Instructions regarding War Diaries and Intelligence Summaries are contained in F. S. Regs., Part II and the Staff Manual respectively. Title Pages will be prepared in manuscript.

(12) Duplicate

WAR DIARY
or
~~INTELLIGENCE SUMMARY~~
(Erase heading not required.)

Army Form C.

Volume II.
155th Fd Coy R E

174

Place	Date	Hour	Summary of Events and Information
	1916 Jan 23		Weather fine & sunny.
			No 1 section 70 working party, 50 carriers & RE nightwork
			Remaining sections as usual.
	24		O C met G O C Division & a/CRE at 7 a m on HULLUCH Road & visited Reserve line, returning at noon. Various details of M G emplacements, their dug-outs & defence of heads of alleys were settled.
			No 1 section 50 carriers with trench boards, 75 making fire steps & clearing N of QUARRY ALLEY
			No 2 section — magazine
			No 3 section Front M G emplacements & T heads, part at night working party 24 on T heads
			No 4 section on M G emplacements, 10 carriers with brick bats.
			J.A.C.

1875 Wt. W593/826 1,000,000 4/15 J.B.C. & A. A.D.S.S./Forms/C. 2118.

Instructions regarding War Diaries and Intelligence Summaries are contained in F. S. Regs., Part II. and the Staff Manual respectively. Title Pages will be prepared in manuscript.

(13)

Duplicate

WAR DIARY

or

~~INTELLIGENCE SUMMARY~~

(Erase heading not required.)

Volume II

155th Fd Coy R E

Army Form C. 2118

175

Place	Date	Hour	Summary of Events and Information	Remarks and references to Appendices
	1916 Jan 23		No 1 section MG Emplacements + completing half finished fire steps. Working party 10 (+ 30 called away after one hours work)	
			No 2 section, 3/4 on magazine, 10 9" frames completed in chamber + centre struts (2 sets) fixed	
			1/4 night shift	
			No 3 section, 14 RE, no working party arrived, work held up. till timber arrived with 20 carriers, work on MG Emplacement + marked out "dogs legs" in dug out for MG in GORDON ALLEY. 10 RE on night work	
			No 4 section 1/2 RE + 1 Offr + 20 men working party on MG Emplacements + completing fire steps, cleaning dug outs. CRE visited section + ordered splinterproof shelters to be provided before dug outs are begun + afterwards loophole for MG	
			All MG emplacements held up for roof girders	
			Weather fine + sunny	
			No 97536 Spr STEEL J wounded slightly in left arm by shell burst outside magazine about 3 pm	
			FAG	

1875 Wt. W593/826 1,000,000 4/15 J.B.C. & A. A.D.S.S./Forms/C. 2118

Instructions regarding War Diaries and Intelligence Summaries are contained in F. S. Regs., Part II. and the Staff Manual respectively. Title Pages will be prepared in manuscript.

(14)

Duplicate

WAR DIARY
or
~~INTELLIGENCE SUMMARY.~~
(Erase heading not required.)

Volume II
155th Fd Coy R.E

Army Form C.

Place	Date	Hour	Summary of Events and Information	Remarks and references to Appendices
	1916 Jan 26		176 Weather dull, sunny at times No 1 Section 20 working party, on 2 M.G Emplacements + Completing half done fire steps. No 2 Section 14 frames in Magazine Chamber No 3 Section 20 Carriers, 20 working party, on 2 M G Emplacements dug-outs + fire-steps. No 4 Section 25 Carriers, 20 working party. Carried 16 girders roofed M G emplacement complete, filled in front with bricks & shaped roof. Fire steps in ~~the~~ BARTS ALLEY and Shelters. O C sent for by C.R.E [illegible] at 7.15 pm to Sgn [illegible] Information received ~~that~~ of an attack by enemy ~~on~~ at 6 pm on KINK + KAISERIN TRENCH (~~evening of the~~ before KAISER'S birthday). Sections 1, 3 + 4 send minimum numbers of R.E to finish off 5 M G emplacements + make them occupiable by morning tomorrow 1/2 R.E to complete finish emplacement + 1/2 in reserve J.A.C	

1875 Wt. W593/826 1,000,000 4/15 J.B.C. & A. A.D.S.S./Forms/C. 2118.

Instructions regarding War Diaries and Intelligence Summaries are contained in F. S. Regs., Part II and the Staff Manual respectively. Title Pages will be prepared in manuscript.

(15)

Duplicate

WAR DIARY
or
~~INTELLIGENCE SUMMARY~~
(Erase heading not required.)

Army Form C.

Volume II
155th Fd Coy RE

17

Place	Date	Hour	Summary of Events and Information
	1916 Jan 21		CRE (D Div) visited billets at 7 pm & further work ordered as situation had quieted down.
			M.G. emplacements in progress to proceed normally with ½ sections
			½ sections in Reserve Day work
			No 1. STANSFIELD ROAD } about 6 men each to dig loop-holed (2)
			No 2. STAFFORD LANE } traverses just behind short "dogs-leg" fork
			No 3. HULLUCH ALLEY } from RESERVE Trg. Picked out "dogs-legs"
			No 4. FOSSEWAY } material provided for blocking way round traverses
			½ sections at work Day work
			No 1 M G Empt / QUARRY ALLEY + 6 Carriers from No 2 Sect
			No 2 Carrying Work on Magazine paid for[?]
			No 3 2 M G Empts GORDON + HULLUCH ALLEYS + 6 Carriers from No 2
			No 4 1 M.G. Empt nearly finished + loop holed (2) traverse at BARTS ALLEY & picked out "dogs-legs"
			Remainder of ½ sections in Reserve night work
			20 dug dogs-legs with 20 men on long leg & 10 on short leg
		3 pm	CRE ordered no heavy work on "dogs legs" & to confine work to M G empts & loop holed traverses
			Dogs legs only possible on STAFFORD LANE & HULLUCH ALLEY - needs shaving
			No 1 Section secured 34 girders for M.G. empts.
			7 a.c.

1873 Wt. W593/826 1,000,000 4/15 J.B.C. & A. A.D.S.S./Forms/C. 2118.

Instructions regarding War Diaries and Intelligence Summaries are contained in F. S. Regs., Part II. and the Staff Manual respectively. Title Pages will be prepared in manuscript.

(14)

WAR DIARY
or
INTELLIGENCE SUMMARY

(Erase heading not required.)

Volume II
155th Fd Coy RE

Army Form C. 2118.

Place	Date	Hour	Summary of Events and Information	Remarks and references to Appendices
			Weather Foggy morning, then sunny, light S.W. wind	
			[illegible] work [illegible] on [illegible] empl [illegible] of QUARRY ALLEY owing to shelling	
			[illegible] ½ RE QUARRY Reserve line, ½ RE STANSFIELD Reserve line	
			70 [illegible] bringing up 40 I girders	
			Preparing for traverse in STANSFIELD ROAD	
			No 2 section ½ RE Magazine 16 frames in chamber, nearly finished	
			½ RE STAFFORD LANE Reserve line, dug-outs (2)	
			No 3 Section RE night work [illegible] digging MILLICH ALLEY	
			70 [illegible] carried up 22 I girders	
			No 4 section RE on M.G empl & BARTS fire steps & Reserve line fire steps. Preparing for traverse in BARTS	
			25 [illegible] party	
			M.G Emplacement nearly finished.	
			[illegible]	

1875 Wt. W593/826 1,000,000 4/15 J.B.C. & A. A.D.S.S./Forms/C. 2118.

Instructions regarding War Diaries and Intelligence Summaries are contained in F. S. Regs., Part II. and the Staff Manual respectively. Title Pages will be prepared in manuscript.

(17) Duplicate

WAR DIARY
or
~~INTELLIGENCE SUMMARY~~
(Erase heading not required.)

Army Form C

Volume II
155th Fd Coy RE

174

Place	Date	Hour	Summary of Events and Information
	1916 7.29 [illegible]		Weather, foggy to sunshine very mild, no wind
			O.C. went round 1st [illegible] Bde M.G. Empls with Bde M G officer planting guns in the loop-holes.
			C.R.E. [illegible] Divn ordered all loop-holes to be cased in timber
			No 1 Section ½ RE M.G Empls (2), ½ RE loopholed traverse STANSFIEL[D]
			25 Carmen carrying timber frames for M.G Empls.
			75 working party fire stepping QUARRY ALLEY all day work
			[illegible] ½ RE loopholed traverse STANSFIELD LANE ½ RE on [illegible] working party [illegible]
			No 3 Section 5 RE on M.G Empl 5 [illegible] [illegible] ALLEY for [illegible], 2 as guides 2 [illegible] working party [illegible]
			[illegible] 15 RE on M.G [illegible] 50 working party carrying [illegible]
			No 4 Section ½ RE fire stepping BARTS [illegible] ALLEY [illegible] M G Empls ½ RE on traverse in BARTS ALLEY & FAS[T]EWAY. 25 working party on whole all day work
			No 98299 Spr GRAY A wounded slightly in back of legs by bullet
			FAE

1875 Wt. W593/826 1,000,000 4/15 J.B.C. & A. A.D.S.S./Forms/C. 2118.

Instructions regarding War Diaries and Intelligence Summaries are contained in F. S. Regs., Part II. and the Staff Manual respectively. Title Pages will be prepared in manuscript.

(18)

WAR DIARY
or
~~INTELLIGENCE SUMMARY.~~
(Erase heading not required.)

Army Form C. 2118.

Volume II
155th Fd Coy R.E.

Place	Date	Hour	Summary of Events and Information	Remarks and references to Appendices
	30		180	
			No 1 Section 33 working party + 25 carriers day + 25 working party night	
			No 2 Section 33 working party day + 25 working party night	
			No 3 Section 25 working party night	
			No 4 Section 33 working party + 25 carriers day + 25 working party night	
			all work as on 29th	
			O.C. attended F.G.C.M. on Cpl MAHER + Spr LEE at SAILLY LA BOURSE. Capt CLIFTON prosecutor	
			New Coy recreation room opened today – also used as medical inspection Room.	
			Weather. dense fog, cold, damp.	
	31		No 1 Section ½ RE on M.G. Empt. ½ RE on STANSFIELD. 25 working party by day + 25 by night	
			No 2 Section ½ RE + 25 working party. Lepford traverse by day	
			½ RE 25 working party, keep bolting + revetting by night	
			No 3 Section ½ RE + 25 carriers with girders + frames for GORDON M.G. Empt + ALLEY traverse by day + night	
			No 4 Section BARTS M.G. Empt + traverse etc. 25 working party day + night 25 carriers day only	
			Weather. foggy, turning to sunshine	
			~~O.C.~~ 8 J. Bremner Capt RE O.C. 155th Fd Coy RE	

1875 Wt. W593/826 1,000,000 4/15 J.B.C. & A. A.D.S.S./Forms/C. 2118.

Instructions regarding War Diaries and Intelligence Summaries are contained in F. S. Regs., Part II and the Staff Manual respectively. Title Pages will be prepared in manuscript.

(1)

WAR DIARY
or
~~INTELLIGENCE~~ SUMMARY
(Erase heading not required.)

Army Form C. 2118

Volume III
155th Fd Coy RE.

Place	Date	Hour	Summary of Events and Information	Remarks and references to Appendices
	1916		153	
PHILOSOPHE	Feb 1		Fighting strength of Coy 6 Offrs 216 O.R.	
			Weather, foggy, cold to sunshine	
			No 3 section 10 R.E. HULLUCH ALLEY traverse + dugs by by day	
			100 Cav carriers with bricks 12 RE on M.G + traverses ~~[illegible]~~ by day	
			No 4 sect ½ R.E, 25 working party, fire steps, M.G + traverses BARTS ALLEY by day	
"	2.		No 1 sect ½ RE by day on M.G's + fire steps of M.G.E.	
			½ RE by nights roofing M.G.E.	
			No 2 section ⅓ RE revetting, firesteps, loopholes by day, STAFFORD LANE	
			⅔ R.E [illegible] by night	
			No 3 section 10 [illegible] HULLUCH + firesteps O.B.1 by day.	
			No 4 section [illegible] BARTS [illegible] by day	

Army Form C. 2

Instructions regarding War Diaries and Intelligence Summaries are contained in F. S. Regs., Part II. and the Staff Manual respectively. Title Pages will be prepared in manuscript.

duplicate (2)

WAR DIARY
or
~~INTELLIGENCE SUMMARY~~
(Erase heading not required.)

Volume III
155th Fd Coy RE

154

Place	Date	Hour	Summary of Events and Information	Remarks and references to Appendices
PHILOSOPHE	1916 Feb 3		No 1 section ½ RE, 25 working party + 50 carriers, M.G's, firesteps, + carrying stores by day 1 RE + 15 working party M.G's, + remainder RE + 10 working party STANSFIELD by night No 2 section 2/3 RE firesteps by day, no working party or carriers by day 1/3 RE Cutting away traverses by night No 3 section ½ RE + 20 working party, loopeholed traverses, firesteps O.B.1 clearing + 25 carriers by day ½ RE + 25 working parties M.G. dogsleg + carrying bricks by night No 4 section 4 carpenters CLARKE'S KEEP on frames for traverse + shelters. 1/3 RE + 20 working party, traverse, firesteps, shelters in BARTS Reserve line 4 RE + 5 working party FOSSEWAY by day ½ RE + 25 working party carrying stores, levelling BARTS parapet, digging shelters, filling in disused trenches by night Weather fine, cold + sunny, strong S.W wind	
"	4		No 1 secn ½ RE + 25 working party by day + night on M.G's. Firesteps by day. No 2 secn 2/3 RE + 20 working party sapping shelters, revetting + loopholes STAFFORD LANE by day 1/3 RE + 25 working party traversing STANSFIELD in addition, by night No 3 secn ½ RE + 25 working party + 25 carriers on M.G's firesteps + traverse in GORDON ALLEY by day + by night (except no 25 carriers) No 4 secn 4 RE FOSSEWAY ½ RE + 6 working party traverses, firebays + shelters by day ½ RE + 6 working party shelters reserve line by night Weather strong S.W. wind fine rain. 7 a.e.	

1875 Wt. W593/826 1,000,000 4/15 J.B.C. & A. A.D.S.S./Forms/C. 2118

Instructions regarding War Diaries and Intelligence Summaries are contained in F. S. Regs., Part II. and the Staff Manual respectively. Title Pages will be prepared in manuscript.

duplicate (3)

WAR DIARY
or
~~INTELLIGENCE SUMMARY~~
(Erase heading not required.)

Volume III
155th Fd Coy R E

Army Form C. 2

Place	Date	Hour	Summary of Events and Information	Remarks and references to Appendices
			155	
PHILOSOPHE	1916 Feb 5		No 1 sect 3 RE + 25 working party on M.G.s QUARRY by day, 3 RE on M.G. by night. Remainder RE + 30 working party carrying wire by night.	
			No 2 sect ⅓ RE revetting 25 working party 25 carriers carrying wire by day. ⅔ RE + 25 working party carried pickets + digging shelters STAFFORD LANE by night.	
			No 3 sect ½ RE on M.G.s + 25 working party + 25 carriers with wire by day. night ½ RE lowering M.G.s + 30 working party with wire + doing dog legs, traverses	
			No 4 sect ½ RE FOSSEWAY + BARTS traverses, firesteps, shelters + 25 working party by day ½ RE + 35 working party wiring GORDON – CENTRAL BOYAU by night	
			Weather, fine, sunny + warm.	
"	6		No 1 sect 6 RE M.G.s + 25 working party + firesteps QUARRY by day, Remainder + 30 working party wiring STANSFIELD by night	
			No 2 sect ⅓ RE revetting traverses + fire steps + 25 working party + 25 carrying timber + wire ⅔ RE (working party sent home, no pickets) on low wire CHAPEL ALLEY.	
			No 3 sect ½ RE + 20 working party firesteps O.B.1, traverse by day M.G.s almost finished. No night work. Working party sent home. No pickets.	
			No 4 sect same as on 5th.	
			Weather cold, strong S W wind, fine rain at night.	
			FAC	

1875 Wt. W593/826 1,000,000 4/15 J.B.C. & A. A.D.S.S./Forms/C. 2118.

Instructions regarding War Diaries and Intelligence Summaries are contained in F. S. Regs., Part II. and the Staff Manual respectively. Title Pages will be prepared in manuscript.

Duplicate (4)

WAR DIARY
or
~~INTELLIGENCE SUMMARY~~
(Erase heading not required.)

Army Form C.

Volume III
155th Fd Coy RE

Place	Date	Hour	Summary of Events and Information 156	Remarks and references to Appendices
PHILOSOPHE	1916 Feb 7		Nos 1 + 4 sects same as 6th except that no night workers arrived.	
			No 2 sect 1/3 RE + 75 working party + 25 Carriers with pickets, revetting by day 2/3 RE wiring by night	
			No 3 sect 1/2 RE firesteps + shelters + 20 working party with timber by day. No night work as no party	
			Practice gas alarm at 7.0 a.m, Coy gas helmets inspected by CRE Div Gas + Div MO	
			Weather wet S.W. wind	
"	8		No 1 sect 6 RE (no working party) on M.Gs 25 Carriers with barbed wire by day.	
			Remainder RE + 20 working party wiring 3 rows of wire about 100x by night	
			No 2 sect 1/3 RE (no working party) revetting OB1 firesteps by day 2/3 RE + 22 working party wiring 3 rows of pickets about 150x by night	
			No 3 sect 10 RE (no working party) (25 Carriers with pickets) firesteps + shelters by day 16 RE + 22 working party wiring HULLUCH – GORDON by night Wiring finished.	
			No 4 sect 1/2 RE (no working party) shelters, firesteps etc by day 1/2 RE + 22 working-party wiring by night	
			CRE 16th Divn visited QUARRY — CHAPEL with OC.	
			Weather alternately wet + sunny. Cold SW wind	
			FAC	

1875 Wt. W593/826 1,000,000 4/15 J.B.C. & A. A.D.S.S./Forms/C. 2118.

Instructions regarding War Diaries and Intelligence Summaries are contained in F. S. Regs., Part II. and the Staff Manual respectively. Title Pages will be prepared in manuscript.

Duplicate (5)

WAR DIARY
or
~~INTELLIGENCE SUMMARY~~
(Erase heading not required.)

Army Form C. 2118

Volume III
155th Fd Coy R E

Place	Date	Hour	Summary of Events and Information 157	Remarks and references to Appendices
PHILOSOPHE	1916 Feb 9		No 1 sect 2 RE + 25 working party on M.G's ~~by day~~ + shelters by day	
			Remainder RE + 30 working party wiring by night, Completed.	
			No 2 sect 1/3 RE + 5 working party revetting O.B.1, 20 working party carried wire by day	
			2/3 RE + 21 working party finished wiring + lowered STAFFORD LANE parapet by night	
			No 3 sect 9 RE + 20 carriers clearing out dug-out + framing by day	
			14 RE + 30 working party on dug-out + shelter + repairs to parapet by night	
			No 4 sect 5 RE + 25 ~~carriers~~ working party + 25 carriers, shelters, traverses, short cut, by day	
			Remainder RE + 25 working party finished wiring by night	
			Weather fine + sunny	
			3 officers 12th Divl Engrs (70th Fd Coy RE) arrived with the news that 155th Coy is to move on 11th.	
"	10		Section officers reporting on state of completion of Reserve line	
			Working parties as usual, finishing off programme of work by day only.	
			O.C. handed over QUARRY – HULLUCH + II JENNINGS STANSFIELD – DEVON LANE to 12th Divl Engrs.	
			Orders received from 16th Divn for Coy to move to HOUCHIN on 11th, NEDON on 12th + BOURECQ on 13th	
			Weather cold + sunny	
			Orders received to proceed to Area E under direction of 47th Inf Bde on 13th instead of to BOURECQ	
HOUCHIN	11		Coy left PHILOSOPHE at 9.30 a.m (pontoons from LABOURSE) + marched to HOUCHIN CAMP (6 miles) + accommodated under canvas for the night; no cooking arrangements	
			Motor lorry did two trips with extra baggage	
			Weather very wet.	
			7 a.c.	

1875 Wt. W593/826 1,000,000 4/15 J.B.C. & A. A.D.S.S./Forms/C. 2118.

Instructions regarding War Diaries and Intelligence Summaries are contained in F. S. Regs., Part II. and the Staff Manual respectively. Title Pages will be prepared in manuscript.

(6)

WAR DIARY
or
~~INTELLIGENCE SUMMARY~~

(Erase heading not required.)

Army Form C. 2118.

Volume III
155th Fd Coy RE

158

Place	Date	Hour	Summary of Events and Information	Remarks and references to Appendices
[N]EDON	1916 Feb 12		Coy left 9.0 a.m. & marched to NEDON (15 miles). Two motor lorries with extra baggage. CRE & Adjt 16th Divl Engrs met Coy at AMETTES. Coy arrived 4 p.m. Capt CLIFFORD arrived 11 p.m. with pontoons after unloading extra stores into two motor lorries at AUCHEL. An officer of R DUBLIN FUSILIERS had arranged billets. Orders received to proceed to MONT CORNET & RANNEVILLE. Weather fine, a few showers	
[RAN]NEVILLE	13		O C & interpreter went ahead at 9.0 a.m. to inspect the two billets, Coy following as far as HURTUBISE. Decided to put whole Coy in RANNEVILLE & Coy brought there 12.30 p.m. (5 miles) Weather very wet. Telephone line laid by 47th Bde Signal Section from Bde H.Q	
"	14		Rest day for all ranks to improve billets & clean up. G O C 47th Inf Bde, CRE & Adjt 16th Divl Engrs visited billets, informally in aft. Weather wet morning, fine afternoon	
"	15		Cleaning harness & wagons & improving roads etc round billets. Received orders to be ready to move at 2 hrs notice as division is reserve to G H Q. Weather fine, strong SW wind	
"	16		Moving animals from paddock into farm yards etc. Preparing men, harness, vehicles & animals for G O C 16th Divn's inspection. Lts HUGHES & MOAKES reconnoitred road to BOURECQ (starting point for emergency move. Received March table from 47th Bde in case of emergency move. Weather: heavy rain & high SW ~~wind~~ gale in morning fine in afternoon.	

7ae

1875 Wt. W593/826 1,000,000 4/15 J.B.C. & A. A.D.S.S./Forms/C. 2118.

Instructions regarding War Diaries and Intelligence Summaries are contained in F.S. Regs., Part II. and the Staff Manual respectively. Title Pages will be prepared in manuscript.

(7) Duplicate

WAR DIARY
or
INTELLIGENCE SUMMARY
(Erase heading not required.)

Volume III
155th Fd Coy RE

Army Form C. 2118

Place	Date	Hour	Summary of Events and Information	Remarks and references to Appendices
	1916 7bre		Coy paraded for inspection by G.O.C. 16th Divon at 11. a m 159	
ANNEVILLE	17		G O C very pleased with turnout of Coy & congratulated them also on their work in the trenches & ordered a whole holiday for next day afternoon making horse lines & cleaning roads etc Weather fine & sunny	
"	18		Holiday for Coy by order of G O C. Interpreter POTEL proceeded on leave Weather very wet & windy	
"	19		Nos 1 & 2 secs Pontooning across pond near billets Nos 3 & 4 secs Brushwood work Weather fine to fine rain	
"	20		Weather fine & sunny Coy drill 9.30 a m – 11.0 a m Officers riding school in afternoon	
"	21		G.O.C 1st Corps inspected Coy with 47th Inf Bde in line on HURTUBISE road at 11 a m & afterwards troops marched past in column of route. No vehicles 2 p m Coy drill 2 N.C.Os sent to LAIRES to assist Lt MOAKES Weather fine & frosty. Sunny	
	20		Lt MOAKES proceeded to Divl Grenade School LAIRES as instructor in M.E. 2 N.C.O.s proceeded to LAIRES for 1 weeks instruction in grenades 7 O C	

Instructions regarding War Diaries and Intelligence Summaries are contained in F. S. Regs., Part II. and the Staff Manual respectively. Title Pages will be prepared in manuscript.

(8)

WAR DIARY
or
~~INTELLIGENCE SUMMARY~~
(Erase heading not required.)

Army Form C.

Volume III
155th Fd Coy R.E.

Place	Date	Hour	Summary of Events and Information
	1917 Feb		159
RAIMBEVILLE	22		Weather, snowing all day.
			9 a.m. Sections doubling up & down road, then knotting & splicing.
			N.C.O.s + cyclists map reading classes under Lts. HUGHES + JENNINGS
			Lt. O'SULLIVAN ill in bed with headache
"	23		Weather snowing all day
			No 1 section firing on 30x picture range
			No 2 section Brushwood hurdles
			No 3 " unloading pontoons
			No 4 " various
			Coy drill 9 a.m - 10 a.m. except No 1 sect.
			O.C. Capt. CLIFFORD & Sergt MEREDITH re-inoculated by Lt BOYD.
"	24		Weather, snow on ground + hard frost
			Nos 2 + 3 sections firing on 30x picture range + afternoon packing No 1 Pontoon wagon
			No 1 + 4 section squad drill. N.C.O.s + cyclists map reading in morning + finding way on maps in afternoon.
			Remainder Brushwood hurdling on H.Q. mule stables
			1 new riding horse received from remounts.
"	25		Weather hard frost, snowing hard + strong N.E. wind
			Nos 1 + 4 sections shooting on 30x range. Nos 2 + 3 squad drill, gas helmet drill + marking & packing tool wagon [illegible]
			N.C.O.s + cyclists map reading class
			Afternoon Whole Coy marched past Gen Sir CHAS MUNRO Cmdg 1st ARMY, at HURTUBISE cross roads in blinding snowstorm.
			Cyclist orderly returning to 47th Bde HQ had to return to Coy HQ owing to snow knee deep on roads.
			Rations sent out by motor lorry turned up at LIVOSSART. No 2 sect with cook's cart + light spring wagon sent out to bring in rations
			Capt CLIFFORD unable to attend trench mortar conference in BETHUNE owing to after effects of inoculation
			F.a.C.

1875 Wt. W593/826 1,000,000 4/15 J.B.C. & A. A.D.S.S./Forms/C. 2118.

Instructions regarding War Diaries and Intelligence Summaries are contained in F. S. Regs., Part II. and the Staff Manual respectively. Title Pages will be prepared in manuscript.

(9)

WAR DIARY
or
~~INTELLIGENCE SUMMARY~~
(Erase heading not required.)

Volume III
155th Fd Coy RE

Army Form C.

161

Place	Date	Hour	Summary of Events and Information
RANNEVILLE	1916 Feb 26		Weather. slight thaw + slight snow showers.
			Morning Nos 2 + 3 secs firing on 30x range.
			Nos 1 + 4 secs clearing snow off HURTEBISE – MONT CORNET road
			NCOs + Cyclists map reading with Lt HUGHES
			afternoon Coy clearing snow from vehicles cleaning + oiling, 3 sappers under Cpl BUXTON
			Lt O SULLIVAN ill in bed all day with eye-headache
			Interpreter POTEL returned from leave 3 pm
			Orders received from 47th Inf Bde + 16th Divl Engrs to move to BOURECQ on 29th
"	27		Weather same as 26th cold
			Coy drill. Then cleaning of vehicles
			Parade of animals harnessed up on vehicles.
			Orders received re supply + transport arrangements for day of move, 29th, also re advance billetting party.
			Lt HUGHES proceeded to 6th CONNAUGHT RANGERS at FEBVIN PALFART + blew up 12 defective detonators.
"	28		Weather slushy thaw, occasional snow
			Coy repairing damages to billets, cleaning up generally, preparatory to move
			6 G.S. Wagons (Divl Train) arrived 1 30 pm + orders received these were instead of 3 motor lorries.
			Orders by wire received from 47th Inf Bde re being in G.H.Q. reserve from today
			7. O. C.

Instructions regarding War Diaries and Intelligence Summaries are contained in F. S. Regs., Part II. and the Staff Manual respectively. Title Pages will be prepared in manuscript.

(10) duplicate

WAR DIARY
or
~~INTELLIGENCE SUMMARY~~
(Erase heading not required.)

Army Form C

Volume III
155th Fd Coy RE

162

Place	Date	Hour	Summary of Events and Information
BOURECQ	1916 Feb 29		Coy left RANNEVILLE 9 am + marched 2½ miles to starting point, where joined by HQ 47th Inf Bde, 6th CONNAUGHT RANGERS + 7th LEINSTERS. Marched as Bde to COTTES, then Coy turned off + arrived BOURECQ at 12.15 pm + settled into billets spread out along the town.
			Weather fine & sunny, light wind
			Capt CLIFFORD reported arrival of Coy personally to Divl HQ at BUSNES
			A.W.J. [signature] Capt RE OC 155th Fd Coy RE

1875 Wt. W593/826 1,000,000 4/15 J.B.C. & A. A.D.S.S./Forms/C. 2118.

16

1553 CRE

Vol 4

Instructions regarding War Diaries and Intelligence Summaries are contained in F. S. Regs., Part II. and the Staff Manual respectively. Title Pages will be prepared in manuscript.

(1) original

WAR DIARY
or
~~INTELLIGENCE SUMMARY~~
(Erase heading not required.)

Army Form C. 2118

Volume IV
155th Fd Coy RE

Place	Date	Hour	Summary of Events and Information	Remarks and references to Appendices
BOURECQ	1916 March 1		Coy Cleaning up + improving billets + stables etc. Lack of stores for same. O.C. arranged for baths for 2nd. Telephone put in from 47th Inf Bde Hdqrs. Weather fine + sunny	
	2		Coy bathing at Bde Baths BOURECQ Improving billets + baths, making straw mats etc. Weather fine, sunny morning, wet afternoon Interpreter visited 156 Coy at BEUVRY	
	3		Weather wet, hail storm in afternoon. Inspection of rifles, identity discs, 1st field dressings + ampoules. Coy drill postponed owing to wet. Carried on with improvements + cleaning billets etc. Bridging wagons exercised in morning (3 miles).	
	4		Weather snowing, turning to wet. New iron rations issued, most of tins of grocery ration faulty.	
	5		Weather wet morning, cold W wind Employed N.C.O.s & men working till 1 p.m. Orders received from HQ RE + 47th Inf Bde for D.C. scheme in case support required for 1st Corps troops in area. Cpls GIBB + THURLOW returned from Bombing school R.A.C.	

1875 Wt. W593/826 1,000,000 4/15 J.B.C. & A. A.D.S.S./Forms/C. 2118.

Instructions regarding War Diaries and Intelligence Summaries are contained in F. S. Regs., Part II. and the Staff Manual respectively. Title Pages will be prepared in manuscript.

(2) original

WAR DIARY
or
~~INTELLIGENCE SUMMARY~~
(Erase heading not required.)

Volume IV
155th Fd Coy RE

Army Form C. 2118

Place	Date	Hour	Summary of Events and Information	Remarks and references to Appendices
BOURECQ	1916 March 6		Weather heavy snow & thaw. Fine afternoon. Work as usual. 7 Reinforcements (6 sappers 1 Pioneer) arrived from ROUEN. Fitting Light Spring Wagon with heavier wheels & axle. Cpl MAHER reduced to ranks for inefficiency from 6/2/16 Inspected new iron rations, in 191 "grocery rations" OXO cubes faulty or deficient, reported to S.O. 47th Inf Bde.	
	7		Weather, snowing lightly all day. Hard frost night before. Coy drill 9-10 am. Lectures on grenades by Cpls GIBB + THURLOW to each ½ Coy, then work as usual. Finished new wheels + axle to Light Spring wagon Mended burst pipe at Bde. Baths. Orders by telephone from 16th Divn & 47th Inf Bde to move to REVEILLON on 8th Detail orders followed late at night	
LE REVEILLON	8		Snowing all night, but thawing after 9 a.m. sunny Coy passed starting-point BOURECQ church at 9.35 a.m. + marched with 47th Inf Bde to LE REVEILLON (6 miles). Lt HUGHES + interpreter went ahead to billet + found LE REVEILLON could not hold Coy + Chateau still occupied by Corps Amm Column. Lt ~~Hug~~ HUGHES met Staff Capt who alotted part of ALLOUAGNE as billets. Coy arrived 11.30 a.m + settled into billets. Section animals in section billets HQ animals picketed in open near wagon park. Temporary officers' mess found for night. JAC	

Instructions regarding War Diaries and Intelligence Summaries are contained in F. S. Regs., Part II. and the Staff Manual respectively. Title Pages will be prepared in manuscript.

(3) original

WAR DIARY
or
~~INTELLIGENCE SUMMARY~~
(Erase heading not required.)

Volume IV
155th Fd Coy RE

Army Form C. 2118

Place	Date	Hour	Summary of Events and Information	Remarks and references to Appendices
LE REVEILLON	1916 March 9		Weather, hard frost at night. Thawing, sunny day. Coy improving + cleaning billets ~~etc~~, vehicles etc No 1 erecting tarpaulins as stables, Nos 2 + 4 making road to HQ picket lines No 3 making sample ovens. Officers' Mess moved to chateau in afternoon.	
	10		Weather fine, thawing. CRE arrived 9.15 a.m in car + took O.C round to see various bits of work to be started. No 1 section digging bombing ground. No 2 road repairs. No 3 Ovens + road repairs No 4 tarpaulin shelter for stables.	
	11		Weather, fine cold dull. Whole Coy, less employed men on ALLOUAGNE – BURBURE road repairs under Lt HUGHES.	
	12		Weather fine, warm sunny. O.C. with CRE + adjt in car out all day visiting various places. No 1 section BURBURE Road repairs, also fitting pump AMETTES baths. No 2 section proceeded to LOZINGHEM for work at 23 CC Stn hut + at AUCHEL 18th Sqn RFC aerodrome, hutting etc. No 3 section proceeded to LILLERS for work on West Riding C.C. Stn hut + baths [initials]	

1875 Wt. W593/826 1,000,000 4/15 J.B.C. & A. A.D.S.S./Forms/C. 2118.

Instructions regarding War Diaries and Intelligence Summaries are contained in F. S. Regs., Part II. and the Staff Manual respectively. Title Pages will be prepared in manuscript.

(4) original

WAR DIARY
or
~~INTELLIGENCE SUMMARY~~
(Erase heading not required.)

Volume IV
155th Fd Coy R.E.

Army Form C. 2118

Place	Date	Hour	Summary of Events and Information	Remarks and references to Appendices
LE, REVEILLON	1916 March 13		Weather, fine warm, sunny. No 1 section on ~~Burbure~~ BURBURE road repairs. Difficulty with wagons, 1st 8 led astray by RE guide, 2nd 8 had to go long way round owing to direct road being closed one way by APM, result only one tip of slag. 6 Carpenters No 1 sect to FAWU LILLERS to make tables + forms No 4 sect proceeded to LABEUVRIERE for work under Lt MOAKES at Divl Grenade School + Rest stn Huts. Working party for No 2 sect (100 men) did not arrive at AUCHEL + lorries had to be sent home.	
	14		Weather brilliant sunny day Work as before.	
	15		3 horses + 4 mules deficient, 3 horses + 1 mule temporarily unfit matter urgently represented to C.R.E, O C went into question of remounts with AA + QMG. No 3 section at work on motor shelter Div HQ + hutting at W Riding C.C. O.C + Lt HUGHES attended demonstration of infantry assault with various kinds of smoke + rocket signals to show progress at Divl Grenade School LABEUVRIERE. Zeppelin reported to have dropped bombs 2 or 3 miles away at 9 pm Weather dull morning, sunny warm afternoon F.a.c	

1875 Wt. W593/826 1,000,000 4/15 J.B.C. & A. A.D.S.S./Forms/C. 2118.

Instructions regarding War Diaries and Intelligence Summaries are contained in F. S. Regs., Part II. and the Staff Manual respectively. Title Pages will be prepared in manuscript.

(5)

original

WAR DIARY
or
~~INTELLIGENCE SUMMARY~~
(Erase heading not required.)

Army Form C. 2118

Volume IV
155th Fd Coy R E

Place	Date	Hour	Summary of Events and Information	Remarks and references to Appendices
LE REVEILLON	1916 March 16		Weather, warm sunny morning, drizzly afternoon.	
			Ditching finished on BURBURE Road.	
			Preparing map of billet area.	
	17		Weather Dull but warm.	
			ST. PATRICK'S day. General holiday for Divn. Bde Sports 12 noon — 5 pm.	
			Maj F.V. Thompson R.E. new Bde Major 47th Inf Bde vice Maj DUNDAS.	
	18		Weather very fine, slight rain at dusk.	
			Wire from C.RE to repair HURIONVILLE – ECQUEDECQUES road. O.C + Lt HUGHES inspected road, found French repairing ECQ.cle end only required. Divl ARTY also asked to repair by Divl H.Q. O.C. + Lt HUGHES rode on to HQ RE + reported facts.	
	19.		Weather very warm + fine.	
			Work as usual except O.C took 18 C.E party to church	
	20.		Weather very sunny + warm. slight rain 6.p.m	
			Work as usual	
			Half No 1 sect. + Drivers bathed at LILLERS.	
	21		Weather dull, cold, inclined to drizzle	
			Work as usual, remainder no 1 section + drivers ~~wa~~ bathed at LILLERS.	
			Orders re taking over 14 Bis sector, centre Divn 1st Corps Front near LOOS.	
			No 86962 Spr BUDD went on leave ~~9 a.m~~ 2.30. a.m 22nd	
			FAE	

1875 Wt. W593/826 1,000,000 4/15 J.B.C. & A. A.D.S.S./Forms/C. 2118.

Instructions regarding War Diaries and Intelligence Summaries are contained in F. S. Regs., Part II. and the Staff Manual respectively. Title Pages will be prepared in manuscript.

(6)

original

WAR DIARY
or
~~INTELLIGENCE SUMMARY~~
(Erase heading not required.)

Volume IV
155th Fd Coy RE

Army Form C. 2118

Place	Date	Hour	Summary of Events and Information	Remarks and references to Appendices
LE REVEILLON	1916 March 22		Weather drizzly all day.	
			O.C. visited Bde HQ by order to discuss trench work. Arranged for No 2 section to proceed to 91st Fd Coy RE PHILOSOPHE on 23rd in motor buses to take over M.G Empts. O.C. also ordered ~~to~~ by CRE to proceed to PHILOSOPHE on 23rd	
	23		Weather dull, cold, some rain. O.C. left in motor car at 8.30 a.m, went to HQ RE for instructions, thence to MAZINGARBE + PHILOSOPHE. Arranged billets for Coy in huts, then to 91st Coy to take over work	
			Lt. JENNINGS + No 2 section arrived by bus, ~~to tak~~ transport by road, billetted + fed by 91st Coy. Lt JENNINGS + small party up the trenches to take over M.G empts	
			Lt O'SULLIVAN + No 3 section returned to REVEILLON from LILLERS + No 4 section from LABEUVRIERE.	
	24		Weather snowing hard morning, some sunshine in afternoon.	
			O.C. up at 4 a.m picked up OC 91st + walked to front line support line, reserve line + village line. Returned 10:15 a.m. Made plan of billets + chalked them, took over more work from 91st Coy after tea	
			Coy cleaning up + packing vehicles + cleaning billets.	
			12 men No 1 section on BURBURE road repairs, no rolling possible	
			FOC	

Instructions regarding War Diaries and Intelligence Summaries are contained in F. S. Regs., Part II. and the Staff Manual respectively. Title Pages will be prepared in manuscript.

(7)

original

WAR DIARY
or
~~INTELLIGENCE SUMMARY~~
(Erase heading not required.)

Army Form C. 2118

Volume IV
155th Fd Coy RE

Place	Date	Hour	Summary of Events and Information	Remarks and references to Appendices
MAZINGARBE	1916 Novr 25		Weather sunny, snow melting, rain in evening. O.C went to see sample concrete M.G. empt with 91st Coy. Then writing programme of work for sections. Took over all plans + correspondence from 91st Coy. Remainder of Coy proceeded to MAZINGARBE, starting 9 a.m. Dismounted under Lt HUGHES marched to LILLERS + entrained for NOEUX-LES-MINES ~~at~~ (10.31 a.m.) arrived NOEUX 11.11 a.m. marched to MAZINGARBE arrived 12.30 p.m. Mounted under Capt CLIFFORD proceeded by road via LOZINGHEM, MARLES-LES-MINES, BRUAY + NOEUX-LES-MINES ~~+~~ (11 miles) arrived 3 p.m. Men accommodated in huts, H.Q drivers in lofts, horses in shelters + stables, officers' mess ~~es~~ + billets in Chateau. LT MOAKES, 8 NCOs & 9 men No 4 section left behind at Divl. School LABEUVRIERE for instruction of infantry.	
	26.		Weather rainy + windy morning fine afternoon. Coy settling into huts + general internal economy Preparing bridging wagons for transport purposes. Section officers up line examining future work. O.C. corrected trench map from air photo. *JAL*	
	27		Weather very wet. S.W. gale. Work commenced in trenches, Sector PUITS 14 BIS, which is the right brigade sector of the Centre Division, occupied by own 16th Div. and extends from just North of LOOS ~~for~~ about 2500 yds almost due North. Coy area of work includes Front line, support line, reserve line & main communication trenches to Village line. Carried on with M.G. empts in front & reserve lines, and cleared mud & water in places in support line & alleys, also commenced deepening same. *ALB*	

1875 Wt. W593/826 1,000,000 4/15 J.B.C. & A. A.D.S.S./Forms/C. 2118.

Instructions regarding War Diaries and Intelligence Summaries are contained in F. S. Regs., Part II. and the Staff Manual respectively. Title Pages will be prepared in manuscript.

(8) original

WAR DIARY
or
~~INTELLIGENCE SUMMARY~~
(Erase heading not required.)

Volume IV
155th Fd. Coy R.E.

Army Form C. 2118

Place	Date	Hour	Summary of Events and Information	Remarks and references to Appendices
MAZINGARBE	28 MAR 1916		Weather fine day, wet night. S. W. Gale	
			O.C. visited both Bn. Hdqrs in Reserve line, also advanced R E dump & Reserve trench, in morning.	
		Parade 6 pm, return 3 am 29th	No 1 Sect clearing mud & water from RAILWAY & GORDON ALLEYS.	
			" 2 " 3 concrete M.G. empts in SCOTS, CHALK PIT & HUGO LANE respectively, in Reserve line. O.P. for D 71 Bty RFA in CHALK PIT alley behind Reserve line, 6 RA party.	
			3 " clearing mud & water from POSEN alley, left support line & continued No 11 MG empt in front line. 50 inf. working party.	
			4 " Deepening & fire bays on south portion of reserve line between ENGLISH & RAILWAY alleys.	
			Wagons bring back Coy from CRUCIFIX at 2 am nightly.	
	29th		Weather fine & sunny. Wind dying down. Frosty night.	
			O.C. at office work & correcting trench map all day.	
			No 1 Sect deepened RAILWAY alley (down end), revetted corner of GORDON alley & support line, cleared GORDON alley, deepened T heads SCOTS alley. 50 Inf. party.	
			2 " excavating 3 MG empts; fixed loophole, revetted front & fixed roof of O.P. 6 RA party	
			3 " cleared front half POSEN alley, repaired Dressing Stn, cleared N. end support line, continued No 12 MG empt in front line. 50 Inf. party.	
			4 " cleared mud & water S. of ENGLISH alley in Reserve line. Deepened Reserve line N. of ENGLISH alley, making fire steps, laying trench boards. 50 Inf party.	
			Commenced road gangs 6 NCOs & 36 Inf in 6 parties each under a sapper for maintaining main alleys.	
			[signature]	

1875 Wt. W593/826 1,000,000 4/15 J.B.C. & A. A.D.S.S./Forms/C. 2118.

Army Form C. 2118

Instructions regarding War Diaries and Intelligence Summaries are contained in F. S. Regs., Part II. and the Staff Manual respectively. Title Pages will be prepared in manuscript.

(9)

original

WAR DIARY
or
~~INTELLIGENCE SUMMARY~~
(Erase heading not required.)

Volume IV
155th Field Coy. R.E.

Place	Date	Hour	Summary of Events and Information	Remarks and references to Appendices
MAZINGARBE	Mar 30th 1916		Weather fine & sunny. SE wind. Frost at night	
		8 am – 2 pm	O.C. visited Bn Hdqrs in Old British front line, CHALK PIT alley, GUN trench, Bn Hdqrs left sub-sector & went round with O.C. Bn to choose Coy. Hdqrs dug-outs in support line near Boy 10 & HUGO LANE respectively, back by HUGO LANE, Reserve line, GUN trench, CRUCIFIX & RAILWAY alley. Visited Bde Hdqrs to check aeroplane photos & trench map, discussing works, etc.	
		6.40 pm – 3 am	No 1 Sect. deepened down end of RAILWAY alley, cleaned front end SCOTS alley & continued T heads in support line; cleared entrance of Boyau 7, cleaned back end GORDON alley. 45 Inf. party.	
			2 " MG. SCOTS alley fully excavated. breaking bricks 5 Inf. party. MG's HUGO LANE & CHALK PIT alley, excavating & deepening trench to latter. O.P. loophole made under & reset for RA. 6 R A party.	
			3 " MG No 12 continued, repaired one covered traverse in Front line. lowered support line Boyaux 13–14 60 yds by 2 ft. lowered GUN alley, POSEN end, 100 yds by 2 ft. 50 Inf. party	
			4 " carried up & laid trench boards in LOOS end of reserve trench, deepened same N. of RAILWAY alley & made fire steps. pumped water out of SCOTS alley in front of reserve line. 50 Inf.	
			AdeYB	
	31st		Weather fine & sunny. no wind. C.R.E visited Coy Hdqrs 4.30 pm & instructed Coy to deepen RAILWAY & CHALK PIT alleys. O.C. drew cash from Field Cashier & men were paid during the afternoon. O.C. visited Bde Hdqrs at 6 pm & discussed trench work with Brigadier 49th Inf Bde who were taking over trenches from 47th Inf. Bde this evening. Nos 1 & 2 Sections bathed in Divl baths MAZINGARBE. No work in trenches owing to Bde reliefs	

1/4/16

AdeY. Brenner
Capt R E
O.C. 155th Fd Coy R E

1875 Wt. W593/826 1,000,000 4/15 J.B.C. & A. A.D.S.S./Forms/C. 2118.

Instructions regarding War Diaries and Intelligence Summaries are contained in F. S. Regs., Part II. and the Staff Manual respectively. Title Pages will be prepared in manuscript.

(1)

WAR DIARY
or
~~INTELLIGENCE SUMMARY~~
(Erase heading not required.)

Volume V XVI
155th Fd Coy R E

Army Form C. 2118

Vol 5

Place	Date	Hour	Summary of Events and Information	Remarks and references to Appendices
MAZINGARBE	1st April 1916	8 am – 2.15 pm	Weather very fine & warm. Light N E wind. OC visited concrete empts. in Reserve line with Bde M G O to choose alternative sites for M G's in connection with dug-outs for same. Visited GORDON & CAMERON alleys, Bn. Hdqrs RIGHT sub-sector & CRUCIFIX R E store.	
		7 pm – 4 am	No 1 Sect RAILWAY alley deepened in several places. SCOTS alley, worked on one Tee head. GORDON alley. Most of mud removed, worked on 50 yds of block to RESERVE Trench. Front line M G Empt No 5, considerably excavated. 50 Inf party.	
			No 2 Sect 3 concrete M G Empts. excavating & breaking bricks. OP – Revetted interior observation room	
			No 3 Sect Continued No 12 M G Empt Front line & repaired one covered traverse. GUN alley (POSEN end) roofed Bomb store & deepened trench 140 yds by 2 ft. 100 Inf party.	
			No 4 Sect Pumped water from CAMERON alley & RESERVE trench here, carried & laid trench boards also in RESERVE trench. Deepened & formed fire steps in RESERVE trench N. of ENGLISH alley & cut electric cables there. 50 Inf party.	AOTYD
	2nd		Weather very fine & warm. No wind. CRE visited billets at 1 pm. Pumped out sewage tank in 111th Fd Amb. Church service by Rev BROWN CF at 3.30 pm. Blew up 5.9" blind shell with 2 lbs guncotton, successfully. OC visited 47th Inf Bde Hdqrs at 5 pm & settled R E trench work with Brigadier.	
		7 pm – 4 am	No 1 Sect SCOTS alley worked on 2 Tee heads. M G Empt No 5 excavating. GORDON alley – all mud removed & passage cleared to RESERVE line, but still requires deepening. 50 Inf party.	
			No 2 Sect M.G. Empt SCOTS alley, carried up cement, stone, sand & mixing gear; Sapping from gun pit to cellar. HUGO & CHALK PIT Empts, excavating. O.P. Framing entrance & revetting above 3' x 2' shaft.	
			No 3 Sect M G Empt No 12. Work stopped owing to hostile Trench mortars. One covered traverse in Front line repaired. Deepened part of Support line & also POSEN alley. 50 Inf party	
			No 4 Sect CAMERON alley. Cleared of water. Deepening RES. line. N of SCOTS alley – deepened, carried up & laid boards in RES line. N of ENGLISH alley, laid boards, deepened, made fire-steps, elbow rests, etc. Cleared mud & water out of SCOTS alley up to Gordon alley. 50 Inf party	AOTYD

1875 Wt. W593/826 1,000,000 4/15 J.B.C. & A. A.D.S.S./Forms/C. 2118.

Instructions regarding War Diaries and Intelligence Summaries are contained in F. S. Regs., Part II. and the Staff Manual respectively. Title Pages will be prepared in manuscript.

(2)

WAR DIARY
or
~~INTELLIGENCE SUMMARY~~
(Erase heading not required.)

Army Form C. 2118

Volume V
155th Fd. Coy. R.E.

Place	Date	Hour	Summary of Events and Information	Remarks and references to Appendices
MAZINGARBE	3rd April 1916		Weather very fine & warm. no wind. O.C. with Bde Major 49th Inf. Bde visited Bn. Hdqrs R. sub-sector & front line. Shelled with 4.2" H.E. down end of GORDON alleys but fortunately two were blind. No 1 Sect. SCOTS alley T heads continued. MG Empts 4 & 5 excavating. No 3 Empt resited in Bay 37/8 & work started. ~~[illegible]~~ No 2 Sect M.G. SCOTS alley - Sapping entrance to cellar & entrance from Trench. MG's HUGO & CHALK PIT - excavating. O.P. - Revetting above shaft & blinding roof & loophole. CRUCIFIX - deepening entrance to RE store No 3 Sect Boyau 6 - Started to straighten trench for loophole traverse. No 4 Sect Forming fire steps & revetting in Reserve Trench. N. of ENGLISH alley & from junction of GORDON in SCOTS alley. No working parties owing to relief of R. Bn. AOH	
	4th	Night work	Weather dull & foggy. Very quiet. O.C. visited Bde Hdqrs & discussed probable crater fighting with G.O.C. No 1 Sect MG Empts Nos 3, 4 & 5 excavating & materials carried up. GORDON alley - Block cleared & made passable. SCOTS alley - T heads continued. 50 Inf party No 2 Sect MG SCOTS No R2. carried up materials. Sapping from entrance to cellar & trench. MG CHALK PIT No R7 } excavating & carried up iron sheets to conceal work. " HUGO LANE No R9 } O.P. Revetting passage to shaft. CRUCIFIX. Deepening entrance. 50 Inf party No 3 Sect M.G. No 12 continued. Carried up timber for M.O's post. Deepening Boyau 6. 50 Inf. No 4 Sect Res. Line (SCOTS) Deepened & laid boards. " " (N. of ENGLISH alley) Deepened, laid boards, made fire step, revetted fire bays & levelled parapet. 75 Inf. AOH	

1875 Wt. W593/826 1,000,000 4/15 J.B.C. & A. A.D.S.S./Forms/C. 2118.

Instructions regarding War Diaries and Intelligence Summaries are contained in F. S. Regs., Part II. and the Staff Manual respectively. Title Pages will be prepared in manuscript.

(3)

WAR DIARY
or
~~INTELLIGENCE SUMMARY~~
(Erase heading not required.)

Army Form C. 2118

Volume V
155 Fld Co R E

Place	Date	Hour	Summary of Events and Information	Remarks and references to Appendices
Mazingarbe	April 5th		Weather dull, with slight mist. No 1 Section Excavating on MG 3.4.5. Continuing construction of T. Heads on SCOTS Alley. Work started on Loophole Traverses in Cameron & Gordon Alleys. No 2 Section Sapping entrance to MG on SCOTS alley, staying out stores for concrete work. Excavating for MG on HUGO Lane & CHALK PIT; roofing in 3'x2' shaft for O.P. No 3 Section Started to clear out BOYAU 11. Began work on M.G. 13 & 14. No 4 Section Deepening & laying racks on Reserve trench near SCOTS Alley. Made firesteps in Reserve trench North of ENGLISH Alley. Bde Major called in the evening & spoke urgent work to be done on shelters for Infantry behind traverses. Capt BRENNER went on leave.	
do	April 6th	Work / Night	Weather dull. G.O.C 49th Bde pointed urgency of roofing in backs of traverses due to large casualties from grenades etc & asked that all work be stopped to do this. He also arranged for a new trench to be dug behind Chalk pit after consultation with G.O.C 16th Div & C.R.E. Infantry practised at marching on to a tape. No 1 Section roofed in one traverse & prepared 4 in F. line N of SCOTS Alley. Difficulties arose with regard to transport of material (Relief night). No 2 Section found emplacement in SCOTS Alley removed by shellfire would therefore do no concreting; excavated on MG HUGO Lane & CHALK PIT alleys. No 3 Section Lt O'Sullivan reconnoitred new trench & found it 260 yds long, needing 250 men in 2 reliefs. Made two emplacements urgently required in case of Mines at Bays 143 & 162. No 4 Section Worked on traverses, as this was very urgent, finished one & prepared four.	

Instructions regarding War Diaries and Intelligence Summaries are contained in F. S. Regs., Part II. and the Staff Manual respectively. Title Pages will be prepared in manuscript.

(4)

WAR DIARY
or
~~INTELLIGENCE SUMMARY~~
(Erase heading not required.)

Army Form C. 2118

Volume V
155th Fd Coy RE

Place	Date	Hour	Summary of Events and Information	Remarks and references to Appendices
MAZINGARBE	1916 April 7		weather fine.	
			CRE called early re new trench + said Pioneers would dig it after Lt. O'SULLIVAN had laid it out, + made arrangements personally with C.O. 11th Hants.	
			No 1 section overhead cover behind traverses in front line.	
			No 2 section M.G. empls SCOTS ALLEY, CHALKPIT ALLEY, + HUGO ALLEY + OP in CHALKPIT ALLEY.	
			No 3 section Marked out new trench from BOYAU No 11 to HUGO ALLEY + cleared approaches. Bringing up timber etc for covered traverses. Completed Medical Aid Post in POSEN ALLEY	
		Night-work	No 4 section Covered in traverses in support line N of SCOTS ALLEY.	
			Capt CLIFFORD returned from leave in evening + took over command of Company.	
	8		Weather fine, moonlight at night.	
			No 1 section overhead cover for traverses in front line.	
			No 2 section as before	
			No 3 section Clearing Boyau 11	
			No 4 section overhead cover for traverses, support line.	
	9		Weather dull but dry.	
			Capt CLIFFORD visited CRA with CRE with reference to Howitzer in CHALKPIT.	
			No work owing to reliefs.	
			35 Infantry joined Coy for mining.	
			F.A.C.	

1875 Wt. W593/826 1,000,000 4/15 J.B.C. & A. A.D.S.S./Forms/C. 2118.

Instructions regarding War Diaries and Intelligence Summaries are contained in F. S. Regs., Part II. and the Staff Manual respectively. Title Pages will be prepared in manuscript.

(5)

WAR DIARY

or

~~INTELLIGENCE SUMMARY~~

(Erase heading not required.)

Army Form C. 2118

Volume V
155th Fd Coy RE

Place	Date	Hour	Summary of Events and Information	Remarks and references to Appendices
MAZINGARBE	1916 April 10		Weather bright + sunny, moonlight night Capt CLIFFORD visited Bde H.Q to see G.O.C. 48th Bde about work he wishes carried out when he comes in. No 1 section Covering in traverses, listening galleries sited. No 2 section M.G Empts + O.P. in CHALKPIT ALLEY. No 3 section Covering in traverses + cleaning out BOYAU 11. No 4 section covering in traverses	
	11	Night work	Weather raining morning, clearing later, moonlight night Nos 1, 3 + 4 sections covering in traverses. No 2 section M.G. Empts + O.P. Listening Galleries started.	
	12.		Weather rainy, stormy. 48th Inf Bde relieved 49th in consequence no work except listening galleries	
	13		Weather, some sun, some showers, stormy, moonlight night Capt CLIFFORD selected sites for 5 M.G. Dug-outs in RESERVE TRENCH, POSEN ALLEY + GUN TRENCH FOSSE 3 heavily shelled + store disorganised in consequence. Listening galleries continued. M.G. Dug-outs started with 10 sappers from Nos 2 + 4 sections + 24 Bde Pioneers. Remainder Nos 1+4 Sections covering in traverses in R sub sector No 3 section covering in traverses L sub-sector, loop-holing traverse + clearing HOWITZER TRENCH No 2 section CHALKPIT ALLEY (No 2R) + HUGO LANE (No 3R) M.G Empts + CHALKPIT ALLEY O.P. TAE	

1875 Wt. W593/826 1,000,000 4/15 J.B.C. & A. A.D.S.S./Forms/C. 2118.

Instructions regarding War Diaries and Intelligence Summaries are contained in F. S. Regs., Part II. and the Staff Manual respectively. Title Pages will be prepared in manuscript.

(6)

WAR DIARY
or
~~INTELLIGENCE SUMMARY~~
(Erase heading not required.)

Army Form C. 2118

Volume V
155th Fd Coy RE

Place	Date	Hour	Summary of Events and Information	Remarks and references to Appendices
MAZINGARBE	1916 April 14	night work	Weather, showery, windy Work continued on Listening-galleries + M.G dug-outs (all No 4 section absorbed by this work) No 1 section roofing in traverses No 3 section " " " + cleaning out HOWITZER TRENCH No 2 section CHALKPIT ALLEY O.P. & started dug-out for MG empl 2R.	
	15		Weather windy, showery some snow Listening-galleries + M.G. Dug-outs continued No 1 section covering in traverses No 2 section O.P. M.G Empts + dug-outs No 3 section covering in traverses + clearing HOWITZER TRENCH	
	16		Weather fine, rain at night Capt BREMNER returned from leave in evening + took command of Coy. No working parties owing to Bn reliefs. Listening-galleries carried on. No 2 section continued with M.G Empts + dugouts } (24 Bde pioneers) No 4 section " " Dug-outs }	

Jae

Instructions regarding War Diaries and Intelligence Summaries are contained in F. S. Regs., Part II. and the Staff Manual respectively. Title Pages will be prepared in manuscript.

(7)

WAR DIARY
or
~~INTELLIGENCE SUMMARY~~
(Erase heading not required.)

Army Form C. 2118

Volume V
155th Fd Coy RE

Place	Date	Hour	Summary of Events and Information	Remarks and references to Appendices
MAZINGARBE	1916 april 17		weather, dull windy, raing	
			Listening galleries continued, during night of 17/18 sounds of picking heard, apparently quite close.	
			No 1 sect covering in traverses (50 inf)	
			No 2 sect O.P., M.G. empts + dug-outs (50 inf + 10 Bde Pioneers)	
			No 3 sect covering in traverses + firestepping CORK TRENCH (80 inf)	
			No 4 sect M.G. Dug-outs (30 inf + 15 Bde Pioneers)	
	18	night work	Weather, raing, windy, cold.	
			Listening Galleries + Dug-outs continued. 24 Bde Pioneers, 40 inf + remains No 4 sect on dug-outs	
			No 1 sect Covered traverses (40 inf)	
			No 2 sect O.P., M.G. empts + dug-outs (40 inf)	
			No 3 sect Covered traverses (40 inf)	
	19		Weather raing windy, very wet night	
			Listening galleries continued (35 inf + 20 sprs of Nos 1+4 sections)	
			M.G. Dug outs continued (24 Bde Pioneers, 10 inf + 10 sprs from Nos 2+4 sections)	
			No 1 section repairing covered traverses, dug out for M.G 207, RAILWAY ALLEY + dug-out for Coy HQ in SUPPORT LINE between ENGLISH + SCOTS ALLEYS. (30 inf)	
			No 2 sect M.G empts + dug outs + O.P. (30 inf + 6 arty)	
			No 3 sect M.G. empt HOWITZER TRENCH, dug-outs CORK TRENCH + BOYAU 14 (45 inf)	
	20		Weather, dull, raing windy	
			Listening galleries continued	
			No 2 sect Continued O.P.	
			No other work as no working parties available on account of Bn reliefs	
			F.a.e.	

1875 Wt. W593/826 1,000,000 4/15 J.B.C. & A. A.D.S.S./Forms/C. 2118.

Instructions regarding War Diaries and Intelligence Summaries are contained in F. S. Regs., Part II. and the Staff Manual respectively. Title Pages will be prepared in manuscript.

(8)

WAR DIARY
or
~~INTELLIGENCE SUMMARY~~
(Erase heading not required.)

Volume V
155th Fd Coy R E

Army Form C. 2118

Place	Date	Hour	Summary of Events and Information	Remarks and references to Appendices
MAZINGARBE	1916 April 21st		Fine morning, wet & windy rest of day & night. Capt CLIFFORD visited 48th Bde Hdqrs re work. OC. 156th Fd Coy RE & officers visited Coy. H.Q. with a view to taking over work from Coy on 23/24th. OC. on light duty. No 1 Sect. covering entrance to Listening gallery No 2. Dug out for MG 7 in Front line N of RAILWAY Alley Coy HQ S. of ENGLISH alley in Support line; also 3 traverses repaired in Support line (50 inf) No 2 Sect 3 concrete MG empts (2 with dug outs) & 2 other M.G. dug outs & O.P. " (50 inf) No 3 Sect clearing bad MG empt HOWITZER trench & starting afresh. MG dug out CORK trench. Work delayed by hostile shelling. (50 inf) No 4 Sect 3 MG dug outs in Reserve line & GUN trench (50 inf)	[illegible]
	22		Wet morning, very wet night. Capt CLIFFORD took O.C 156th Fd Coy round trenches to take over work. No 1 sect Dug-outs & covered traverses No 2 sect M.G. Empts, dug-outs + O.P. No 3 sect Clearing GALWAY TRENCH, M.G. Empt & dug-outs No 4 sect M.G. dug outs	
	23		weather fine (EASTER DAY) Coy completed handing over to 156 Coy. No work at night by order of G.O.C Divn.	
	24		Weather fine. O.C. left for NOEUX-LES-MINES to take over duties of CRE (on leave). Capt CLIFFORD left in command of Coy No 1 sect ballasting railway (40 inf + 6 G.S wagons) No 2 sect O.P + M.G empts CHALKPIT ALLEY (no inf arrived) No 3 sect Pipe line FOSSE 3 to FOSSE 7 (40 inf) No 4 sect miscellaneous. J.A.C.	

1875 Wt. W593/826 1,000,000 4/15 J.B.C. & A. A.D.S.S./Forms/C. 2118.

Instructions regarding War Diaries and Intelligence Summaries are contained in F. S. Regs., Part II. and the Staff Manual respectively. Title Pages will be prepared in manuscript.

(9)

WAR DIARY
or
~~INTELLIGENCE SUMMARY~~
(Erase heading not required.)

Army Form C. 2118

Volume V
155th Fd Coy RE

Place	Date	Hour	Summary of Events and Information	Remarks and references to Appendices
MAZINGARBE	1916 april 25		Weather fine	
			Work as before. Party for No 2 sect again did not arrive + party for No 3 sect went to wrong rendezvous.	
	26		weather fine	
			Work as before. again no party for No 2 sect.	
	27		Weather fine hot slight Easterly breeze in morning	
		a.m	Hostile gas attack.	
		4.30	men warned	
		4.15–5.0	Officers wakened by heavy firing, largely with tear-shells.	
		5.10	Warning sounded by "Strombus" horn.	
		5.20	Warning received by telephone.	
		6.50	gas cloud arrived at MAZINGARBE, pretty thick at first but thinning pretty rapidly.	
		7.30	air clear again	
		8.0	Firing practically ceased.	
			Intermittent shelling of Fosse 3 + neighbourhood during morning.	
			Company standing-by all day.	
		p.m 6.55	second gas alarm (Strombus horn) but wind Northerly.	
			10 men No 1 sect, repairing road-bridge + railway near POSEN STATION. Jae	

1875 Wt. W593/826 1,000,000 4/15 J.B.C. & A. A.D.S.S./Forms/C. 2118.

Instructions regarding War Diaries and Intelligence Summaries are contained in F. S. Regs., Part II. and the Staff Manual respectively. Title Pages will be prepared in manuscript.

(10)

WAR DIARY
or
~~INTELLIGENCE SUMMARY~~
(Erase heading not required.)

Army Form C. 2118

Volume V
155th Fd Coy R.E.

Place	Date	Hour	Summary of Events and Information	Remarks and references to Appendices
MAZINGARBE	1916 April 28		Weather fine, wind easterly.	
			Nos 1+2 sections detailed to assist 156th Coy repairing front line 14 bis sector by night, good progress made.	
			Nos 3+4 sections detailed to assist 157th Coy repairing front line HULLUCH sector by night. No work done owing to gas alarm.	
		p.m 8.45	Intensive bombardment started.	
		9.5	Gas alarm sounded.	
		9.30	2nd gas alarm sounded, warning received by 'phone. Intensive bombardment ceased	
	29		Weather fine, wind easterly.	
		a.m 4.0	Gas alarm, intensive bombardment	
		4.10	alarm by 'phone.	
		4.45	Fire slackened.	
			Demonstration of wire-cutting by "Bangalore torpedo" arranged for midday for G.O.C. Divn to see. Quite successful. F.a.C	
	30		Weather fine wind north-easterly	
			No 1 Sect repaired railway + RAME dug out PHILOSOPHE	
			No 2 Sect O.P+M.G empls CHALKPIT ALLEY, Well.	
			No 3. Pipe-line	
			No 4. Miscellaneous.	
			F a clifford Capt RE O.C 155th Fd Coy RE	

Instructions regarding War Diaries and Intelligence Summaries are contained in F. S. Regs., Part II. and the Staff Manual respectively. Title Pages will be prepared in manuscript.

(1)

WAR DIARY
or
~~INTELLIGENCE SUMMARY~~
(Erase heading not required.)

Army Form C. 2118

Volume VI
155th Fd Coy R.E.
Vol 6

XVI

Place	Date	Hour	Summary of Events and Information	Remarks and references to Appendices
MAZINGARBE	1916 May 1		Weather fine, wind north-easterly.	
			5 O.R. (oxy-acetylene personnel) sent to base leaving strength of Company	
			6 officers + 218 O.R including following not with Company	
			1 Officer acting C.R.E.	
			1 " on leave	
			1 " + 6 O.R at Divl Grenade school.	
			6 O.R at H.Q.R.E.	
			1 O.R attached 48th Inf Bde.	
			1 O.R. " A.S.C.	
			1 O.R. at Bomb store, MAZINGARBE.	
		night - work	No 1 sect repaired + ballasted Railway, repaired R.A.M.C dug-out PHILOSOPHE + repaired road bridge nr PHILOSOPHE Railway Crossing (40 inf)	
			No 2 sect. Excavating O.P., deepening sap to M.G empt, fixing windlass at well. PHILOSOPHE water supply	
			No 3 sect Dug-out No 78 (continuous work). Pipe line, FOSSE 3 to FOSSE 7 (250 ft done to date) (40 inf	
			No 4 sect. MAZINGARBE bomb store + miscellaneous.	
	2		Weather dull, a little rain in morning, clearing in aft, wind South-westerly.	
			No 1 sect. work as before (40 inf)	
			No 2 sect Work as before	
			No 3 sect Dug-out 78 completed, 500 ft pipe-line ~~comp~~ (40 inf)	
			No 4 sect. completed rack MAZINGARBE bomb-store + miscellaneous	
			F.a.c.	

Instructions regarding War Diaries and Intelligence Summaries are contained in F. S. Regs., Part II. and the Staff Manual respectively. Title Pages will be prepared in manuscript.

(2)

WAR DIARY
or
~~INTELLIGENCE SUMMARY~~
(Erase heading not required.)

Army Form C. 2118

Volume VI
155th Fd Coy RE

Place	Date	Hour	Summary of Events and Information	Remarks and references to Appendices
MAZINGARBE	1916 May 3		Weather fine wind mainly westerly.	
		a m 1·45	Gas alarm by telephone	
		2·10	" " Cancelled " "	
		p m 9·5	" " by telephone.	
		night work	No 1 sect ballasting & repairing railway, R.A.M.C dug-out PHILOSOPHE, 2 bridges near Railway completed (40 inf)	
			No 2 sect O.P. CHALKPIT ALLEY, well, M.G. empls. CHALKPIT ALLEY	
			No 3 sect Pipe line (40 inf)	
			No 4 sect miscellaneous. JAC	
	4		Weather fine to cloudy, wind east to South-west.	
			No 1 sect work as before (40 inf)	
			No 2 sect " " " + O.P. in Village line (30 inf)	
			No 3 sect Pipe line (40 inf)	
			No 4 sect miscellaneous JAC	
	5		Weather dull, hot, dusty, a little rain in aft. wind changeable.	
			Company ordered to vacate huts & take over filthy billets.	
			Work as before.	
			Handing over to 157th Fd Coy RE.	
	6.		Weather dull, some rain, wind variable.	
			Taking over line from 157th Coy. No work owing to Brigade change.	
			Decided to put men in tents in garden of VILLA ARNOULD	
			Lt O'SULLIVAN went on leave. JAC	

1875 Wt. W593/826 1,000,000 4/15 J.B.C. & A. A.D.S.S./Forms/C. 2118.

Instructions regarding War Diaries and Intelligence Summaries are contained in F. S. Regs., Part II. and the Staff Manual respectively. Title Pages will be prepared in manuscript.

(3)

WAR DIARY
or
~~INTELLIGENCE SUMMARY~~
(Erase heading not required.)

Army Form C. 2118

Volume VI
155th Fd Coy R.E.

Place	Date	Hour	Summary of Events and Information	Remarks and references to Appendices
MAZINGARBE	1916 May 7		Weather cloudy, some rain, wind variable. Lt HUGHES returned from leave. Company fixing up tents and shelters in garden at VILLA ARNOULD. No work at night owing to Brigadier ~~changing plans~~ upsetting plans lat in afternoon. r.a.c	
	8	Continuous work	Weather cloudy some rain, strong W wind. No 1 sect. Listening Gallery No 17, Dug-out in Reserve line between POSEN ALLEY and VENDIN ALLEY. No 2 sect "The Daisy" O.P. WINGS WAY + Dug-out in RESERVE line between POSEN + VENDIN, ALLEYS No 3 sect 3 dug-outs in RESERVE line between POSEN + VENDIN ALLEYS. No 4 sect Listening Gallery No 18, 2 Dug-outs in SUPPORT LINE between TREE LANE and 20th AVENUE. Sounds of picking heard from L.G No 18.	
	9.		Weather dull, wet, cold. 2/Lt HEGARTY, RE(T.C) joined Company Work as before Plan + instructions received re consolidation of Craters r.a.c	

1875 Wt. W593/826 1,000,000 4/15 J.B.C. & A. A.D.S.S./Forms/C. 2118.

Instructions regarding War Diaries and Intelligence Summaries are contained in F. S. Regs., Part II. and the Staff Manual respectively. Title Pages will be prepared in manuscript.

(4)

WAR DIARY
or
~~INTELLIGENCE SUMMARY~~
(Erase heading not required.)

Army Form C. 2118

Volume VI
155th Fd Coy RE

Place	Date	Hour	Summary of Events and Information	Remarks and references to Appendices
MAZINGARBE	1916 May 10	night work	Weather fine.	
			Portions nos 1, 2, 4 sections Crater-work	
		continuous work	Remainder nos 1 + 4 Listening Galleries.	
			Remainder no. 2. O.P. "The Daisy"	
			No 3 Dug-outs, RESERVE LINE	
			1 Spr wounded (slightly) by shrapnel in trenches	
	11		Weather dry	
			Heavy shelling of PHILOSOPHE + neighbourhood in afternoon.	
			Orders received to cancel work for night. F.a.C	
	12	continuous work	Weather dry	
			Work as on 10th.	
	13		Weather raining. Capt BREMNER returned + took command of Coy.	
			Work as on 10th. KINGSBRIDGE stn opened.	
	14		Weather fine, but dull. Tried mule drawing trucks along tramway, quite successful.	
			Crater + Listening Gallery parties turned back from Tenth Avenue on account of 'strafe' on 15th Divn front, Lts HUGHES + JENNINGS reported all quiet on our front	
	15.		Weather very wet early, fine later with strong S.W wind.	
			Work as usual but pushing party reported to 156 Coy until put right at 9.p.m. Mule tried for pulling trucks along line to QUARRY DUMP, quite successful	
			Lt JENNINGS went on leave. F.a.C	

1875 Wt. W593/826 1,000,000 4/15 J.B.C. & A. A.D.S.S./Forms/C. 2118.

Instructions regarding War Diaries and Intelligence Summaries are contained in F. S. Regs., Part II. and the Staff Manual respectively. Title Pages will be prepared in manuscript.

(5)

WAR DIARY
or
~~INTELLIGENCE SUMMARY~~
(Erase heading not required.)

Volume VI
155th Fd Coy RE

Army Form C. 2118

Place	Date	Hour	Summary of Events and Information	Remarks and references to Appendices
MAZINGARBE	1916 May 16		Weather fine & hot.	
			Brigade side stepped to south, taking up front VENDIN ALLEY to ENGLISH ALLEY.	
			Reorganised store arrangements, Right Bns drawing material from CRUCIFIX STORE + left from QUARRY DUMP	
			Section work organised as follows, each section to do any work required in its sector.	
			No 1 section frontage H. 19.6 — H 19.2 & VENDIN ALLEY	
			No 2 section " H. 19.1 — H 25.6 & POSEN ALLEY	
			No 4 section " H 25.5 — Boyau 52 + CHALKPIT ALLEY	
			No 3 section " Boyau 52 — H 31.6 + RAILWAY ALLEY	
			Working on dug-outs in Front, Support & Reserve lines	
			No 4 section also on new defences CHALKPIT Salient	
			No 3 section also on Listening Galleries nos 2+3 (new numbers 16+17)	
			All sections going round trenches to find actual site of work.	
			1st shift for Listening Galleries ~~started~~ left at 8 p.m	
	17		Weather lovely + warm, no wind.	
			O.C arranged carrying parties etc with 48th Inf Bde	
			Lt. O'SULLIVAN returned from leave	
			sections assisting Infantry with dug outs by day + night	
	18		Weather very hot, foggy early.	
			O.C went sick in afternoon	
			Work as before.	
			FAE	

1875 Wt. W593/826 1,000,000 4/15 J.B.C. & A. A.D.S.S./Forms/C. 2118.

Instructions regarding War Diaries and Intelligence Summaries are contained in F. S. Regs., Part II. and the Staff Manual respectively. Title Pages will be prepared in manuscript.

(6)

WAR DIARY
or
~~INTELLIGENCE SUMMARY~~
(Erase heading not required.)

Volume VI
155th Fd Coy RE

Army Form C. 2118

Place	Date	Hour	Summary of Events and Information	Remarks and references to Appendices
MAZINGARBE	1916 May 19		Weather very hot & sunny Work as usual O.C in bed (sick) 48th Bde want us to dig new trench N of PAT TRENCH, matter referred to CRE	
	20		Weather very fine + warm. O.C. recovering G.O.C ordered 48th Bde to dig trench themselves, Bde wants 2 RE officers to superintend the work, only Lt HUGHES available. No work on dug outs at night owing to Bn reliefs.	
	21		Weather very fine + warm, night foggy. O.C. still on sick list Report sent to CRE with reference to Lt HUGHES work on new trench. Work as usual.	
	22		Weather very fine morning, dull afternoon. O.C resumed control of company but is ordered to avoid physical fatigue. Work as usual.	
	23		Weather very fine & warm. Bde ordered 1 officer + 3 OR to accompany a raid for night 23/24. Lt HUGHES warned for it as it is in his sector but he is very tired, having been up the trenches all day. 2/Lt HEGARTY volunteered to accompany him. Bde postponed raid as weather unsuitable. Work as usual.	
	24		Weather, fine morning, drizzly aft. O.C. Lts HUGHES + HEGARTY being to preparation of charges for raid but raid cancelled. Work as usual. F.O.C.	

1875 Wt. W593/826 1,000,000 4/15 J.B.C. & A. A.D.S.S./Forms/C. 2118.

Instructions regarding War Diaries and Intelligence Summaries are contained in F. S. Regs., Part II. and the Staff Manual respectively. Title Pages will be prepared in manuscript.

(7)

WAR DIARY
or
~~INTELLIGENCE SUMMARY~~
(Erase heading not required.)

Volume VI
155th Fd Coy RE

Army Form C. 2118

Place	Date	Hour	Summary of Events and Information	Remarks and references to Appendices
MAZINGARBE	1916 May 25		Weather, wet morning, fine afternoon.	
			Work as usual.	
			Capt. CRICHTON R.M.F. in charge of work on dug-outs ~~[illegible]~~ for 47th Bde arranged with us for work on dug-outs as follows:–	
			11 dug outs in support line, 12 in reserve line, with 42 RE + 92 infantry which gives, 1 RE + 2 Infantry on each shaft except for No 3 section who are doing Nos 16 + 17 (old 2 + 3) Listening Galleries. Work by day ~~[illegible]~~ only on dug-outs	
	~~26~~ 26		Weather fine + sunny. Cool.	
			Work carried on as detailed above	
	27		Weather sunny but cool.	
			Lt JENNINGS returned from leave.	
			Work as on 26th. All dug-outs now numbered.	
			CRE rang up at 8 pm + ordered all parties for tonight to be cancelled owing to rumours of possible hostile attack.	
		10.30 pm	received orders from 47th Inf Bde to take 100 5th Northants Pion + firestep FOREST TRENCH. Made all preparations + referred matter to Adjt RE who, after speaking to G.S.O.1 cancelled it all as party would not have been able to get to site of work before daylight.	
			FAE	

1875 Wt. W593/826 1,000,000 4/15 J.B.C. & A. A.D.S.S./Forms/C. 2118.

Instructions regarding War Diaries and Intelligence Summaries are contained in F. S. Regs., Part II. and the Staff Manual respectively. Title Pages will be prepared in manuscript.

(8)

WAR DIARY
or
~~INTELLIGENCE SUMMARY~~
(Erase heading not required.)

Volume VI
155th Fd Coy RE

Army Form C. 2118

Place	Date	Hour	Summary of Events and Information	Remarks and references to Appendices
MAZINGARBE	1916 May 28		Weather fine & hot No 4 sect fire-stepped nearly all FOREST TRENCH by day. Other work on dug-outs & Listening Galleries as usual, but no carrying or pushing parties. J.A.C.	
	29		Weather very hot & sunny, rain at night Fire stepping FOREST TRENCH & working on dug-outs by day. Lt HUGHES placed Norton tube pump in fallen in well in SUPPORT LINE S of BOYAU 66. J.A.C.	
	30		Weather fine & warm Work as 29th but only half dug-out infantry were available & at 9.30 am instead of 7.15 am owing to their having been on carrying last night. and No 2 section with 50 inf firestepping MEATH TRENCH & No 4 section had 50 inf for FOREST TRENCH J.A.C.	
	31		Weather fine & sunny, cool West breeze. Work continued on Dug-outs & Listening Gallery No 17(3), L.G. No 16(2) Completed. 11 sprs No 2 sect firestepping MEATH TRENCH No 4 section clearing parapet of FOREST TRENCH by night. J.A.C. A.J. Brenner Capt RE O.C. 155th Fd Coy R.E. 1/6/16	

Instructions regarding War Diaries and Intelligence Summaries are contained in F. S. Regs., Part II. and the Staff Manual respectively. Title Pages will be prepared in manuscript.

(1)

WAR DIARY
or
~~INTELLIGENCE SUMMARY~~
(Erase heading not required.)

XVI

Volume VII
155th Fd Coy RE

Army Form C. 2118

Vol 7

Place	Date	Hour	Summary of Events and Information	Remarks and references to Appendices
MAZINGARBE	1916 June 1		Weather, warm sun, cool west breeze Handed over No 16 Listening Gallery (completed) to 47th Inf Bde. Lt. O'SULLIVAN detailed to assist Inf on SUPPORT LINE S of RAILWAY ALLEY. Coy working on dug-outs + started Nos 29 + 29A R. Sub sect + No 3A L Sub-sect.	
	2		Weather, warm sun, cool West Breeze. O.C handed over work on 14 bis sector to O.C. 156th Fd Coy + took over reserve work as from night of 4/5. ~~Sp~~ 1. O.R. wounded severely in leg + eye by shell at junct RAILWAY + ENGLISH ALLEYS. Work as on 1st	
	3		Weather as 2nd Work as before. Section officers handing over to section officers of 156th Coy. all carrying parties cancelled for night. JAE	
	4		Weather as on 1st King's Birthday honours. Capt BREMNER (O.C) Military Cross. ~~Work~~ Coy went into Reserve + took over work as below No 1 section Repair of railways as required, Ballasting wooden track beyond 2100x (Inf 1 ofr 40 OR + 6 G Swagons) completing digging new ADS 350x up CHALKPIT ALLEY (12 men 7th SUFFOLKS) No 2 section RAILWAY ALLEY M.G. Empts. V3 + V4 not yet started. V5 Concreted wall up to 3'6" no dug-out V6, frame up 8'2" x 6'10", revetted partly. No dug-out. V8 CHALKPIT ALLEY Provide screen for loophole. V9 hit by shell, wants cutting away + remaking. Wants table. Inf party 2 N.COS 25 O.R. No 3 section Survey O.P. Carry on with dug-out. 65-Metre Redoubt convert 4 shafts into 2 dug-outs + 2 shafts into 1 provision + SAA store. Laying 2" pipe FOSSES 7-3 2/3 completed. Maintenance of water supply to trenches. 7th Suffolks 16 men per relief parading 8:30 am 1.00 pm + 5:30 pm. No 4 section LENS RD REDOUBT making new dug-out as provision store. New OP in Water Tower for D/180, C/77 + 177 Heavy RGA Battys. JAE	

1875 Wt. W593/826 1,000,000 4/15 J.B.C. & A. A.D.S.S./Forms/C. 2118.

Instructions regarding War Diaries and Intelligence Summaries are contained in F. S. Regs., Part II. and the Staff Manual respectively. Title Pages will be prepared in manuscript.

(2)

WAR DIARY
or
~~INTELLIGENCE SUMMARY~~
(Erase heading not required.)

Volume VII
155th Fd Coy R.E.

Army Form C. 2118

Place	Date	Hour	Summary of Events and Information	Remarks and references to Appendices
MAZINGARBE	1916 June 5.		Weather wet & windy, clearing later Work as usual above. SUFFOLKS to exchange with 5th BERKS from midday tomorrow FAC	
"	6th		Weather wet & windy, clearing later Lt. O'Sullivan, 2 N.C.O's & 6 men proceeded to Bethune to witness trials with pipe pusher Capt Clifford went on leave 7th–17th. Lt Hughes doing his work (whilst on leave) Sapper Kathro's F.G.C.M. charged with striking L.Cpl Pow was acquitted. No 4 Sect: restarted a new dugout in Lens Rd Redt S Face otherwise work as usual. O.C visited Hdqrs R.E. ACH	
	7th		Weather sunny but cold. Sections erecting corrugated shelters against shell splinters Sap: Ivory sent to Cookery class at Divl School; he should have proceeded yesterday. Work as usual. Watercart returned after repair by I.O.M. New G 1098 War Equip: Fd Coy received 4 light spring wagon, 2 horses, 1 driver etc cut out. No 2 Party reported at 156 Hdqrs. No 11 Party did not arrive. ACH.	
"	8th		Weather fine. Wet at night. O.C & Lt Hegarty went to HQRE at 9.30 a.m. Lt H sent off to see 6. Prean Water Tower. OC discussed Fd Coy personnel with CRE staff at 6.30pm with Lt Voce 229th Fd Coy RE & deposited Lt V with 70th Bde at Abattoir. Noeux-les-Mines Road shelled all day. Parties No's 2 & 11 went to 156 HQ. No 1 Sect had 8 RAMC carrying stores for A.D.S. Chalkpit Alley. Lt Hughes reports existing A.D.S near Chalk Pit Alley will have to be rebuilt. ACH.	

—1875 Wt. W593/826 1,000,000 4/15 J.B.C. & A. A.D.S.S./Forms/C. 2118.

Instructions regarding War Diaries and Intelligence Summaries are contained in F. S. Regs., Part II. and the Staff Manual respectively. Title Pages will be prepared in manuscript.

Original

(3)

WAR DIARY
or
~~INTELLIGENCE SUMMARY~~
(Erase heading not required.)

Army Form C. 2118

Volume VII
155th Field Co RE

Place	Date	Hour	Summary of Events and Information	Remarks and references to Appendices
MAZINGARBE	1916 June 9th		Weather fine & sunny. O.C busy helping 229th Fd Coy to settle into billets. 113th F.A put 15 horses & drivers into Villa Compound. Parties for 65 [illegible] point now & future from 11th Middlesex. Work as usual except for parties No 2 & No 11 which did not turn up. 1 Carpenter to fix Survey Co direction [illegible] man repairing Tanks Posen Alley. Reported to C.R.E re new O.P. & instructed to carry on with brick tower inside end of present building. A.S.H.	
	June 10th		49th Inf Bde relieving 47th in Left Subsector. Weather Thundering [illegible]. Leave reduced to 7 days from Pont [illegible] Depot. Parties Nos 2 & 11 promised at 8.15 pm at Philosophe Cross roads. O.C visited billets of 229th Co & gave advice. Boring pipe in Brewery repaired by Sergt Davies. Work went on as usual & an O.P started in same House as existing one in Manor & at [illegible] Water Tower. Party shelled with 5.9's. A.S.H.	
	June 11th		Weather wet & thundering. Service & H.C by Clergy Padre at 10.30 am in Brewery. C.R.E & Adjt visited billets 4.30 pm & stated that 1 Coy 12th Yorks will come for instruction & work on 14th–22nd. Work to be 2nd entrance to [illegible] store in Lens Rd redoubt, dig out Reante's Passage to 6' deep & also Evacuation Trench. Ordered to report on dug-outs in Duke St. CSM detailed. Sergt [illegible] & L/Cpl Pope off on leave. Finished repairing Watercart. A.S.H.	
	June 12th		Weather wet. C.S.M visited Duke St to report on dug outs. All parties from 11th Middlesex cancelled from tonight owing to their departure. [illegible] Brig 49th visited Coy & arranged for a class of 12 Y Officers, taken out of trenches, to report here for instruction daily 9.30 am to 12.30 & 2–3 pm. C.R.E called & arranged for 2 N.C.O & 20 men from 48th to make collapsible wire entanglements in the grounds. C.R.E ordered us to put [illegible] down in Fosse 3 & put up 5 Rendezvous boards in Philosophe. A.S.H.	

1875 Wt. W593/826 1,000,000 4/15 J.B.C. & A. A.D.S.S./Forms/C. 2118.

Instructions regarding War Diaries and Intelligence Summaries are contained in F. S. Regs., Part II. and the Staff Manual respectively. Title Pages will be prepared in manuscript.

(4)

Original

WAR DIARY
or
~~INTELLIGENCE SUMMARY~~
(Erase heading not required.)

Army Form C. 2118

Volume VII
155th Field Co R.E.

Place	Date	Hour	Summary of Events and Information	Remarks and references to Appendices
MAZINGARBE	June 13th		Weather wet. No wire party arrived. 5 Officers 7th R.I. Fus arrived & erected 3 bays of shelter under C.S.M. C.R.E. & Adjt called & discussed several points. Lt Shaw Y Coy 12th Yorks Pion. called & O.C. arranged for their work from 5th onwards. O.C. X Coy also came about Stores. Shifted Spray baths from 5th Northants huts. 4 N.C.O's & men returned from Anti-gas School Vaquin. Work much as usual. no parties for Bryants or Dressing stations. A.H.	
	June 14th		Weather hot morning relieving later. 6 Officers & class building bay shelter under Maj Wilson 7th R.I.F. O.C. 7th R.I.F. visited them in the morning. 2 N.C.O's & men of 48th Bde making up collapsible wire entanglements. C.R.E. said Y & Yorks to put one Platoon on trench boarding London Rd working back from North St. O.C. rearranged programme of work & sent it to Y Coy. C.R.E. ordered at 8 p.m. 6th Pioneers ready for work tomorrow at 1 p.m. so that they could not be available for a day or two to move by Coys on as but they can without parties. Lt Williamson & Coy exercising horses. [illegible] returned. A.P.M. informed search party sent out. At 11 p.m. all watches put on one hour.	
	June 15th		Weather cold but fine. Company ordered by C.R.E. to stand to at 8.30 p.m. for night work. C.R.E. came & held a Conference at Villa Arnold for all 3 Coys. A.H. & 2 Coys 12 Yorks Pioneers arranged work for night. The White Coy & 104 12th Yorks excavating in front line for 354 Equipment boxes between Bryans 46 & 51. 64 12th Yorks & 3 A.S.C. Wagons went to LOOS to carry up 42 Boxes to Bryan 51-52 arrived there 3 a.m. Straw issued by A.S.C. for lining round boxes.	
	June 16th		Weather fine, hot sun in afternoon. Reported to C.R.E. results of work. Trouble experienced with parapets falling in. C.R.E. & Adjt arrived at 2.30 for conference. Gas alert ordered at 6 p.m. No 1 Sect 5 G.S. Wagons 91 X Coy 12th Yorks No 2 Sect 4 G.S. Wagons & 90 X Coy No 3 Sect 4 Wagons & 90 6th Lon Rangers No 4 Sect 7 G.S. Wagons & 90 6th Lon Rangers.	

1875 Wt. W593/826 1,000,000 4/15 J.B.C. & A. A.D.S.S./Forms/C. 2118.

Instructions regarding War Diaries and Intelligence Summaries are contained in F. S. Regs., Part II. and the Staff Manual respectively. Title Pages will be prepared in manuscript.

(5)

Original

WAR DIARY
or
~~INTELLIGENCE SUMMARY~~
(Erase heading not required.)

Army Form C. 2118

Volume VII 155th Field Coy RE

Place	Date	Hour	Summary of Events and Information	Remarks and references to Appendices
MAZINGARBE	June 17th		Weather fine sunny Wind NE-S.W. 218 boxes carried up & 133 fixed. CRE & Adjt arrived at 10 am & settled work for night No1 Sect 26 Men of 229th Fld Coy & 36 X Coy 12th Yorks, No2 16 men 229th Fld Coy & 18 X Coy No3 Sect 19 men 229th & 12 X Coy No4 33 men 229th & 90 men X Coy 106 LOOS WALLERS to be carried up & 2 RE per Coy left for placing them. ABH	
	June 18th	Night Work	Capt Bremner left for Casualty Clearing Station. CRE called to arrange work. Weather bright & sunny. No1 Sect No parties Total = 86 boxes fixed No2 sect 8 Pioneers Total boxes = 76 fixed No3 helping No4 No4 Sect 36 of 229 Field Coy & 20 Pioneers Parties of 229th stayed up for fixing LOOS WALLERS ABH	
	June 19th		Weather fine & sunny No4 Sect completed boxes = 96 Total Guides for 229th supplied in the evening O.C 157th Field Coy called re handing over ABH	
	June 20th		Weather dull & some Rain. CRE went up trenches with Lt HUGHES. Nos 1.2 & 3 Sects taking over from 157th ABH	
	June 21st		Weather fine Capt Clifford visited trenches with O.C 157th. No2 Sect went out to start work on craters but no work done owing to misunderstanding ABH	
	June 22nd		Weather fine dull later Nos 1 & 4 Sects working on dugouts No3 on dugouts & M G empl No2 on craters, G.O.C enquiry that no work was done on Craters 2 Lt Hegarty went on leave. 100 men Y Coy 12th Yorks sent out to deepen Piccadilly but no work done. Bde Major visited billets in evening & arranged work. ABH	

1875 Wt. W593/826 1,000,000 4/15 J.B.C. & A. A.D.S.S./Forms/C. 2118.

Instructions regarding War Diaries and Intelligence Summaries are contained in F. S. Regs., Part II. and the Staff Manual respectively. Title Pages will be prepared in manuscript.

(6) Original

WAR DIARY
or
~~INTELLIGENCE SUMMARY~~
(Erase heading not required.)

Army Form C. 2118

Volume VII
155th Field Coy

Place	Date	Hour	Summary of Events and Information	Remarks and references to Appendices
MAZINGARBE	June 23rd		Weather dull, heavy Thunderstorms. Work as before. Sites for new dugouts chosen with N.G.O & Coy 12th Yorks. Stopped the deepening Boy 42 & 46 so work done. AH	
	June 24th		Weather dull some rain. CRE & Adjt visited billets. Work as before but no Inf. working parties. 12th Yorks working on craters with No 2 Sect & clearing Boy 46. Bde Major 47th Inf Bde visited billets in afternoon. AH	
	June 25th		Weather dull. Nos. 1, 3 & 4 Sections work as before. Orders received that no work was to be done in front of Village Line. Lt Jennings sent for by C.R.E. re consolidation of new craters on same night. Nos. 2 & 3 Sections detailed. Lt Jennings & O'Sullivan reconnoitred work.	
	June 26		Weather dull & showery. 6 Men from No 1 & 6 from No 4 were detailed to accompany raiding party with explosives. Remainder No 1 & 4 on shelters & shifting in preparation for consolidation. AH	
	June 27th		Weather dull & showery. Mines exploded at 12.15 a.m. & raiders went across to German trenches at 12.30. No 2 started consolidating near portion of Harrisons crater & made bombers post & sap to it. No 3 were to do the same for new Hart's but new crater was a failure & most of party got lost owing to mistaken orders. Old saps were cleared & repaired. Total casualties were one killed, 2 seriously wounded, 5 wounded & one missing. Nos 1 & 4 (Remainder) went out to continue crater work at night. AH	Orders appendix A. Report on operations appendix B
	June 28th		L/Cpl Sidnall & Sap Bickerstaffe & Ballingall died, the latter being previously missing. Nos 1 & 3 Sections working on craters at night with 50 Infantry. Nos 2 & 4 Sections with 100 Inf clearing front line between Gordon & Cameron Alleys.	
	June 29th		Weather fine. No 3 Section on craters at night, no Infantry available. A Shell landed in stables & killed 3 horses & wounded 2 drivers.	

Instructions regarding War Diaries and Intelligence Summaries are contained in F. S. Regs., Part II. and the Staff Manual respectively. Title Pages will be prepared in manuscript.

Original (7)

WAR DIARY

or

~~INTELLIGENCE SUMMARY~~

(Erase heading not required.)

Volume VII
155th Field Coy R.E.

Army Form C. 2118

Place	Date	Hour	Summary of Events and Information	Remarks and references to Appendices
MAZINGARBE	June 30th		Weather fine with some rain Nos 1, 2 & 4 Sections working by day on dugouts & M.G. Emplts. No work at night. 3 Sappers buried in MAZINGARBE cemetery in afternoon.	
			F. A. Clifford Capt R.E. O.C. 155th Fd Coy R.E.	

1875 Wt. W593/826 1,000,000 4/15 J.B.C. & A. A.D.S.S./Forms/C. 2118.

APPENDIX A

S E C R E T.

47th Infantry Brigade Raid Scheme.

A. PERSONNEL.

No.1 Party	Front line Right.	1 Off'cr	25 O.R.	2 R.E.	
No.2 Party	Support line right.	1 "	25 "	2 R.E.	
No.3 Party	Front line left.	1 "	25 "	2 R.E.	
No.4 Party	Support Line left.	1 "	25 "	2 R.E.	
No.5 Party	Right Support.	1 "	20 "	2 R.E.	
No.6 Party	Left Support.	1 "	20 "	2 R.E.	
Party A.	Consolidation Right.	(1 "	15 "	R.E.	
		(1 "	52 "	Infantry.	
Party B.	Consolidation Left.	(1 "	15 "	R.E.	
		(1 "	52 "	Infantry.	
Party C.	Relief covering party) right)	1 "	15 "	Infantry	
Party D.	Relief covering party) left.)	1 "	15 "	Infantry	
Torpedo parties.	... .	2 N.C.Os	18 "		
Reserve party	... .	1 Officer	60 O.R.		

B. TASKS.

No.1 Party (Front line Right) 2/Lieut. HICKMAN and 25 O.R.
Objective Front line, enter enemy trench at A to form block (1) with 1 N.C.O. and 4 men. Bomb down enemy front line from A to K. 1 N.C.O. and 6 men detailed to bomb trench H to C.

No.2 Party (Support line Right) Lieut. JOHNSTONE and 25 O.R.
Objective Enemy Support line, enter trench at A, bombs trench A to B form block (2). Bombs trench from B to D forms block (3) bombs trench D,E,K, returned by Sap at K.

No.3 Party (Front line left) Capt. LYNCH and 25 men.
Objective. Enemy front line, enters enemy trench at H, bombs trench H to K forming block (7) with 1 N.C.O. and 4 men, returning by sap at K.

No. 4 Party (Support line left) 2/Lieut. HODGSON and 25 O.R.
Follows No.3 enters trench at H, bombs trench H to C forms block(5) with 1 N.C.O. and 4 men. Bombs trench G to E dropping dropping 1 N.C.O. and 4 men to form block (4) bombs trench E to K returning by sap K.

No.5 Party (right Support Party) 2/Lieut. FIELD and 20 O.R.
To protect R.E. consolidating party. Round up any enemy in the area of the new crater. To evacuate wounded and prisoners. If necessary to support Raiding Parties.

No. 6 Party (Left Support Party) 2/lieut. DUFFIELD and 20 O.R.
Duties similar to Right Support Party.

Party A. see Appendix 1.
Party B. see Appendix 1.
Party C. to relieve No.5 party after return of Raiders and to continue to cover party A until dawn.
Party D. to relieve No.6 Party after return of Raiders and continue to cover Party B until dawn.

Capt, LEACROFT controls parties No.1, 2, 5, A and C.
Capt. PHILLIPS controls parties 3, 4, 6, B and D.

Torpedo Parties. 2 N.C.Os and 18 men. Objective. To destroy enemy wire, three groups of 6 men will each place and explode torpedo in enemy wire.

Reserve Party. Lieut. STUDHOLME and 60 O.R. to be held in immediate readiness to reinforce or support the Raiding Parties.

	Officers	O.R.
Total	9	220.
	13	338

Machine Gun action. Machine guns will be placed in advanced positions to strengthen the support and to cover the flanks, Lieut. Furney, 8th Munsters and 2/lieut. MOSS, 7th Leinsters will occupy positions on new crater and assist with Lewis guns.

R.E. There will be 2 R.E. with each of parties 1, 2, 3, 4, 5, 6 carrying explosives. One man of each party will be deatailed as an extra carrier. The duties of the R.E. will be to destroy obstacles and trench mortars.

C. Sequence of events.

12.15 a.m. Two mines explode forming craters as shown on sketch. Artillery barrage on front line. Parties at Assembly Post.

12.18 a.m. Artillery lift to enemy's support line forming box barrage.
Raiding parties enter enemy's front line.
Torpedo parties move forward to cut gaps at X.

12.30 a.m. Artillery lift to enemy's reserve lines. Stokes guns and Machine guns co-operate on flanks.
Raiding parties bomb towards enemy's support line.
Support parties take up position and consolidation parties commence worl vide Appendix 1.

1.0 a.m. Raiding parties expected to return.
Arrangements made to inform artillery when parties have returned.
If a raiding party is checked and unable to advance, it will return by the route it entered.

D. Notes for raiders.

1. All telephone wires to be cut.
2. Any check to be cleared at once by getting outside trench and taking the enemy in flank and rear.
3. Blocks to hold on until ordered to withdraw.

Evacuation. Prisoners, trophies and wounded to be passed back through the support parties.
O.C.Enterprise. Major LEONARD, 7th Leinsters, will be at Coy. H.Q. in SUNKEN ROAD
Assembly Posts, for forming up and returning to, marked on ground by placards.
Aid Posts, marked on ground.
Collecting posts for Prisoners Marked on ground
Traffic. Up and Down trenches arranged by O.C. ENTERPRISE.
Bombs. Dumps to be arranged at the forward Assembly Post.
R.E.Dumps. Near Assembly Posts and marked on ground.
~~R.E.Stores. Dumps at assembly posts.~~
Signals. Telephones to be arranged by Signal Officer 7/Leinsters.
Very Light Signals arranged. Recall for stragglers arranged.

[signature]

Major,
Brigade Major, 47th Infantry Brigade.

26-6-16.

App I

S E C R E T.

CONSOLIDATING OF NEW CRATERS.

1. Parties.

A. New HARRISON'S CRATER.

1 R.E. Officer .... Lieut. R.B.JENNINGS.

15 O.R.

6/Connaughts.- 1 Officer Lieut. L.G.D'ARCY.

15 O.R. to dig.

37 -25 O.R. to carry & 12 to carry timber

Covering Party No. 5, Lewis guns and Stokes.

B. New HART'S CRATER.

1 R.E. Officer ... Lieut J.O'SULLIVAN.

15 O.R.

6/Connaughts 1 Officer ... 2/Lieut. J.F.BLAKE O'SULLIVAN.

15 O.R. to dig.

37 25 " to carry.

Covering Party. Party No. 6, Lewis gun and Stokes.

2. Object. To establish a post for 6 bombers on the near lip of each crater and to dig a communication trench from the posts to our front system.

3. Position of assembly.

Party A in rear of Party 5.

Party B in rear of Party 6.

4. Action by artillery.

12.15 a.m. mines explode.

Artillery bombard front line.

12.18 Artillery lift on to Support line.

12.25 30 " " Reserve line.

A box barrage is formed.

5. Action by Infantry. 12.15 a.m. Parties 1,2,3,4 advance across new CRATERS and enter enemy's trenches. Parties 5 and 6 act as covering parties. When raid is finished covering parties 5 and 6 remain out and may be relieved by new parties C and D (8/Munsters) At dawn the covering parties and consolidation parties A and B will withdraw and bombers 8/Munsters will hold the posts made.

5. Action by parties A and B. These follow immediately in rear of Parties 5 and 6. The R.E. officer in charge will first select the bombers post and commence work on it without delay. The remainder will dig a trench from the post to our front system.

It is essential to completethe post and to make some kind of trench to it before dawn. The post must have some splinter proof cover. A wiring party will place steel knife rests on the flanks of the posts.

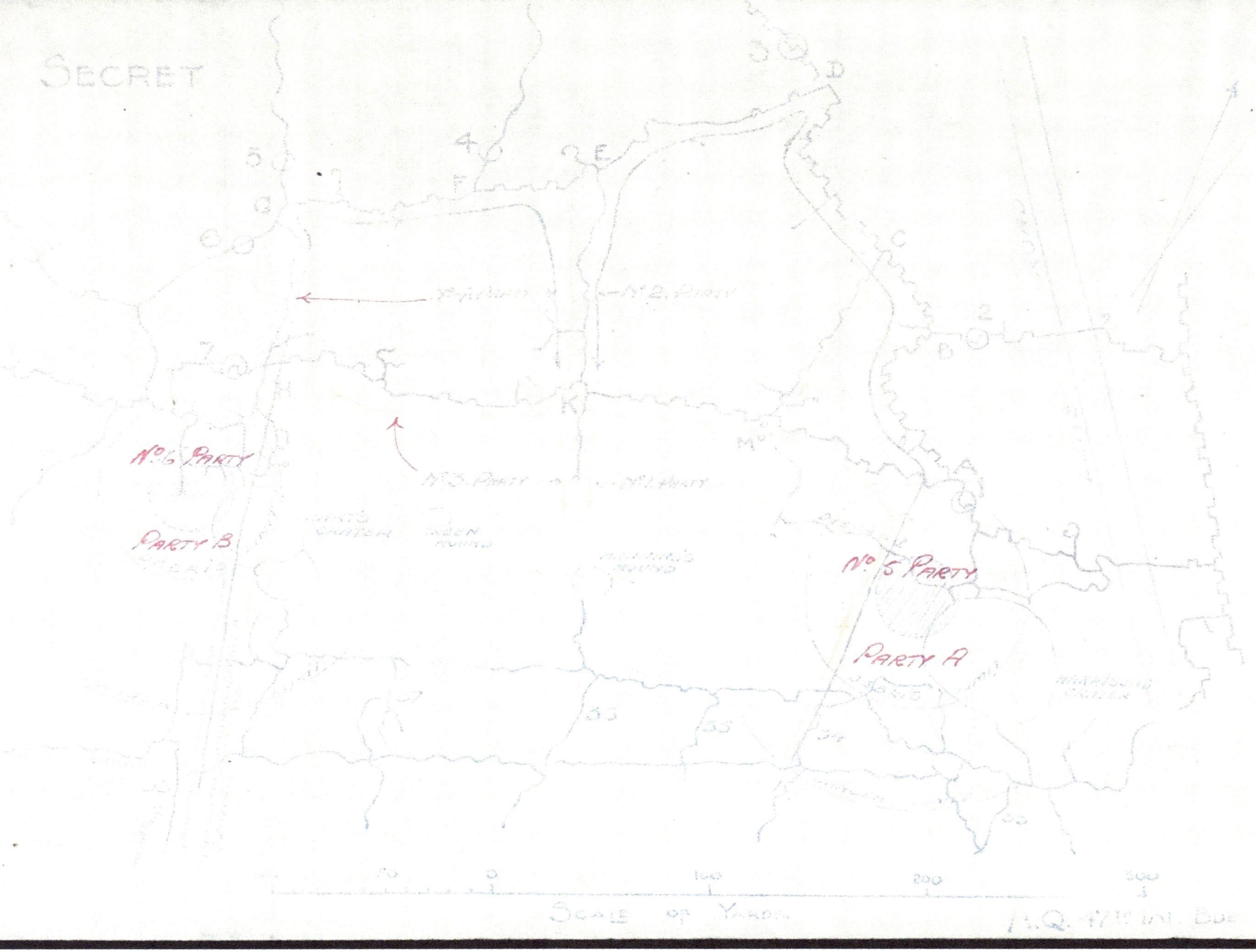
SECRET
No. 6 PARTY
PARTY B
No. 5 PARTY
PARTY A
No. 2 PARTY
SCALE OF YARDS
50
0
100
200
300

APPENDIX B

Report of Occurrences on night of 26/27 June 1916

A RE with Raiding parties

No 1 Party (Right) sappers Brown, Perrin, Fearnley & McLean

This party went across to German front line but sappers were ordered not to get into the trench until the bombing had eased off a bit, on account of the danger of getting the guncotton hit, they were also told they had better throw away their guncotton but did not do so. Later they were told that there was no chance of their getting into the German trench to demolish anything and that they had better come back. Some of the infantry got into the German front line but were unable to proceed. The RE came back bringing ~~with~~ their guncotton & a wounded Leinster with them.

No 4(?) Party (Left) Sprs Hall, Lewis, Corrance & Side

This party got into the German front line and proceeded along it driving the Germans before them. The covering party got separated from the RE who had to drop their guncotton & throw bombs for their own protection. Later when they retired to the place where they had ~~too~~ left the guncotton & where they were going to demolish some dug outs, there were too many of our men passing for them to do any demolitions & they finally withdrew with the infantry.

No 5 Party (Right Support) Pioneer Ferme & Spr ~~[illegible]~~ Hanson.

This party went astray, the RE got separated from the rest of their party & when they were out in the open Spr Hanson was hit, he went on for a while but was finally unable to proceed so ~~[illegible]~~ Pioneer Ferme brought him back.

Party Unknown possibly No 3 (Left) Sprs Richards & Bickerstaffe,

This party proceeded across rather to their right, then got the order to lie down & open rapid fire, they stayed there for about ten minutes & then went across towards their left & on coming to the German wire they halted & threw bombs. The RE were ordered to drop their guncotton & throw bombs too

On the way back, after they had reached our own trenches Spr Bickerstaffe was wounded by shell splinters & has since died of these wounds.
It will thus be seen that not a single one of the charges of guncotton was used + that the only chance that occurred of using them was for blowing in dug-outs where they would probably have done very little damage.

B Work on HARRISHON'S CRATER

I have received the following report on this work from Lieut R B JENNINGS. R.E.

"My party consisting of 25 R.E. + 52 6th CONNAUGHTS
" under 2 Lt DARCY followed party No 5 out to
" front wire, seeing that the crater was a long
" way to the right I returned to front line
" and ran along it and up the left hand sap of the
" old crater to what I thought was the best position
" to start. I went up + picked the place for the bomber's
" post + left 2/Cpl BRICKWOOD with 6 RE to
" get to work. 2/Lt DARCY was then getting his
" diggers out + we lined them up on their job. The
" wirers got a bit delayed by their heavy burdens
" so I ran back to beat them up + shewed 2/Lt DARCY
" + Cpl SIDNELL where to get the wire out, which
" was done very quickly. Seeing all was proceeding
" well on the crater I went off to get the party with
" the shelter frames but could only find one sapper
" of them in support line so I told him to keep on
" looking for them + bring them up to the front
" line near crater. I then returned to crater
" + found the wiring party ready + remained there.
" I found it advisable to shift the right hand
" wire a bit further to the right flank. Fearing
" that I shouldn't find my party with timber I got
" a party to get any available timber + full sandbags
" from the old front line and saps. Spr WILD, my
" orderly was absolutely invaluable in finding

"material & guiding men to it & getting them
"off to the bombers' post, as it was most important
"not to delay the Sappers in the post a minute. I
"had the shelter about half made when the
"frames arrived nailed together but I found it
"would be impossible to try to use them on account
"of their size, so I broke them up & used them in
"the roof. By this time the wire was finished
"and I told 2/Lt DARCY to get them on the old
"Front line & sap & have it cleared out, they
"also relieved some of the men in the new trench
"who were played out. Sapper SOUSTER had
"~~dug~~ worked himself to a standstill. By 2 AM it had
"become very trying and several men were hit
"carrying materials up to the post as we couldn't
"use the trench, for fear of stopping the work.
"I cleared the men off the top as the shelter
"was finished & continued working on the trench and
"post. It was at this time that Sprs GARLAND and
"MEHAFFEY were hit while in the new trench, so
"I made them keep down low. L/cpl SIDNELL was
"hit on top & Pion HANNA went out after him but
"couldnt get him in & shouted for help. Spr
"MILLETT jumped up from the trench & was killed
"immediately. I don't know what happened then as HANNA
"seems to have lost his head. I cleared all the
"men out then & reported to CAPT LEACROFT 7th
"LEINSTERS all finished & his party occupied
"the post. This was at 2.30 am I was held up
"in support line by a barrage & reported to Bn HQ
"instead of the ENCLOSURE.
"The CONNAUGHTS worked splendidly — every man of them.
"2/Lt. DARCY was always on the spot & was of
"the greatest help in keeping his men going & getting
"them on their work. I can't mention any of
"them as I don't know them individually except

"his N.C.O's, Sergt DUNLOP with the diggers, sergt
"DIVER & L/cpl DORAN with the wire
"The Connaught RANGER who went out & fetched in
"Spr MILLETT is worthy of notice."

C. Work on HARTS CRATER

I have received the following report on this work from Lt J O'SULLIVAN. RE
"My scheme to get my party to work was:-
"On the order to advance all men were to advance
"to the front line in rear of party No 6. On
"getting on to the front line 1 N.C.O. + 4 sappers
"already detailed were to advance with me
"to make a bombing post when I had decided on
"the site 2/Lt BLAKE O'SULLIVAN was to come
"with me so as to know the ground. The
"remainder of the party were to remain in
"the front line trench until 2/Lt BLAKE O'SULLIVAN
"or I came back to get them on to the work.
"On the order to advance given by CAPT PHILLIPS
"I ordered my men to advance keeping in touch
"with Capt PHILLIPS, taking my orders from him.
"On getting to the front line I ordered my party
"to halt except for the forward party above
"mentioned, I advanced with with this party
"as directed by Capt PHILLIPS to his position.
"While reconnoitring the ground word was brought
"to me that my party had been given orders to
"retire. I immediately ~~deputed~~ deputed 2/Lt
"BLAKE O'SULLIVAN with my orderly to collect
"the party. He ~~[illegible]~~ succeeded in getting
"a few men together after a considerable time.
"I reported the matter immediately to Capt
"PHILLIPS and told him what work I intended
"to carry out and offered to assist him
"in any way I could as my party was
"then too depleted to do any extensive work

(5)

"During my preliminary reconnaissance of the
"crater I could not discover any new crater
"and came to the conclusion that the explosion
"had taken place in or near the centre of the
"old crater.

"With the help of some men 2/Lt BLAKE O'SULLIVAN
"had collected, I carried out the following work,
"I cleared out & deepened two of the old saps which
"had been blown in, repaired two covered shelters,
"a sniper's post and put in a bomber's post.

" At 2.50 I discovered a mound to the left
" of the old crater, close to the enemy's lines.
"This mound from what I could see
"in the bad light, did not appear to be a
"large one. With the help of some men of my
"party which 2/Lt BLAKE O'SULLIVAN had
"again collected & brought to me, I put up a
"temporary sniper's post so as to cover the
"ground between the mound and our lines.
"I reported to CAPT PHILLIPS and withdrew
"my party at 3.20 a.m.

"I should like to ~~call~~ draw attention to
the excellent work done by 2/Lt BLAKE O'SULLIVAN
"of the 6th CONNAUGHT RANGERS in collecting
"scattered ~~portion~~ portions of my working
party & getting them on the work. His
"assistance was most invaluable to me. By
"his coolness & disregard of danger he infused
"confidence into his men & kept them to their work."

The whole of this work was carried out under
a very heavy fire of all sorts, it being probably
heaviest at HARRISONS CRATER.
I am sending separately a list of those whom I consider
have particularly distinguished themselves

2.8.6.16

F A Clifford Capt R.E.
O C 155th Fd Coy R.E.

W A R   D I A R Y

155th Field Coy
Royal Engineers

1st. July to 31st. July 1916.

VOLUME No. 8.

16 July
155 F.C.R.E.
Vol 8

Instructions regarding War Diaries and Intelligence Summaries are contained in F. S. Regs., Part II. and the Staff Manual respectively. Title Pages will be prepared in manuscript.

(1)

WAR DIARY
or
~~INTELLIGENCE SUMMARY~~
(Erase heading not required.)

Army Form C. 2118

Volume VIII
155th Fld Co RE

Place	Date	Hour	Summary of Events and Information	Remarks and references to Appendices
MAZINGARBE	July 1st		Weather fine 2Lt Hegarty returned from leave. Stables shelled killing 3 & wounding 7 mules. 1 & 4 Sects & part No2 on dugouts remainder No2 with 40 Inf repairing front line between GORDON & CAMEROON ALLEYS No3 on Craters. 1 NCO & one sapper from Nos 3 & 4 with 40 Inf repairing front line near CAMERON. ASH	
	July 2nd		Weather fine No 1, 2 & 4 Sects on dugouts. No2 repairing front line with 15 Inf in CAMERON. No 3 & 50 Inf on Craters. ASH	
	July 3rd		Weather fine Work as yesterday except that No4 Sect relieved & changed with No 3. C.R.E. visited Works. ASH	
	July 4th		Weather dull heavy rain & thunder in afternoon. Nos 1 & 2 Sections on dugouts. Nos 3 & 4 helping Inf redig front line. ASH	
	5.		Weather dull, rainy, thundery. Half of each of nos 1, 2, 3, sections on dugouts by day, remainder nos 1 + 2 + all no 4 sections on Craters at night. Party for HART'S Crater not allowed through. Party on HARRISON'S Crater had to stop work ~~& the~~ + throw + carry bombs for about 1½ hours on account of a hostile bombing attack.	
	6		Weather dull, some rain. No 3 section on dugouts by day remaining sections on Craters by night. No 98082 Spr CHALMERS A.J. + No 98040 Pion ANDERSON. R. <u>Killed</u> No 96401 Spr LEE. P. + No 65318 Spr PEARMAN H. <u>Wounded</u>	
	7		Weather dull, showery. Work as before. Light, Spring wagon sent away to THEROUANNE. JAC	

1875 Wt. W593/826 1,000,000 4/15 J.B.C. & A. A.D.S.S./Forms/C. 2118.

Instructions regarding War Diaries and Intelligence Summaries are contained in F. S. Regs., Part II. and the Staff Manual respectively. Title Pages will be prepared in manuscript.

(2)

WAR DIARY
or
~~INTELLIGENCE SUMMARY~~
(Erase heading not required.)

Army Form C. 2118

Volume VIII
155th Fd Coy RE

Place	Date	Hour	Summary of Events and Information	Remarks and references to Appendices
MAZINGARBE	1916 July 8		Weather fine. No 3 section on dugouts by day. Nos 1+2 sections on Craters by night. Lt. O'SULLIVAN + 2/Lt. HEGARTY with Nos 3+4 sections went to billet in LOOS in evening	
	9		Weather fine. Bt. Major H. R. P. REYNOLDS R.E. arrived + took command of Coy. No 3 section on dug-outs by day. Remaining sections on Craters by night	
	10		Weather fine. Work as usual.	
	11		Weather dull & cold. Work as usual. zae	
	12		Weather dull & cold, some rain, Work as usual zae	
	13		Weather dull, cold. Work as usual zae	
	14		Weather fine. Work as usual. zae No 23251 Pion HALL C. W + No 98034 Spr FERRIS S.C. awarded Military Medals zae	APPENDICES C 49th Inf Bde scheme D 155th Fd Coy Scheme E. Plan of probable Craters F Report by Maj Reynolds RE G Report by 49th [illegible]
	15		Weather fine. No 3 section, work as usual + returned to MAZINGARBE in evening. ~~Lt~~ Lt. HUGHES + 2/Lt HEGARTY, with parties from Nos 1+4 sections, consolidated new SEAFORTH CRATERS. No 98226 Spr BROWN. S. Killed No 98327 Spr SADLER. W. T. Wounded No 59627 Sergt MEREDITH R Wounded, at duty. zae	
	16.		Weather dull, rain in afternoon. 156th Fd Coy RE took over LOOS Sector. zae	
	17		Weather wet, afternoon dry but dull. No 3 section on dug-outs 65 METRE POINT REDOUBT, remainder working in camp. zae	

1875 Wt. W593/826 1,000,000 4/15 J.B.C. & A. A.D.S.S./Forms/C. 2118.

Instructions regarding War Diaries and Intelligence Summaries are contained in F. S. Regs., Part II. and the Staff Manual respectively. Title pages will be prepared in manuscript.

(3)

WAR DIARY
or
~~INTELLIGENCE SUMMARY.~~
(Erase heading not required.)

Volume VIII
155th Fd Coy RE

Army Form C. 2118.

Place	Date	Hour	Summary of Events and Information	Remarks and references to Appendices
	1916 July			
MAZINGARBE	18		Weather fine. No 3 section as before. No 4 section Bomb store FOSSE 3 & Dug-outs NORTHERN SAP REDOUBT. No 2 + No 1 working at VILLA ST. ARNOULD. ZAC	
	19		Weather, bright sun. No 1 Sect VILLA ST ARNOULD. No 2. M.G. Dug-out CHALKPIT ALLEY. No 3 as before also No 4. ZAC	
	20		Weather, bright sun. No 1 sect. laying trenchboards LONDON ROAD, a pike line N. Sap Redoubt. No 2 as before. No 3 as before. No 4 as before. ZAC	
	21		Weather bright sun, work as before No 4 section also O.P MAROC & Water supply. Northern SAP REDOUBT. Lt HUGHES went to Special Works Park RE for course in Concealment. Parchment certificates received from G.O.C. Divn for:- Lt O'SULLIVAN, Lt JENNINGS, No 96409 Spr PERRIN, No 98252 Spr WILD, No 97662 Spr WALSH, No 98034 Spr FERRIS. No 23251 Pion HALL. No 59627 Sergt MEREDITH, No 97803 2/Cpl BUXTON, No 96459 L/Cpl BRICKWOOD. (2) ZAC Lt HUGHES went to Special Works Park for course in Concealment. ZAC	
	22.		Weather bright sun. Work as before. ~~New System~~ C.R.E. explained new system of Field Company work in Divn. viz, all 3 companies in line all the time with one section resting for a week at a time. 155th Coy allotted Northern portion of line (Boyaux 94 inclusive to 78 exclusive). ZAC	

T2134. Wt. W708-776. 500000. 4/15. Sir J. C. & S.

Instructions regarding War Diaries and Intelligence Summaries are contained in F. S. Regs., Part II. and the Staff Manual respectively. Title pages will be prepared in manuscript.

(4)

WAR DIARY
or
~~INTELLIGENCE SUMMARY.~~
(Erase heading not required.)

Volume VIII
155th Fd Coy RE.

Army Form C. 2118.

Place	Date	Hour	Summary of Events and Information	Remarks and references to Appendices
	1916 July			
MAZINGARBE	23		Weather fine. Lt O'SULLIVAN, JENNINGS & HEGARTY reconnoitred front line & support line. No 1 sect. laying trench boards LONDON ROAD. No 2 sect. Dug-out NORTHERN SAP REDOUBT., No 3 Dug-outs 65 METRE POINT REDOUBT. No 4 Dug-out & Water supply NORTHERN SAP REDOUBT. FAC	
	24.		Weather dull in morning, fine later. No 1 as before No 2 as before. No 3 & 4 as before. FAC	
	25		Weather fine, took over allotted bit of line, 48th Inf Bde in. Work allotted as follows. No 2 section front line, No 3 Support line, No 4 Curly Crescent. No 1 at rest at Billets. Nos 2 & 3 sections getting stores up to new dump. FAC	
	26		Weather fine. No 2 section on Craters. No 3 section shelters in support line. No 4 section on shelters in CURLY CRESCENT for forward section, helped by 9 men No 1 section. FAC	
	27		Weather dull. O.C. selected new sites for forward sections in O B 4 + O.B 5 + new site for dump in disused trench on railway near O.B.1. No 2 section consolidated by night new crater blown by enemy in afternoon. Other work as 26th. FAC Lt. HUGHES returned from Special Works Park. FAC	

T2134. Wt. W708–776. 500000. 4/15. Sir J. C. & S.

Instructions regarding War Diaries and Intelligence Summaries are contained in F. S. Regs., Part II. and the Staff Manual respectively. Title pages will be prepared in manuscript.

(5)

WAR DIARY
or
~~INTELLIGENCE SUMMARY.~~
(Erase heading not required.)

Army Form C. 2118.

Volume VIII
155th Fd Coy RE.

Place	Date	Hour	Summary of Events and Information	Remarks and references to Appendices
	1916 July			
MAZINGARBE	28.		Weather fine & hot. No 2 section on Craters. No 3 section on shelters in Support line, but unable to get any work done owing to stores not arriving. No 4 section cleaning out & repairing dug-outs in O.B.5. JAC	
	29		Weather fine & hot. Work as intended for 28th. No 3 section took up quarters in dug-outs in O.B.5. JAC	
	30.		Weather, hot sun. No 2 section cleared 46 emplacements for gas cylinders between Boyaux 78 & 79. Nos 3 & 4 sections as before.	
	31		Weather hot sun. Work as on 29th. Parchment Certificates received from G.O.C. Divn for:- Lt. HUGHES, 2/Lt. HEGARTY. No 59627 Sergt MEREDITH, No 99919 Sergt TONKS, No 97674 Cpl ADDISON. No 103875 2/Cpl DUNNING, No 97907 Spr SIDE. JAC	
			[signature] Major O.C. 155th Fd Coy RE. 31.7.16.	

T2134. Wt. W708-776. 500000. 4/15. Sir J. C. & S.

APPENDIX F

Report on Consolidation of two new Craters at old Seaforth Crater, carried out at the same time as 49th Infantry Bde Scheme at 11 pm on 15th July 1916

1. 11 pm. The two mines were exploded. Directly after explosion the consolidation parties (each consisting of 1 R.E. Officer, 1 R.E N.C.O., 4 Sappers, 1 Infantry N.C.O. & 4 men) started for the lips of the craters.

Lieut Hughes was in command of Right party & 2nd Lieut Hegarty of Left party. The saps to the two craters were dug by 2 parties, each consisting of 1 Infantry Officer
2 — " — N.C.O's
3 Sappers
25 Infantry men

These went out at about 11.5 pm. The officers i/c going out first with each of the R.E. officers and then going back for their parties.

The Saps were so placed as to be as much as possible in dead ground from the flanks. The positions of bombing posts were chosen with the same object in view and also so as to allow sentries close to them to get as good views as possible into the craters.

2. Conditions:

All the work was done in very bright lights.

Both sapping parties worked under fairly good cover. The 2 parties making Bombing Posts were both subjected to M.G. fire from left flank & to grenade fire from other side of craters. Sniper on camouflet to right was active & apparently a good shot.

Pieces of shells which burst in front line worried parties a good deal.

3. Results:

Bombing Post on right was finished at 12·30 am.

Bombing Post on left at 12·45 am.

Sap on right was finished about 12·50 am.

Sap on left was probably finished about 1·30 am.

Work being somewhat delayed by shortage of men.

In both saps barbed wire was encountered about 1 ft down from the surface of the ground, close to front trench, which caused considerable delay. The saps were dug to about 3 feet depth.

4. Opposite the end of Seaforth Alley an old sap existed running towards the crater. It was hoped to utilize this in making the new approach, but in the end it was not used owing to difficulties in lining out the men.

5. Bombing Post on right was put in a good position except that it was found afterwards that it was visible from the German Lines to the Northward. Today it was destroyed by hostile gun fire and is being re-sited and rebuilt by 156th Coy R.E.

6. It was arranged with O.C. 8th Inniskillings that R.E. were not responsible for the saps. But assistance was given by R.E. officers where necessary.

7. Two or three individuals did exceptionally good work — reports on their conduct follow.

8. Rough Sketch attached

9. Bombing posts consisted of 4 mine frames (4' x 2') each Covering over with half sleepers & chalked, & revetted round outside with sandbags.

M.M. Meynold [?]
Major
O.C. 155th Field Co R.E.

16.7.16

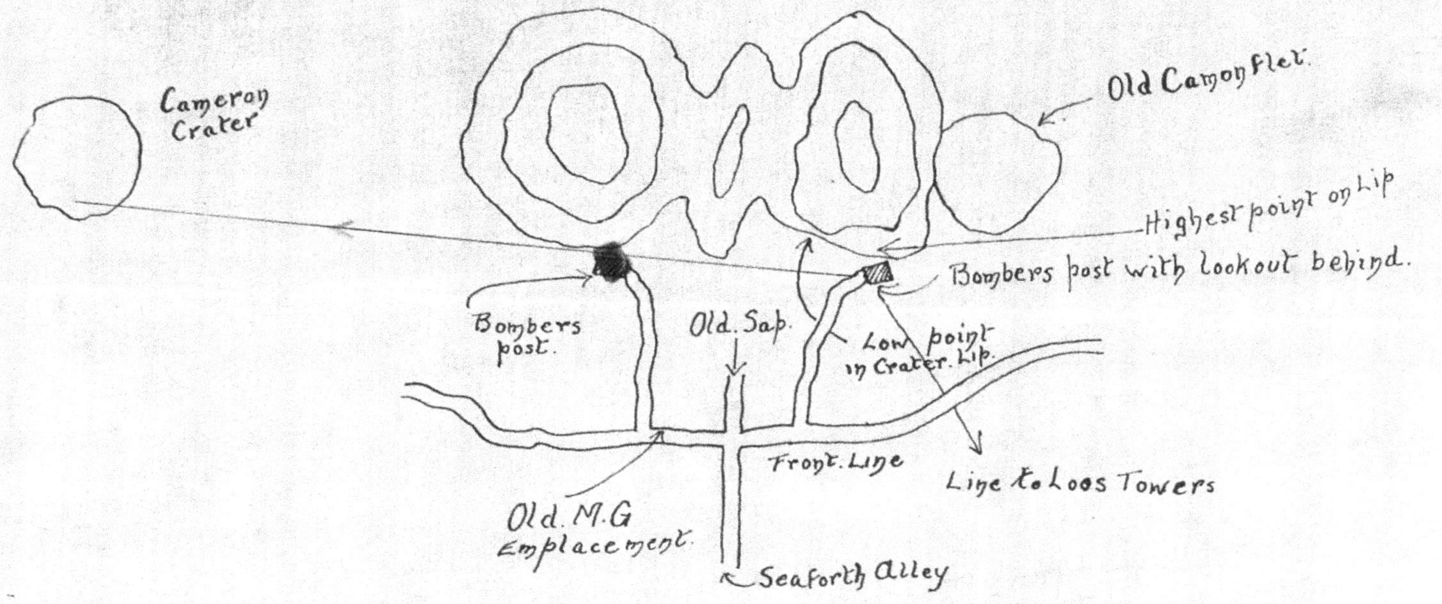
Cameron Crater
Old Camonflet.
Highest point on Lip
Bombers post with lookout behind.
Bombers post.
Old. Sap.
Low point in Crater. Lip.
Front. Line
Line to Loos Towers
Old. M.G Emplacement.
Seaforth Alley

Vol 9

W A R D I A R Y.

155th Field Co. R.E.

MONTH OF AUGUST, 1916.

VOLUME:- 9.

Army Form C. 2118.

Instructions regarding War Diaries and Intelligence Summaries are contained in F. S. Regs., Part II. and the Staff Manual respectively. Title pages will be prepared in manuscript.

(1)

WAR DIARY
or
~~INTELLIGENCE SUMMARY.~~
(*Erase heading not required.*)

Volume IX
155th Fd Coy RE

Place	Date	Hour	Summary of Events and Information	Remarks and references to Appendices
	1916 August			
MAZINGARBE	1		Weather fine, No3 section on Craters, No 4 on Support line. No2 work at VILLA ARNOULD	ZAC
	2		Weather fine, work as before also No1 section on shelters in LONE TRENCH. ZAC	
	3.		Weather fine, work as before ZAC	
	4		Weather fine, work as before. Officers of 15th Coy (8th Div) taken round line. ZAC	
	5.		Weather fine, work as before. ZAC	
	6		Weather fine, work as before. ZAC	
	7		Weather fine, very hot. Company holiday. Changed over to HULLUCH Section. ZAC	
	8		Weather hot. No 4 section on Craters, No1 T.M. emplacements. No 2 Shelters LONE TRENCH. No 3 'rest' section went to gas demonstration ZAC	
	9.		Weather very hot, work as 8th. ~~No~~ No 62148 Spr MEREDITH. G. wounded by shell near billet ZAC	
	10		Weather, raining in morning, dull all day. Work as before. ZAC	
	11		Weather fine + hot. Work as before. ~~ZAC~~ ~~No 3 section started work on~~ ZAC	
	12		Weather fine + hot. Work as before but no Crater work on account of reliefs. No 3 section started work on Bomb store Fosse 3 ~~ZAC~~ Lt O'SULLIVAN went to First Army School ZAC	
	13.		Weather fine. No4 section on Craters + dismantling mono-rail. No1 on T.M. Emplts, No 2 work in + around 10th AVENUE. No 3 (REST Section) on Bomb Store Fosse 3 ZAC	

T2134. Wt. W708-776. 500000. 4/15. Sir J. C. & S.

Instructions regarding War Diaries and Intelligence Summaries are contained in F. S. Regs., Part II. and the Staff Manual respectively. Title pages will be prepared in manuscript.

(2)

WAR DIARY
or
~~INTELLIGENCE SUMMARY~~.
(Erase heading not required.)

Army Form C. 2118.

Volume IX
155th Fd Coy RE

Place	Date	Hour	Summary of Events and Information	Remarks and references to Appendices
	1916 August			
MAZINGARBE	14		Weather fine. 36 men sent to assist specialists to let off gas but wind was not favourable. Some work done on T.M. empts, & 10th avenue & Fosse 3 bomb store. ZAC	
	15		Weather fine, work & gas attempt as 14th. ZAC	
	16		Weather fine, work & gas attempt as 14th. ZAC	
	17		Weather, heavy showers, work & gas attempt as 14th ZAC	
	18		Weather fine but showery, No 1 section on Craters, No 2 on T.M. Empts, No 3 on Shelters etc 10th Avenue, No 4 (Rest Section) at work at R.A. ~~Ctr~~ Ammunition store VERMELLES & general work at VILLA ST ARNOULD	
	19		Weather Dull & rainy. Work as 18th. ZAC	
	20		Weather Dull, work interfered with by 36 men being taken to assist Gas Company letting off Gas. ZAC	
	21		Weather fine. Work as before. sections ~~now~~ at night changing to No 2 Frontline No 3 Support, No 4 reserve & No 1 rest. ZAC	
	22		Weather fine. Work as before with sections changed as above. ~~ZAC~~ No 99919 Sergt C.S TONKS, No 103875 2/cpl DUNNING J & No 97907 Spr ~~A~~ SIDE A.E. awarded MILITARY MEDAL. ZAC	

T2134. Wt. W708–776. 500000. 4/15. Sir J. C. & S.

Instructions regarding War Diaries and Intelligence Summaries are contained in F. S. Regs., Part II. and the Staff Manual respectively. Title pages will be prepared in manuscript.

(3)

WAR DIARY
or
~~INTELLIGENCE SUMMARY.~~
(Erase heading not required.)

Volume IX
155th Fd Coy RE

Army Form C. 2118.

Place	Date	Hour	Summary of Events and Information	Remarks and references to Appendices
	1916 August			
MAZINGARBE	23		Weather dull. Received orders to move to VERQUIN tomorrow. Men withdrawn from trenches & packing transport. 2/Lt. T. C V. HEGARTY awarded MILITARY CROSS. ZAC	
VERQUIN. ~~VERQUIN.~~	24		Weather fine. Marched to VERQUIN. Pontoons started 3.30 a.m. so as to be in NOEUX-LES-MINES before ~~by~~ daylight, awaited rest of transport there. Advance party (cyclists with Interpreter) left at 7.0 a.m. Tool carts left at 10.00 a.m. & joined Pontoons in NOEUX. Remainder transport left 10.45 a.m. picked up pontoons & toolcarts in NOEUX & all proceeded together. Dismounted left at 11.0 a.m. & arrived at VERQUIN at 1 p.m. About 6 p.m. received orders to proceed ~~now~~ to CAUCHY-A-LA-TOUR on 25th. ZAC	Orders for move Appendix H.
CAUCHY-A-LA-TOUR	25.		Marched to CAUCHY-A-LA-TOUR. Advance party (as before) started at 6.45 a.m. Remainder (transport behind dismounted) started 7.0 a.m. Marched via LABUISSIERE, BRUAY, MARLES-LES-MINES, LOZINGHEM & AUCHEL. arrived CAUCHY-A-LA-TOUR about 12.15 p.m. Road hilly but no trouble with transport. Weather fine in morning, showery in afternoon. ZAC	Orders for move Appendix J
	26		Weather showery. Inspections of arms equipment, feet, & general arrangements ZAC	

Instructions regarding War Diaries and Intelligence Summaries are contained in F. S. Regs., Part II. and the Staff Manual respectively. Title pages will be prepared in manuscript.

(4)

WAR DIARY
or
~~INTELLIGENCE SUMMARY.~~
(Erase heading not required.)

Volume IX
155th Fd Coy RE

Army Form C. 2118.

Place	Date	Hour	Summary of Events and Information	Remarks and references to Appendices
	1916 August			
CAUCHY-A-LA-TOUR	27		Weather fine, some showers. All men cleaning up billets etc TAC	
	28		Weather fine, Route march at 10.30 a.m TAC.	
	29		Packed transport.	Orders see appendix K
		4pm	Paraded in Heavy thunderstorm. 430 started march to FOUQUEREUIL, arrived 9. pm, raining nearly all the way. Entrained, + train left at 12.12 pm	
CORBIE ~~FOUQUEREUIL~~	30.		Arrived LONGEAU about 9. a.m. Detrained + marched to CORBIE March started 10.50 a.m, arrived about 3.30 pm. Raining the whole way Very bad billets in ETAMPES nr CORBIE.	
SANDPIT CAMP E.24, b.1.1	31		Weather fine. Left billets just before 10. a.m, marched via CORBIE MERICOURT, just outside MEAUTE to ~~sand~~ SANDPIT Camp arrived about 4 pm. Bivouac with a few tents just off ALBERT—BRAY road.	Orders see appendix L

J A Clifford capt RE
for O.C. 155th Fd Coy RE

T2134. Wt. W708–776. 500000. 4/15. Sir J. C. & S.

Appendix K

S E C R E T.   16th Divn No. 7371.

H.Q.

....

48 Bde

....

Reference attached programme of entrainment

1. First Column "No of Train" is the order in which Trains go, i.e. First Train from FOUQUEREUIL; Second Train from CHOCQUES; and Third Train from LILLERS; Fourth Train from FOUQUEREUIL and so on.

Trains will go at three hours interval from each Station.

The time of departure of First Train will be notified as soon as known, and from this the hour of departure of each Train can be calculated.

2. Trains from FOUQUEREUIL and CHOCQUES will go to LONGUEAU, those from LILLERS to SALEUX.

The journey will be about 7 hours.

3. All Trains are "Type Combattant" unless marked "PARC". Composition as under :-

Type Combattant......33 Covered Trucks
14 Flats.
1 Officers' Carriage.

Type Parc............24 Covered Trucks.
23 Flats.
1 Officers' Carriage

Covered Trucks take 8 horses or 40 men - latter is very full. 3 Men can go in each horse truck.

4. Units will be at the Station 3 hours before the time of departure of train, except in the case of Infantry, when the transport and a strong loading party of 100 men from each Battalion will be at the station 3 hours and the remainder of the Battalion 1¼ hours before departure of trains.

5. Entraining States shewing Men, Horses, Vehicles (G.S., 4 wheeled limbered, and 2 Wheeled) will be handed to R.T.O. 3 hours before departure of train.

6. Breast and Head Ropes for tying horses must be provided by Units, but the Railway Authorities provide lashings for vehicles.

7. R.F.A. will unship traversing handspikes.

8. In mixed trains the senior officer proceeding by the train will be responsible that a loading party is told off to load all horses and vehicles going by that train.

9. Officers in 3 reliefs to assist the R.T.O. will be detailed for duty at each Station as under :-

3 Officers	- LILLERS -	to be detailed by C.R.A.
3 Officers	- CHOCQUES -	to be detailed by Brig: 47th Infy Bde.
3 Officers	- FOUQUEREUIL -	to be detailed by Brig: 49th Infy Bde.

P.T.O.

The Officers should know the billets of all Units entraining at the Station and will have a copy of the entraining Programme.

They will also have means of communicating with these Units.

One of these Officers will be present at the Station during the whole time of the entrainment.

10. Baggage and Supply wagons will entrain with their Units.

11. Troops will entrain daily with supplies for consumption the following day. Detailed instructions as to this will be issued separately.

12. The R.T.O. is responsible for loading the trains and all his orders will be carried out and every assistance given to him.

[signature] Maj

/o. Lieut Colonel,

25th August, 1916. A.A. & Q.M.G., 16th Division.

S E C R E T.

PROGRAMME OF MOVE OF 16TH DIVISION FROM FIRST TO FOURTH ARMY.

FOUQUEREUIL.

No: of Train.	Serial No:	Unit.	Time of Dept:
1.	30.	H.Q. 49th Inf: Bde:	
	36.	Bde: M.G. Co:	
	37.	Light T.M. Battery.	
	35.	Sec: Div: Sig: Co:	
4.	34.	8th Royal Inniskilling Fusiliers.	
7.	32.	8th Royal Irish Fusiliers.	
10.	33.	7th Royal Inniskilling Fusiliers.	
13.	31.	7th Royal Irish Fusiliers.	
16.	04.	11th Hants (Pioneers). Less Personnel of 1 Company.	
19.	86.	157th Field Co: R.E.	
	04.	11th Hants (Pioneers) 1 Company Personnel only.	
22.	93.	113th Field Ambulance.	
25.	84.	155th Field Co: R.E.	
	94.	Sanitary Section.	
28.	92.	112th Field Ambulance.	
31.	85	156th Field Co: R.E.	
	83.	H.Q. Divl: Engineers.	
	87 to 90.	½ Men Divisional Train.	
34 (Parc)	87 to 90.	Divisional Train.	
37.		SPARE.	

CHOCQUES.

2.	10.	H.Q. 47th Inf: Bde:	
	15.	Sec: Div: Sig: Co:	
	16.	Bde: M.G. Co:	
	17.	Light T.M. Battery.	
5.	11.	6th Royal Irish Regt:	
8.	12.	6th Connaught Rangers.	
11.	14.	8th Royal Munster Fusiliers.	
14.	13.	7th Leinster Regt;	

CHOCQUES (Contd)

No: of Train.	Serial No:	Unit.	Time of Dept:
17.	20.	H.Q. 48th Inf: Bde:	
	26.	H.Q. M.G. Company.	
	25.	Sec: Div: Sig: Co:	
	01.	Divisional H.Q.	
	05.	H.Q & No: 1 Sec: Div: Sig: Co:	
	27.	Light T.M. Battery.	
20.	21.	7th Royal Irish Rifles.	
	26A.	Sec: Bde: M.G. Company.	
23.	22.	1st Royal Munster Fusiliers.	
	26B.	Sec: Bde: M.G. Company.	
26.	24.	9th Royal Dublin Fusiliers.	
	26C.	Sec: Bde: M.G. Company.	
29.	23.	8th Royal Dublin Fusiliers.	
	26D.	Sec: Bde: M.G. Company.	
32.	91.	111th Filed Ambulance.	
	09.	Salvage Company.	
35. (Parc)	82.	½ No: 4 Section D.A.C.	
38. (Parc).	82.	½ No: 4 Section D.A.C.	

LILLERS.

3.	40.	H.Q. 177th Bde: R.F.A.	
	44.	✓ 'D' Battery, 177th Bde: R.F.A. (How)	
	80.	¼ No: 2 Section D.A.C. *	
6.	42.	'B' Battery, 177th Bde: R.F.A.	
	80.	¼ No: 2 Section D.A.C. *	
9.	43.	'C' Battery, 177th Bde: R.F.A.	
	80.	¼ No: 2 Section D.A.C. *	
12.	41.	'A' Battery, 177th Bde: R.F.A.	
	80.	¼ No: 2 Section D.A.C. *	
	18.	Medium T.M. Battery.	
15.	02.	H.Q. Divl: Artillery.	
	73.	'C' Battery, 77th Bde: R.F.A.	
	79.	¼ No: 1 Section D.A.C. *	
18.	70.	H.Q. 77th Bde: R.F.A.	
	74.	'D' Battery, 77th Bde: R.F.A. (How).	
	79.	¼ No: 1 Section D.A.C. *	
21.	71.	'A' Battery, 77th Bde: R.F.A.	
	79.	¼ No: 1 Section D.A.C. *	
	28.	Medium T.M. Battery.	

LILLERS (Contd).

No: of Train.	Serial No:	Unit.	Time of Dept:
24.	72.	'B' Battery, 77th Bde: R.F.A.	
	79.	¼ No: 1 Section D.A.C. *	
27.	50.	H.Q. 180th Bde: R.F.A.	
	54.	'D' Battery, 180th Bde: R.F.A. (How)	
	81.	¼ No: 3 Section D.A.C. *	
30.	52	'B' Battery, 180th Bde: R.F.A.	
	81.	¼ No: 3 Section D.A.C. *	
33.	53.	'C' Battery, 180th Bde: R.F.A.	
	81.	¼ No: 3 Section D.A.C. *	
36.	51.	'A' Battery, 180th Bde: R.F.A.	
	81.	¼ No: 3 Section D.A.C. *	
	38.	Medium T.M. Battery.	
39.	78.	H.Qrs: D.A.C.	
(Parc)	80.	No: 2 Section D.A.C. - 6 G.S. Wagons for S.A.A. with Drivers & Horses.	
	81.	No: 3 Section D.A.C. - 6 G.S. Wagons for S.A.A. with Drivers & Horses.	
	95.	Mobile Veterinary Section.	
	79	No. 1 Section D.A.C. 6 G.S Wagons for S.A.A. with Drivers & Horses	

* Exclusive of 6 G.S. Wagons for S.A.A.

Note:- All trains TYPE COMBATTANT unless PARC is shewn under the number of train.

J.H.C.J. Hildyard
Lieut: Colonel.
A.D.R.T.,I.

-thune.
-/8/16.

Bde 77.

No. 7371.

SECRET.

....

Hd

....

18 Bde

....

Reference my 7371 dated 25thinstant relating to Entraining Programme.

1. Following is the time ofdeparture of the various trains.

FOUQUEREUIL.

NO OFTRAIN.	TIME OF DEPARTURE. HOUR	DATE.
1	12.10 a.m.	29th August.
4	3.10 a.m.	"
7	6.10 a.m.	"
10	9.10 a.m.	"
13	12.10 p.m.	"
16	3.0 p.m.	"
19	6.10 p.m.	"
22	9.10 p.m.	"
25	12.10 a.m.	30th August.
28	3.10 a.m.	"
31	6.10 a.m.	"
34	9.10 a.m.	"

CHOCQUES.

2	1.12 a.m.	29th August
5	4.12 a.m.	"
8	7.12 a.m.	"
11	10.12 a.m.	"
14	1.2 p.m.	"
17	4.12 p.m.	"
20	7.12 p.m.	"
23	10.12 p.m.	"
26	1.12 a.m.	30th August.
29	4.12 a.m.	"
32	7.12 a.m.	"
35	10.12 a.m.	"
38	1.2 p.m.	"

LILLERS.

3	2.1 a.m.	29th August.
6	5.1 a.m.	"
9	8.1 a.m.	"
12	10.31 a.m.	"
15	2.1 p.m.	"
18	5.1 p.m.	"
21	8.1 p.m.	"
24	11.1 p.m.	"
27	2.1 a.m.	30th August.
30	5.1 a.m.	"
33	8.1 a.m.	"
36	10.31 a.m.	"
39	2.1 p.m.	"

It will be noticed that certain trains do not follow each other at 3 hours interval as previously stated.

2. The first five trains from FOUQUEREUIL will proceed to HEILLY and not LONGUEAU taking about 8 hours over the journey.

3. Forage wagons of the Train will entrain with units as under:-

Each Infantry Brigade............	1 Wagon.
Each Artillery Brigade...........	4 Wagons.
"A" Echelon, D.A.C...............	2 Wagons.
"B" Echelon, D.A.C...............	1 Wagon.
16th Divisional Train............	2 Wagons.

for Lieut Colonel,
A.A. & Q.M.G., 16th Division.

27th August, 1916.

16th Divn No. 7371.

SECRET.

O.C.

155th Coy R.E.

Reference my 7371 dated 27th August, Times of departure of Trains - para 2.

All trains from FOUQUEREUIL will now proceed to LONGEAU.

The first five trains from CHOCQUES will proceed to HEILLY.

[signature] Maj
for Lieut Colonel,
A.A. & Q.M.G., 16th Division.

27th August, 1916.

W A R   D I A R Y

155th Field Company R.E.

FOR   MONTH   OF   SEPTEMBER,   1916.

VOLUME 10

Vol 10

Instructions regarding War Diaries and Intelligence Summaries are contained in F. S. Regs., Part II. and the Staff Manual respectively. Title pages will be prepared in manuscript.

(1)

WAR DIARY
or
~~INTELLIGENCE SUMMARY.~~
(Erase heading not required.)

Volume X
155th Fd Coy RE

Army Form C. 2118.

Place	Date	Hour	Summary of Events and Information	Remarks and references to Appendices
	1916 Sept			
SANDPIT CAMP E.24.B.1.1.	1		Weather fine. Fixing up camp. Zae	
	2		Weather fine, fixing camp. Lt J.C. MOAKES rejoined from leave. 2/Lt B.W HOLMAN joined from base. Orders received in evening for Brigade Group to move up into Corps Reserve Zae	M
Nr BILLON FARM	3		Weather fine. Marched to near BILLON FARM. Made boxes for brigade to carry petrol tins full of water. Bde moved forward about 6 pm to neighbourhood of CARNOY into Reserve to 20th Divn. Zae	N
MINDEN POST	4		Weather fine. Squaring up camp. 6.10 pm marched to MINDEN POST, reported to CRE 20th Divn for work with his Coys. Sent up to help in consolidation of ~~Guilleme~~ GUILLEMONT. Night very wet, no-one knew way about & no work done. Lt HUGHES knocked over by shell & shaken but otherwise unhurt. Zae	
	5		CRE 16th Divn took over from CRE 20th Divn. Coy ordered to take over from 83rd Coy & work with 48th Bde on consolidation of GUILLEMONT. No infantry carrying or working parties available. Coy improved existing trench. Lt J.C. MOAKES & No 145324 Spr HILL E killed by shell. No 98282 Spr JONES W.E, No 98231 Spr FEARNLEY J, No 120825 Spr BROWN F, No 65318 Spr PEARMAN H, No 83039 ~~Spr~~ Pion WAITTAKER, J wounded by shellfire. No 103875 Spr DUNNING J; No 97933 Spr CORRANCE H wounded at duty shell fire Zae	O & P.

T2134. Wt. W708–776. 500000. 4/15. Sir J. C. & S.

Instructions regarding War Diaries and Intelligence Summaries are contained in F. S. Regs., Part II. and the Staff Manual respectively. Title pages will be prepared in manuscript.

(2)

~~Duplicate~~

WAR DIARY
or
~~INTELLIGENCE SUMMARY.~~
(Erase heading not required.)

Volume X
155th Fd Coy RE

Army Form C. 2118.

Place	Date	Hour	Summary of Events and Information	Remarks and references to Appendices
	1916			
CARNOY	Sept 6		Weather fine. Coy withdrawn from 48th Bde & put in Reserve. 1 section working on DHQ camp. Lt HUGHES went to CRE to be Assistant-Adjutant by way of a rest. Coy moved to Dugouts in CARNOY TAC	Q
	7		Weather fine, 1 section on DHQ camp 1 section clearing up infantry bivouac alongside, remainder working at own camp.	
		4.10 pm	Got orders to ~~form~~ proceed to GUILLEMONT & form part of garrison with 156 & 157 under command of O.C. 11th Hants Pioneers.	R.
		6 pm	2/Lt HOLMAN & 4 men went in advance to find out about accommodation	
		8 pm	Coy marched off with packs. Dixies & water in Cooks-cart as far as MONTAUBAN from which point they were carried TAC	
	8	1 am	Coy remained in trench by railway E of TRONES WOOD while O.C. went on to report to O.C. 11th Hants. Coy eventually got up to 157 HQ at about 6 a.m. About 9.30 am took over own trenches to N of 157, between them & 11th Hants. Trenches merely three disconnected scratches & not nearly in line. Coy worked on these & made them into trenches. Found excellent old dug-out behind centre of line & made it Coy H.Q. TAC	

T2134. Wt. W708–776. 500000. 1/15. Sir J. C. & S.

Instructions regarding War Diaries and Intelligence Summaries are contained in F. S. Regs., Part II. and the Staff Manual respectively. Title pages will be prepared in manuscript.

(3)

WAR DIARY
or
~~INTELLIGENCE SUMMARY.~~
(Erase heading not required.)

Volume X
155th Fd Coy RE.

Army Form C. 2118.

Place	Date	Hour	Summary of Events and Information	Remarks and references to Appendices
GUILLEMONT	1916 Sept 8 contd		Weather fine, intermittent shelling all day + night	
		4pm	Orders received that we would be relieved that night by 49th Inf Bde + would be in Divl Reserve at BERNAFAY WOOD zac	S.T.U. V
BERNAFAY WOOD	9		Weather fine. Marched off from GUILLEMONT about midnight + reached BERNAFAY WOOD about 4 a.m. Quartered in old German dug outs. Hostile shelling of wood with lachrymatory + H.E. shells from 2 pm till 4.45 pm when offensive started. Very little shelling after zac	
MORLANCOURT	10		Weather fine. Paraded 5.45 + marched back to MINDEN POST.	
		1pm	Marched back to MORLANCOURT arriving about 4 pm. Received orders to march to CORBIE tomorrow. zac	W. X.Y
CORBIE	11		Weather cloudy, started for CORBIE at 3.45 pm but much delay, did not ~~get~~ arrive until about 8.15 pm. zac	
	12		Weather fine. Coy resting. zac	
	13		Weather, slight rain in morning. Route march in skeleton equipment at 11. a.m. zac	
	14		Weather fine. Coy bathing. zac	

T2134. Wt. W708-776. 500000. 4/15. Sir J. C. & S.

Instructions regarding War Diaries and Intelligence Summaries are contained in F. S. Regs., Part II. and the Staff Manual respectively. Title pages will be prepared in manuscript.

(4)

WAR DIARY
or
~~INTELLIGENCE SUMMARY.~~
(Erase heading not required.)

Army Form C. 2118.

~~B~~ Volume X
155th Fd Coy R.E.

Place	Date	Hour	Summary of Events and Information	Remarks and references to Appendices
	1916 Sept			
CORBIE	15		Weather fine. Route march in skeleton equipment in mng, drill + arms inspection in afternoon. FAC	
	16		Weather fine. Work etc as 15th. FAC	
	17		Transport + cyclists, with Capt CLIFFORD + 2/Lt HOLMAN, started about 1.45pm for LA CHAUSSÉE (about 20 miles) marched with 48th Bde. at DAOURS 47th Bde, having taken wrong road broke into middle of 48th Bde. Arrived at PICQUIGNY + billetted about 11 pm. FAC Weather fine.	Z. 1.
LIMEUX	18		~~No order~~ Weather very wet. No orders as to time of starting or destination arrived for transport, so left without any for HALLENCOURT where found Coy was billetting at LIMEUX, arrived about 8.30pm (about 20 miles). Dismounted left billets ~~abou~~ 10 45 a.m, marched to LANEUVILLE + got on board motor-buses about 1.pm arrived LIMEUX about 6.15 pm. Lt O'SULLIVAN rejoined from 1st Army School. FAC	2. 3
	19		Weather fine but dull. Received orders re entrainment from both 47th + 48th Bdes, we are apparently to entrain with 47th Group but no orders received on the subject. Entrainment to start about midnight tonight but postponed a day. Coy resting. 9 reinforcements arrived. FAC	

Instructions regarding War Diaries and Intelligence Summaries are contained in F. S. Regs., Part II. and the Staff Manual respectively. Title pages will be prepared in manuscript.

(5)

WAR DIARY
or
~~INTELLIGENCE SUMMARY.~~
(Erase heading not required.)

Volume X
155th Fd Coy RE

Army Form C. 2118.

Place	Date	Hour	Summary of Events and Information	Remarks and references to Appendices
	1916 sept			
LIMEUX	20		Weather fine. Coy route-marching + drilling. Received 1 reinforcement bringing coy up to strength also received 1 LD horse as well as 1 LD horse received in exchange for 1 charger sent away sick. FAE	
	21		Weather fine. Cleaned up billets. Marched ABBEVILLE starting 3·30 pm, arrived about 6·45 pm. Entrained. Train started 9.40 pm	4, 6.
KEMMEL	22		WEATHER fine. Arrived BAILLEUL 7.a.m. Received orders billets cancelled. Marched – starting 9.a.m – to billet near KEMMEL. Billet occupied by 12th Canadian Fd Coy. 157 Coy also there. Bivouacked in open. 2/Lt HEGARTY went to take charge of RE Park.	5.
	23		Weather fine. Section officers went round line with Canadian officers in morning Moved into Canadian billets in afternoon.	
	24		Weather fine. In afternoon section officers went to trenches to arrange for work. Heard of redistribution of Brigades. NOS 2.3.4 Sections working in line by night with 60 infantry. Lt JENNINGS appointed Drainage Specialist. FAE	

Instructions regarding War Diaries and Intelligence Summaries are contained in F. S. Regs., Part II. and the Staff Manual respectively. Title pages will be prepared in manuscript.

(6)

WAR DIARY
or
~~INTELLIGENCE SUMMARY.~~
(Erase heading not required.)

Volume X
155th Fd Coy RE.

Army Form C. 2118.

Place	Date	Hour	Summary of Events and Information	Remarks and references to Appendices
	1916 Sept			
KEMMEL	25		Weather fine. C.R.E. held conference of Company Commanders. Nos 2, 3, 4 sections working in trenches by night with 50 infantry. No 1 section working in camp. 2/Lt HEGARTY admitted to HOSPITAL. zac	
	26		Weather fine. Lt. HUGHES sent to replace 2/Lt HEGARTY. Work as 25th. Sergt BRICKWOOD went on leave. zac	
	27.		Weather fine. Work as 25th. Sergts MEREDITH & BRICKWOOD awarded retrospective MILITARY MEDALS. C.S.M ARGYLE admitted to hospital. zac	
	28		Weather fine. Work as 25th. zac	
	29		Rain in morning. Work as 25th. ~~but~~ but no working parties zac	
	30		Weather fine. Work as 25th with 80 infantry. Lt O'SULLIVAN went to ~~x~~ CANADA CORNER in evening to replace Lt. HUGHES. zac	

M.H. Meredith Major
O.C 155 Co. RE

T2134. Wt. W708-776. 500000. 4/15. Sir J. C. & S.

W A R D I A R Y

MONTH OF OCTOBER, 1916.

A.Q. No. 11 16th DIVISION

VOLUME 11

155th Field Co. R.E.

Vol 11

Instructions regarding War Diaries and Intelligence Summaries are contained in F. S. Regs., Part II. and the Staff Manual respectively. Title pages will be prepared in manuscript.

(1)

WAR DIARY
or
~~INTELLIGENCE~~ SUMMARY.
(*Erase heading not required.*)

Volume XI
155th Fd Coy RE.

Army Form C. 2118.

Place	Date	Hour	Summary of Events and Information	Remarks and references to Appendices
	1916 Oct			
KEMMEL	1		Weather fine. No 2 section on drainage, Nos 3, 4 + part of No 1 on General trench repairs. Lt. HUGHES returned from CANADA CORNER: Maj REYNOLDS went on leave. Capt CLIFFORD took over command of Coy. Zac	
	2		Weather wet, work as 1st. Zac	
	3		Weather wet, work as 1st Zac	
	4		Weather wet, work as 1st Zac	
	5		Weather dull, dry work as 1st. Zac	
	6		Weather dull, dry, work as 1st. Cpl SALTER went on leave Zac	
	7		Weather showery, work as 1st Zac	
	8		Weather showery C.R.E came round billets + dump with Lt. Col BUTTERWORTH DSO R.E. Men exchanged billets with 157 Fd Coy RE. Sergt BRICKWOOD returned from leave: Zac	
	9		Weather, dull, dry. No 2 section on drainage, Nos 3 + ~~No~~ 1 on General trench repairs, No 4 working on hutting BEAVER FARM. Lt-Col PALMER left + Lt Col BUTTERWORTH became C.R.E. Zac	

T2134. Wt. W708-776. 500000. 4/15. Sir J. C. & S.

Instructions regarding War Diaries and Intelligence Summaries are contained in F. S. Regs., Part II. and the Staff Manual respectively. Title pages will be prepared in manuscript.

(2)

WAR DIARY
or
~~INTELLIGENCE SUMMARY.~~
(Erase heading not required.)

Army Form C. 2118.

Volume XI
155th Fd Coy RE

Place	Date	Hour	Summary of Events and Information	Remarks and references to Appendices
	1916 Oct			
KEMMEL	10		Weather dull dry windy, work as 9th Zae	
	11		Weather as 10th. Work as 9th. CRE. held conference of Coy Commanders in morning. In afternoon all odd men from CANADA CORNER etc returned to Coy + No 3 section went back to SCHARPENBERG for hutting. No 2 section on drainage, No 1 section General trench repairs, No 4 hutting BEAVER FARM. Zae	
	12		Weather ~~Zae~~ as 10th, work as 11th. 2/Lt HEGARTY returned from Hospital to CANADA CORNER. Zae	
	13.		Weather as 10th work as 11th Zae Maj REYNOLDS' leave extended to 20th by W.O. Zae	
	14		Weather dull dry. a/2/cpl HARRIS slightly wounded by shell Zae	
	15.		Weather variable, some showers. Work as 11th. Zae	
	16		Weather dull, dry. Work as 11th Zae	
	17.		Weather fine morning, wet afternoon. Work as 11th. Cpl Salter returned from leave Zae	
	18		Weather dull, inclined to rain. Work as 11th. CQMS COKER went to base for transfer to England. Zae	

T2134. Wt. W708-776. 500000. 4/15. Sir J. C. & S.

Instructions regarding War Diaries and Intelligence Summaries are contained in F. S. Regs., Part II. and the Staff Manual respectively. Title pages will be prepared in manuscript.

(3)

WAR DIARY
or
~~INTELLIGENCE SUMMARY~~.
(Erase heading not required.)

Army Form C. 2118.

Volume XI
155th Fd Coy RE

Place	Date	Hour	Summary of Events and Information	Remarks and references to Appendices
	1916 Oct			
KEMMEL	19		Weather very wet all day. Work as 11th. [initials]	
	20		Weather fine cold, N to N W wind, frost at night. Work as 11th II/Lt HEGARTY went on leave. [initials]	
	21		Weather as 20th Work as 11th. Maj. REYNOLDS returned from leave. [initials]	
	22		Weather as 20th. Work as 11th. Reported gas attack to North [initials]	
	23.		Weather fine & cold. Orders received for Capt CLIFFORD to return to England & report to War Office. Work as before. Nos 1 & 3 Sects changed over. [initials]	
	24.		Weather fine & cold CAPT CLIFFORD left company in the afternoon. Work as usual. Pioneer Officer visited trenches to look at site of proposed new Communication trench arrangements made for him to clear Canada drain which had fallen in. Work begun at night [initials]	
	25		Weather dull & showery. New trench abandoned temporarily on account of the state of Canada drain. Other work as usual. C.R.E visited camp re new trench. [initials]	
	26.		Weather fine all day, raining at night. Work as usual No 4 Sect started taking over from remaining No 2 Sect with drainage. [initials]	
	27.		Weather dull & showery. MAJOR REYNOLDS visited trenches with Brigadier & inspected progress of work. Another communication trench joining the centre of OAK TRENCH.	

Instructions regarding War Diaries and Intelligence Summaries are contained in F. S. Regs., Part II. and the Staff Manual respectively. Title pages will be prepared in manuscript.

(4) Original

WAR DIARY
or
~~INTELLIGENCE SUMMARY~~.
(Erase heading not required.)

Army Form C. 2118.

Volume XV
155th Field Coy. RE

Place	Date	Hour	Summary of Events and Information	Remarks and references to Appendices
	Oct 1916			
KEMMEL	27 (cont)		to FRONT LINE + PARK LANE arranged for & work started. aH	
	28th		Weather rainy & windy, clearing towards dusk. work as before. Notice received that BOULOGNE was closed till further orders & leave stopped aH.	
	29th		Weather rainy with high wind. C.R.E visited & inspected all billets & buildings. Work as usual. Raid carried out by 49th Bde assisted by 48th. aH	
	30th		Weather showery work as before. O.C visited gunners billets with a view to assisting them. aH	
	31st		Weather fine & windy occasional showers. C.R.E demonstrated use of tubes of Ammonal — for making quick communication trenches, at Divisional School. Work as usual. aH	

J.M. McReynolds[?] Major
O.C. 155 Field Co. R.E.

W A R D I A R Y .

F O R

MONTH OF NOVEMBER, 1916.

VOLUME 12.

155th Field Coy. R.E.

Vol 12

Instructions regarding War Diaries and Intelligence Summaries are contained in F. S. Regs., Part II. and Staff Manual respectively. Title pages will be prepared in manuscript.

(1) Original

WAR DIARY
or
~~INTELLIGENCE~~ SUMMARY.
(Erase heading not required.)

Army Form C. 2118.

Volume XII
155th Field Coy RE

Place	Date	Hour	Summary of Events and Information	Remarks and references to Appendices
KEMMEL	Nov 1916 1		Weather showery Work as before ½ Nos 2 & 4 Sections on drainage & half on camp duties No 3 Section working in trenches No 1 back at BU ZON hutting. Work in hand consists of the following:-	
			1 AID POST 2 C.H.Q.s T.M. Emplacements & a new trench from PARK LANE to FRONT LINE & an O.P.	a.H.
	Nov 2		Weather as yesterday, work as above.	a.H.
	Nov 3		Weather fine with occasional showers. Work as 1st CAPTAIN VARLEY Chaplain C.E. joined ~~this~~ unit for rations. a.H.	
	Nov 4		Weather fine short intense bombardment in afternoon. DUKE of CONNAUGHT visited the Division watched the Bombardment from KEMMEL HILL work as 1st a.H.	
	Nov 5th		Weather fine C.R.E visited billets in the morning & took O.C back with him to his office work as 1st	a.H.
	Nov 6th		Weather showery Nos 1 & 3 changed over No 3 returning to BU ZON for hutting work as before. Sergt Ayris joined from 130th Field Coy as mounted sergeant.	a.H.
	Nov 7th		Weather very wet enough a slight thunderstorm towards evening No 1 Section working in the line 47th Inf Bde made a raid in early hours of morning.	a.H.
	Nov 8th		Weather fine showery later. O.C visited Machine gunners in trenches with a view of helping them	a.H.

T2134. Wt. W708–776. 500000. 4/15. Sir J. C. & S.

Instructions regarding War Diaries and Intelligence Summaries are contained in F. S. Regs., Part II. and the Staff Manual respectively. Title pages will be prepared in manuscript.

Original ②

WAR DIARY
or
INTELLIGENCE SUMMARY.
(Erase heading not required.)

Army Form C. 2118.

Volume XII
155th Field Coy RE.

Place	Date	Hour	Summary of Events and Information	Remarks and references to Appendices
KEMMEL	Nov 1916 9th		Weather fine work as before. ARH.	
	10th		Weather fine O.C visited gunners to help them with Camouflage for the fronts of their gunpits. camouflage arranged. work as before ARH.	
	11th		Weather fine slight mist in evening. work as before ARH	
	12th		Weather fine C.R.E came, visited KEMMEL with O.C watched demonstration on baby Elephant shelter by 157th Coy. RE. ARH	
	13th		Weather fine. C.R.E visited billets in morning. O.C visited miners in line re their stores. work as before. C.R.E mentioned O.C might have to take over C.R.E temporarily ARH.	
	14th		Weather fine. work as before. ARH.	
	15th		Weather fine. Work started on special job of demolishing an old house in KEMMEL. Colonel Haynes president of Trench Tramways called. ARH.	
	16th		Weather fine & very cold. Sapper sent back to help gunners ~~make~~ improve their camp. work as before ARH	
	17th		Weather fine & very cold. O.C visited Brigade & marked out rifle range near Loore. ARH.	
	18th		Weather wet work as before. ARH.	
	19th		Weather wet C.R.E came in afternoon & spoke of a trench mortar show which was come off & made arrangement about Trench mortar emplacements. Nos 1 & 3 Sections changed over	

Instructions regarding War Diaries and Intelligence Summaries are contained in F. S. Regs., Part II. and the Staff Manual respectively. Title pages will be prepared in manuscript.

③ Original

WAR DIARY
or
~~INTELLIGENCE SUMMARY.~~
(Erase heading not required.)

Army Form C. 2118.

Volume XII
155th Field Coy RE.

Place	Date	Hour	Summary of Events and Information	Remarks and references to Appendices
KEMMEL.	19th (cont)		No 1 returning to Du ZON camp. Afternoon parties stopped in consequence. No 3 took over trench work. ARH	
	20th		Weather fine. 2nd Lieut H. TAYLOR reported for duty. & took charge of No 3 Section. O.C. visited line to inspect positions of parapet loopholes to be erected by Special Works park etc. Large stock of steel Cupolas arrived for us, allowing numerous jobs to proceed. work as before ARH	
	21st		Weather fine & misty. work started on framework for special parapet O.Ps for Special works park otherwise work as usual ARH	
	22nd		Weather fine & warmer. C.R.E visited billets also Adjutant & S.O.R.E. Great scarcity of 3" timber of all kinds. Further supply of Cupolas arrived. 4 Carpenters sent to 157 for work on T.M.S work as before. ARH	
	23rd		Weather fine work as before. Great shortage of all sorts of timber in Corps area ARH	
	24th		Weather fine in the morning wet mist towards evening 2nd Lieut T. C. V. HEGARTY struck off the strength of the unit by authority of 2nd Army work as before ARH	
	25th		Weather very wet materials for conversion of Pontoon wagons into mechanical draught arrived. work as before. Pumping plant at KEMMEL taken over from 156. ARH	
	26th		Weather fine wet towards evening. work as before. ARH	

T2134. Wt. W708-776. 500000. 4/15. Sir J. C. & S.

Instructions regarding War Diaries and Intelligence Summaries are contained in F. S. Regs., Part II. and the Staff Manual respectively. Title pages will be prepared in manuscript.

(4) Original

WAR DIARY
or
~~INTELLIGENCE SUMMARY.~~
(Erase heading not required.)

Army Form C. 2118.

Volume XII
155th Field Coy. R.E.

Place	Date	Hour	Summary of Events and Information	Remarks and references to Appendices
KEMMEL	27th		Weather fine C.R.E. visited billets in morning + inspected Stables & Mounted men's billets work as before. Bde require ~~at~~ 6 Stokes & 2 medium emplacements made + completed at short notice, sites chosen & taped. 157th Coy are going to put in the frames + make emplacements, we dig the holes 2 more Carpenters sent to 157th Coy. ADH	
KEMMEL	28th		Weather cold & misty. C.R.E called on return from trenches. work as before. ADH.	
"	29th		Weather cold & misty work as before ADH	
	30th		Weather cold + misty C.R.E called for conference of 3 O.Cs in afternoon Lieut KENRICK S.W. Park called re parapet O.P's work satisfactorily arranged for evening ADH	

[signature]
O.C. 155th Field Coy. R.E.

T2134. Wt. W708-776. 500000. 4/15. Sir J. C. & S.

WAR DIARY FOR MONTH OF DECEMBER, 1916.

VOLUME 13.

155th Field Coy. R.E.

Vol 13

Instructions regarding War Diaries and Intelligence Summaries are contained in F. S. Regs., Part II. and the Staff Manual respectively. Title pages will be prepared in manuscript.

(1) Original

WAR DIARY
or
~~INTELLIGENCE SUMMARY.~~
(Erase heading not required.)

Army Form C. 2118.

Volume XIII
155th Field Company, RE.

Place	Date	Hour	Summary of Events and Information	Remarks and references to Appendices
Near KEMMEL	1·12·16		Weather frosty. Work as usual. Parapet O.P. fixed but ~~[illegible]~~ not satisfactorily finished.	MMM
—"—	2·12·16		Weather frosty. Work as usual. Parapet O.P. finished. Lt Hughes went on leave	MMM
—"—	3·12·16		—"— . Lt Hughes authorized to wear Captain's badges in Div orders. Work as usual. Orders for Bde to take over section to North, now held by 47th Bde as well as half our present section; — change to take place on night of 4/5th	MMM
—"—	4·12·16		All Officers inspecting new piece of Line. Work as usual. New Line in very bad condition throughout. Weather milder & wet in afternoon. One man sent on leave in afternoon.	MMM
—"—	5·12·16		Raining for large part of day. Work started in new line. Lot of trouble with working parties. — Party left working on new Aid Post in Via Gellia (now in 49th Bde area) owing to temporarily unsafe state of ~~new~~ uncompleted entrance — Sent Officer to give advice re new Brigade rifle range.	MMM

T2134. Wt. W708–776. 500000. 4/15. Sir J. C. & S.

Instructions regarding War Diaries and Intelligence Summaries are contained in F. S. Regs., Part II. and the Staff Manual respectively. Title pages will be prepared in manuscript.

(2) Original

WAR DIARY
or
~~INTELLIGENCE~~ SUMMARY.
(Erase heading not required.)

Volume XIII
155th Field Coy RE

Army Form C. 2118.

Place	Date	Hour	Summary of Events and Information	Remarks and references to Appendices
Nr. KEMMEL	6.12.16		Weather mild & damp. Further reconnaissance of new area. Work as usual on old front, new work under way. O.C. attended G.O.C.'s conference of Battalion Commanders. One man went on leave.	JMcM
— " —	7.12.16		Weather damp & foggy. Work going well in new area. Two reinforcements arrived. ~~Suggested~~ Proposal for forming Brigade Pioneer Company to work under R.E. brought up & approved at conference last night.	JMcM
— " —	8.12.16		Damp & foggy. Work as usual. Put storeman in advanced dump at Rossignol	JMcM
— " —	9.12.16		Raining hard. Work as usual. Started new shelter for storeman at Rossignol. A number of men going sick with colds etc.	JMcM
— " —	10.12.16		Damp & cold. Work as usual — Battalion relief day. Two men went on leave.	
— " —	11.12.16		Rain & mist. Work as usual. One man wounded, one suffering from Shell Shock	JMcM
— " —	12.12.16		Snow & Sleet all day. Work as usual. Started on front line shelters for the infantry. — Very badly wanted.	JMcM
— " —	13.12.16		Misty but brighter. Work as usual. Capt Doran 9th R.D.F. arrived with a view to preparing for & taking command of the new Pioneer Company. Two men went on leave.	JMcM

Instructions regarding War Diaries and Intelligence Summaries are contained in F. S. Regs., Part II. and the Staff Manual respectively. Title pages will be prepared in manuscript.

(3)

Original

WAR DIARY
or
~~INTELLIGENCE SUMMARY.~~
(Erase heading not required.)

Army Form C. 2118.

Volume XIII
155th Field Coy RE

Place	Date	Hour	Summary of Events and Information	Remarks and references to Appendices
Nr Kemmell	14.12.16		Mild & Damp. New Company H.Q. started. Otherwise work as usual. Captain Hughes returned from leave in evening.	MWM
— " —	15.12.16		Mild & Damp. O.C. visited trenches. Work as usual. Heavy shelling of front line	MWM
— " —	16.12.16		Weather fine. Work as usual. Lt Jennings went on leave. Front line shelled again. Sergt Pollard promoted a/C.S.M.	MWM
— " —	17.12.16		Weather fine — Sent Officer to investigate how Decauville track (unused) there ~~[illegible]~~ is in the area. Otherwise work as usual.	MWM
— " —	18.12.16		Weather fine — Work as usual	MWM
— " —	19.12.16		— " — & cold — " — . Snow on ground	MWM
— " —	20.12.16		— " — " — " — Two men went on leave	MWM
— " —	21.12.16		Showery. Work as usual	MWM
— " —	22.12.16		Very wet day. Battalion relief. Great shortage of working parties. Otherwise work as usual. G.O.C. 48th Bde inspected work	MWM
— " —	23.12.16		Gale Blowing. C.R.E. visited billet. Two men went on leave. Work as usual	MWM
— " —	24.12.16		Windy & some rain. Work as usual.	MWM
— " —	25.12.16		Wet early — fine later. Div. Commander visited billet. C.R.E. came twice. Captain Doran went on leave. — No work.	MWM

T2134. Wt. W708–776. 500000. 4/15. Sir J. C. & S.

Instructions regarding War Diaries and Intelligence Summaries are contained in F. S. Regs., Part II. and the Staff Manual respectively. Title pages will be prepared in manuscript.

(4)

Original

WAR DIARY
or
~~INTELLIGENCE SUMMARY~~.
(Erase heading not required.)

Army Form C. 2118.

Volume XIII
155th Field Coy RE

Place	Date	Hour	Summary of Events and Information	Remarks and references to Appendices
Nr KEMMEL	26.12.16		Weather fine. C.R.E. visited camp. Bde informed us that Pioneer Company will be formed on evening of 29th. G.O.C. 28th Bde visited billet. Work as usual. Two men went on leave.	MM
— " —	27.12.16		Weather fine. Sent officer begin reconnoitring wire. Trench mortar bombardment of enemy lines in afternoon. Work as usual	MM
— " —	28.12.16		Fine again, hard frost in morning. Work as usual. Lt Jennings returned from leave. Colonel Stocker, who is now to take charge of Pioneer Company, visited billet & Pioneer Farm. Made & sent in designs for dugouts in conjunction with O.C. 157 Co	MM
— " —	29.12.16		Fine, except for rain in morning. Work as usual. ~~Gen~~ Brigadier went round some of the works. No 3 Section relieved No 1 in the evening. Pioneer Company assembled at Pioneer Farm in evening.	MM
— " —	30.12.16		Fine weather, though very heavy rain in early morning. Pioneer Co. started work. One man went on leave	MM
— " —	31.12.16		Fine weather. Work as usual. One man of Pioneer Co. admitted to Field Ambulance with shell shock	

M.M. Meynell [signature]
Major RE
O.C. 155 Field Co RE

T2134. Wt. W708—776. 500000. 4/15. Sir J. C. & S.

W A R D I A R Y for month of JANUARY, 1917.

VOLUME 14

Royal Engineers 155th Field Compy.

Vol 14

Instructions regarding War Diaries and Intelligence Summaries are contained in F. S. Regs., Part II. and the Staff Manual respectively. Title pages will be prepared in manuscript.

(1) Original

WAR DIARY
or
~~INTELLIGENCE SUMMARY~~.
(Erase heading not required.)

Volume XIV
155th Field Coy RE

Army Form C. 2118.

Place	Date	Hour	Summary of Events and Information	Remarks and references to Appendices
Nr KEMMEL	1-1-17		Weather fine — Bombardment (Trench mortars etc) of enemy's line at 8 am. Work as usual. ~~to~~ Received orders in evening for Major REYNOLDS to proceed to Aldershot for Senior Officers' Infantry Course. Lt Holman went on leave.	[illegible]
— " —	2-1-17		Fine weather. Work as usual. Completed reconnaissance of wire in sector. C.R.E visited billet. Four men went on leave.	[illegible]
— " —	3-1-17.		Fine weather – work as usual. Major Reynolds to C.R.E in evening — Leaves Bailleul tomorrow to proceed to England. Handing over Company to Captain Hughes.	[illegible]
— " —	4-1-17.		Weather Fine. Major Reynolds left for England. Major Stocker O.C Pioneer Company also left on duty for England. Pioneer Company taken over by Captain O'Carroll 8 R.D.F. B.G.C 48th visited billets in afternoon re work. Work as usual. 2nd Lieut Johnstone joined unit from No 4 G.B.D.	[illegible]
— " —	5.1.17.		Weather bright & sunny. Work as usual. G.O.C visited this sector with B.G.C. A state of how [illegible] was employed rendered to CRE. 4 men went on leave. Work as usual.	[illegible]
— " —	6.1.17		Weather stormy some rain. Work as before. Lieut Jennings handing over to Lieut. JOHNSTONE	

T2134. Wt. W708-776. 500000. 4/15. Sir J. C. & S.

Instructions regarding War Diaries and Intelligence Summaries are contained in F. S. Regs., Part II. and the Staff Manual respectively. Title pages will be prepared in manuscript.

(2)

Original

WAR DIARY
or
INTELLIGENCE SUMMARY.
(Erase heading not required.)

Volume XIV

155 Fd Coy R.E.

Army Form C. 2118.

Place	Date	Hour	Summary of Events and Information	Remarks and references to Appendices
KEMMEL	6.1.17 (cont)		who took command of No 4 Section. Special working party put on Vattery street.	ABH
— " —	7.1.17	~~(cont)~~	Weather fine. Work as before. Lieut Jennings left for 16th Div School as instructor.	ABH
— " —	8.1.17		Weather light & windy. 4 men went off on leave. Raining towards evening. Work as usual.	ABH
— " —	9.1.17		Weather fine. Enemy shelled vicinity of billets with 77mm putting about 20 rounds in the field just beyond. CAPTAIN PAKENHAM-WALSH arrived with CRE to take command of Company. Work as usual. Dummy raid carried out at 7 p.m. by 41st Division. B.G.C rang up at 10 p.m. to say front line had been obliterated & ordered a special working party to go up ~~unparentated~~ unparented also an officer. Repairs completed.	ABH
— " —	10.1.17		Weather fine. O.C visited Battalion HQrs & front trenches to look at work. ~~[illegible]~~ Work as usual.	ABH
— " —	11.1.17.		Weather fine. O.C visited left subsector trenches with O.C. Left Subsector. 2 men went on leave. Work as usual	RPW
— " —	12.1.17		Weather fine. Damage to old and new support trenches in Left subsector by enemy T Ms. Damage cleared. Work as usual	RPW
— " —	13.1.17		Snow and heavy rain. 2/Lt Holman returned from leave. O.C. saw B.G.C, 48th Bde at Bde H.Q. re work in afternoon. 1 man went on leave. Work as usual	RPW

T2134. Wt. W708-776. 500000. 4/15. Sir J. C. & S.

Instructions regarding War Diaries and Intelligence Summaries are contained in F. S. Regs., Part II. and the Staff Manual respectively. Title pages will be prepared in manuscript.

(3)
original

WAR DIARY
or
INTELLIGENCE SUMMARY.
(Erase heading not required.)

Army Form C. 2118.

Volume XIV
155 Fd Coy R E

Place	Date	Hour	Summary of Events and Information	Remarks and references to Appendices
KEMMEL	14.1.17		Foggy. O.C visited Trenches in centre of sector. Considerable flooding in various parts. O.C went with other O.s C. companies to C.R.E's office for instructions as to guards and drills etc. Work as usual	RPM
— " —	15.1.17		Fine weather. C.R.E visited billet and trenches in afternoon with O.C. Enemy T.Ms bombarded support line of left subsector. 4 men went on leave. Work as usual.	RPM
— " —	16.1.17		Snow in the morning. O.C visited ~~Bde~~ 48th Bde H.Q to arrange with O.C as to new scheme of work & rest day. Work as usual	RPM
— " —	17.1.17		Snow lying 2" deep & falling. O.C. visited trenches in morning. C.R.E visited billet. 4 men went on leave. Work as usual.	RPM
— " —	18.1.17		Snow lying but thawing. Work as usual.	RPM
— " —	19.1.17		Fine. Thawing. 35 men of 11th Labour Battn reported for work under instructions from C.R.E. One of these wounded by Shrapnel. O.C. visited trenches. New method of rapid repair of breastworks experimented with fair success	RPM
— " —	20.1.17		Frosty. Work as usual. 4 men went on leave.	RPM
— " —	21.1.17		Only a few men employed on important work in trenches remainder remained in	

T2134. Wt. W708-776. 500000. 4/15. Sir J. C. & S.

Instructions regarding War Diaries and Intelligence Summaries are contained in F. S. Regs., Part II. and the Staff Manual respectively. Title pages will be prepared in manuscript.

(4)

WAR DIARY
or
INTELLIGENCE SUMMARY.
(Erase heading not required.)

Army Form C. 2118.

Original

Volume XIV

155 Fd Coy. R.E.

Place	Date	Hour	Summary of Events and Information	Remarks and references to Appendices
KEMMEL	21.1.17	(cont)	Camp for cleaning repairing and inspection of kit etc. Parade under C.R.E at de ZON CAMP of sections on huttings and all available officers for presentation of parchment certificates and badges awarded by G.O.C Divn. for devotion to duty. Parchments & badges awarded in 155 Fd Coy to – 2/Lt. B.W. HOLMAN, No 97857 Sgt A THURLOW, No 61174 Cpl C NORGATE, No 101552 2/Cpl E.W. HARRIS, No 81663 L/Cpl J. HORNBY. 1.45 pm. O.C inspected the Company	[initials]
—	22.1.17		Sharp Frost. New system of employment started. Area divided into Front, Middle, & Rear, sections, to be worked respectively by each section. No. 2 Section relieved No 1 section at fir hutting at CANADA CORNER, leaving distribution for next fortnight No 1 Section, Rear; No 2 Section, Canada Corner; No 3 Section, Front; No 4 Section Middle. O.C visited left sub section with Battn. Commander. Considerable hostile T.M. activity.	[initials]
—	23.1.17		Still freezing. Ground very hard. Orders. Rough line of levels in HARINGHEBEEKE taken with a view to inundation. 4 men went on leave. Work as usual	[initials]
—	24.1.17		Still freezing. Work hampered by scarcity of timber scantling. Report on all	

T2134. Wt. W708–776. 500000. 4/15. Sir J. C. & S.

Instructions regarding War Diaries and Intelligence Summaries are contained in F. S. Regs., Part II. and the Staff Manual respectively. Title pages will be prepared in manuscript.

(5)

Original

WAR DIARY
or
~~INTELLIGENCE~~ SUMMARY.
(Erase heading not required.)

Army Form C. 2118.

Volume XIV

155 Fd Coy R.E.

Place	Date	Hour	Summary of Events and Information	Remarks and references to Appendices
KEMMEL	24.1.17	(cont)	Dugouts etc in area sent to C.R.E. Work as usual.	RPTD
"	25.1.17		C.R.E. visited billet. O.C. interviewed O.C. 1st Entrenching Battalion to arrange hours of work. Work as usual. Weather freezing.	RPTD
"	26.1.17		Freezing but fine. Leave stopped owing to congestion of Traffic. Work as usual. LIEUT JENNINGS returned from Divisional School.	RPTD
"	27.1.17		Freezing but fine. Divl G.O.C. went round part of Sector with C.R.E. and called at Billet. Work as usual much hindered by frost.	RPTD
"	28.1.17		Freezing and clear. Only important new work in trenches. Company inspected by O.C. 11.10 am. Church Parade 11.30 am. Sections otherwise at disposal of Sections officers for inspection etc. 11.30 am several time H.E. shells burst over billet. One N.C.O. Reinforcement arrived.	RPTD
"	29.1.17		Freezing & clear. Owing to reorganization of Divisional front, the Company took over R.E. charge of an extended front to coincide with new 46th Inf Brigade Front. VIERSTRAAT – WYTSCHAETE Road (exclusive) to BROADWAY & LEAMING LANE (inclusive). O.C. visited new area & Right subsection Work. Work as usual.	RPTD
"	30.1.17		Freezing but not so settled, a little snow. Lt JENNINGS interviewed at BAILLEUL	

T2134. Wt. W708–776. 500000. 4/15. Sir J. C. & S.

Instructions regarding War Diaries and Intelligence Summaries are contained in F. S. Regs., Part II. and the Staff Manual respectively. Title pages will be prepared in manuscript.

(6)

Original

WAR DIARY
or
INTELLIGENCE SUMMARY.
(Erase heading not required.)

Vol XIV

155 Fd. Coy. R.E

Army Form C. 2118.

Place	Date	Hour	Summary of Events and Information	Remarks and references to Appendices
REMMEL	30.1.17	(contd)	with view to transfer to Field Survey Coy. Work as usual	[illegible]
— " —	31.1.17		Thaw threatening but not commenced. O.C. visited left subsection Trenches in morning. C.R.E. called at Billet. Work as usual	
			A.P. Pakenham Walsh Capt R.E O.C. 155 Fd. Coy. R.E	

T2134. Wt. W708–776. 500000. 4/15. Sir J. C. & S.

W A R D I A R Y.

FOR MONTH OF FEBRUARY, 1917.

VOLUME 15

UNIT:- 155th Field Coy R.E.

Vol 15

Instructions regarding War Diaries and Intelligence Summaries are contained in F. S. Regs., Part II. and the Staff Manual respectively. Title pages will be prepared in manuscript.

(1)

Original

WAR DIARY
or
INTELLIGENCE SUMMARY.
(Erase heading not required.)

Army Form C. 2118.

Volume XV

155 Fd Coy. R.E

Place	Date	Hour	Summary of Events and Information	Remarks and references to Appendices
KEMMEL	1.2.17		Freezing. Some signs of thaw. Arrangements for construction of baths at PIONEER FARM. Chief new ~~fo~~ work in hand new Trench from CORNTRENCH to VAN REEP. new Trench OAK TRENCH to Front Line (FIR LANE). CHINESE WALL. new DUG OUTS etc. Gas proofing doors to Dugouts etc. Maintenance and drainage. O.C visited B.G.C at Bde H.Q and discussed relative precedence of new work etc. Work as usual	[illegible]
— " —	2-2-17		Freezing. O.C accompanied C.R.E round right subsector and Tunnels, and then visited other work. Work as usual.	[illegible]
— " —	3.2.17		Freezing. O.C went to VIERSTRAAT with R.A Officer re construction of new O.P. Order received for 2nd Lt HOLMAN to join 176th Drainage Coy, to be replaced by 2/Lt ~~[illegible]~~ LEACH of that Company. Work as usual. 2/Lt TAYLOR & 1 man went on leave	[illegible]
— " —	4.2.17		Freezing. Only important trench work carried out. Church Parade. No.1 Section then paraded & checked Coolcart.	[illegible]
— " —	5.2.17		Freezing. 2nd Lt HOLMAN left for 176th Drainage Coy. C.R.E visited billet to discuss various matters with ~~C.R.E~~ O.C. Work as usual	[illegible]
— " —	6.2.17.		Freezing. Work as usual. Report received from Dvl Train that Pioneer Pearson, attached to the train died on a wagon last night. Matter being investigated.	[illegible]

T2134. Wt. W708-776. 500000. 4/15. Sir J. C. & S.

Instructions regarding War Diaries and Intelligence Summaries are contained in F. S. Regs., Part II. and the Staff Manual respectively. Title pages will be prepared in manuscript.

(2)

Original

WAR DIARY
or
~~INTELLIGENCE SUMMARY.~~
(Erase heading not required.)

Volume XV

155 Fd. Coy. RE

Army Form C. 2118.

Place	Date	Hour	Summary of Events and Information	Remarks and references to Appendices
KEMMEL	7-2-17		Freezing. O.C visited trenches and on way back reported serious damage to A Frames by troops to O.C Left Subsector. ~~Also~~ Also repeated same in afternoon to Bde Major at Bde H.Q. 2 shells (77 mm) fell in billet about 3.30 pm. One entered grooms quarters but failed to explode. Another burst in field by road. Enemy damaged hedge in front of BRYKERIE Trench by shell fire in afternoon. Work as usual.	[illegible]
"	8.2.17		Freezing. Acting B.G.C visited billet ref Gas proof doors to dug-outs. 2 men went on leave. Work as usual. No men of Entrenching Battalion available.	[illegible]
"	9.2.17		Freezing & fine. Work as usual no entrenching battalion. Three huts in Bde Pioneer Coy billet at PIONEER FARM destroyed by fire between 8 & 9 a.m. 2nd Lt G.B. LEACH R.E. arrived to replace 2/Lt HOLMAN. C.R.E. visited billet in evening.	[illegible]
"	10.2.17		Freezing & fine. Work as usual. No men of Entrenching Battalion available.	[illegible]
"	11.2.17		Slight thaw. Fine. ~~At~~ Only important work on Trenches. Parade Service 11.30. No 4 Section checked tool cart & Nos 1 & 3 Sections, arting as drill 12.15 pm. C.R.E. inspected Camp and Sections on parade 12.15 pm. No 3 Section relieved No. 2 at DEZON Camp. Divisional Artillery bombarded PETIT BOIS & STANBROEKMOELEN at 12 noon & 3 pm respectively.	[illegible]
"	12.2.17		Slight thaw. Fine ~~a[illegible]~~ Section Relief. No 1. Middle Section No. 2 Back Section. No. 3	

T2134. Wt. W708-776. 500000. 4/15. Sir J. C. & S.

Instructions regarding War Diaries and Intelligence Summaries are contained in F. S. Regs., Part II. and the Staff Manual respectively. Title pages will be prepared in manuscript.

(3)

Original

WAR DIARY
or
~~INTELLIGENCE SUMMARY.~~
(Erase heading not required.)

Army Form C. 2118.

Volume XV

155th Fd Coy. RE

Place	Date	Hour	Summary of Events and Information	Remarks and references to Appendices
KEMMEL	12.2.17	(cont)	Section at DE ZON Camp for hutting No 4 Section Front Section. O.C went round trenches with 2/Lt LEACH. Principal important new work on FIR LANE, NEW SUPPORT trench, new trench WATSONVILLE to BYRON FARM, CHINESE WALL.	RAMD
"	13.2.17		Slow thaw. Work as usual.	RAMD
"	14.2.17		Fine, slow thaw, freezing at night. CAPT O'CARROLL R.D.F returned from leave and reassumed command of Pioneer Company from 2/Lt MAITLAND. M.C, R.I.R. who returned to his battalion. O.C saw B.G.C at Bde H.Q with O.C Sect 250th Tunnelling Company re clearing of spoil bags from shaft in ROSSIGNOL to CHINESE WALL. Work as usual.	RAMD
"	15.2.17		Fine slow thaw. O.C. visited trenches and arranged for C H Q in S.P 13 to move temporarily into Adv. Battn. H.Q in Mine Gallery in S.P 13. Battery about 400 yards E of Billet bombarded in morning and afternoon with 4.2" & 5.9" including gas shells, the gas from which was carried past the billet. One Sapper (Sapr. FENNE) slightly wounded in the knee with a splinter from one of these shells. O.C visited Bde. H.Q to discuss certain matters. Work as usual.	RAMD

T2134. Wt. W708-776. 500000. 4/15. Sir J. C. & S.

Instructions regarding War Diaries and Intelligence Summaries are contained in F. S. Regs., Part II. and the Staff Manual respectively. Title pages will be prepared in manuscript.

(4)

Original

WAR DIARY
or
INTELLIGENCE SUMMARY.
(Erase heading not required.)

Army Form C. 2118.

Volume XV

155 Fd Coy R.E

Place	Date	Hour	Summary of Events and Information	Remarks and references to Appendices
KEMMEL	16.2.17		Thawing. Fine. Frost at night. O.C visited Left Bn HQ re strengthening of ROSSIGNOL ESTAMINET Work as usual. 2nd Lt. TAYLOR returned from leave	R.R.A.
"	17.2.17		Thaw more rapid, misty. O.C Reconnoitred BYRON FARM and old Support line in the neighbourhood. Thaw traffic restrictions imposed. Work as usual	R.R.A.
"	18.2.17		Thaw Fine. Only important trench work. No 2 Section Toolcart inspected. Other Sections on antigas drill. IX Corps H.A. + 16th Divn. F.A bombarded in afternoon and evening. Our G.S. Wagons turned out at 10.30 pm to salve H.A. Ammn from a upset lorry.	R.R.A.
"	19.2.17		Fine but Misty. C.R.E. went round ground by BYRON FARM and called at Billet on return. S.O.C.E. IX Corps called at Billet, also a/B.G.C. the latter to arrange about working party for repair of NEW SUPPORT trench off WATLING ST.	R.R.A.
"	20.2.17		Showery but fairly clear. IX Corps Heavy Arty + 16th Divn. F.A bombarded enemys position around BLACK COT and NANCY CRESCENT in afternoon. Enemy's retaliation about 5 pm breached PARK AVENUE in 7 places, some hits on CHINESE WALL (and FENNE) caused no damage. Work as usual	R.R.A.
"	21.2.17		Very Foggy. O.C. went with C.R.E round the defences of VIERSTRAAT and the right of the 47th Divn. area to see how the system of defences	

T2134. Wt. W708-776. 500000. 4/15. Sir J. C. & S.

Instructions regarding War Diaries and Intelligence Summaries are contained in F. S. Regs., Part II. and the Staff Manual respectively. Title pages will be prepared in manuscript.

(5) Original

WAR DIARY
or
~~INTELLIGENCE~~ SUMMARY.
(Erase heading not required.)

Army Form C. 2118.

Volume XV
155 Fd. Coy. R.E.

Place	Date	Hour	Summary of Events and Information	Remarks and references to Appendices
KEMMEL	21-2-17	(cont)	Co-ordinated. O.C visited Bde H.Q ~~to~~ at 7.30pm to arrange about hours of withdrawal of working parties during bombardment arranged for 22-2-17. Work as usual. 2 of Bde P.W. Coy wounded at FIR LANE.	R.A.A.
— " —	22.2.17		Very Foggy. Bombardment arranged for morning postponed owing to fog. O.C. visited ~~work~~ trenches in morning. Repairs to PARK AVENUE & work in front area delayed by trenches being cleared. Ground very soft on surface, but not thawed underneath. With above exceptions work as usual	R.A.A.
— " —	23.2.17		Very Foggy. Bombardment again postponed. One of our guns dropped a shell just in front of CHINESE WALL at a.m. 2/Lt LEACH reported matter to Coy. H.Q at HARLEY HOUSE & recovered the nose cap as evidence. 125 Entrenching Battalion unexpectedly reported for work. All employed in rear section owing to proposed bombardment.	R.A.A.
— " —	24.2.17.		Fine. Fairly clear in morning. Orders received to keep Front line clear 9am to 7pm. So employed all (including 165, Entrenching Battn) in area behind HARINGHEBEEKE. Only worked till noon and arranged to work next	

T2134. Wt. W708-776. 500000. 4/15. Sir J. C. & S.

Instructions regarding War Diaries and Intelligence Summaries are contained in F. S. Regs., Part II. and the Staff Manual respectively. Title pages will be prepared in manuscript.

(6) Original

WAR DIARY
or
~~INTELLIGENCE SUMMARY.~~
(Erase heading not required.)

Vol XV
155 Fd Coy R.E.

Army Form C. 2118.

Place	Date	Hour	Summary of Events and Information	Remarks and references to Appendices
KEMMEL	24-2-17	(cont)	afternoon. In reply to a morning bombardment Enemy shelled SP12, 4 13 and surrounding area. At 4.55 pm enterprise by 124 Bde 41st Div. on our left with heavy artillery support.	
	25.2.17		Weather fine but misty, Work as usual in afternoon on account of yesterday. ADH	
	~~—~~		No 4 Section relieved No 3 at Canada lines. No 1 Section started work in front line No 2 centre No 3 taking over back areas. MAJOR WALSH left for 10 days course of instruction at RE School.	
	26.2.17.		Weather light & fine work carried on as usual under new arrangements. Enemy shelled Reserve areas CORK TRENCH blown in for about 20 yds. ADH	
	27.2.17.		Weather fine but foggy with slight rain, Work as before. CRS visited billets. ADH	
	28.2.17		Weather fine but dull. Working party from entrenching Battalion reduced by thirty men Work started on repairs to floor of SIEGE FARM also firestepping in VIERSTRAAT SWITCH. Otherwise work as usual. ADH	

A D Hughes Capt RE
O.C. 155th Field Coy RE

W A R D I A R Y

FOR MONTH OF MARCH, 1917.

VOLUME 16

U N I T :- 155th Field Company R.E.

WO 95/2216

Instructions regarding War Diaries and Intelligence Summaries are contained in F. S. Regs., Part II. and the Staff Manual respectively. Title pages will be prepared in manuscript.

WAR DIARY
or
~~INTELLIGENCE~~ SUMMARY.
(Erase heading not required.)

Original (1)

Army Form C. 2118.

Vol XVI
155th Field Coy R.E.

Place	Date	Hour	Summary of Events and Information	Remarks and references to Appendices
KEMMEL.	1.3.17.		Weather fine but dull, work as usual ie No 1 section front line No 2 Section centre section No 3 Sect rear section. [illegible]	
	2.3.17		Weather misty slight rain later work as before. artillery fairly active [illegible]	
	3.3.17		Weather fine, Hants Pioneers started work on the front line near Mayo St. C.R.E. visited billets in morning. Work as before new Baby elephant dugouts (4) put in hand for T.M. Battery [illegible]	
	4.3.17		Weather fine Company rest day ½ No 2 Sect working & allow of baths for pioneers on Tuesday. II Corps HA. just right of our front. Lieut Taylor took over from Lieut Culver the work on VIERSTRAAT SWITCH.	
	5.3.17		Weather fine about 1" of fresh snow on ground in morning yesterdays bombardment continued. Entrenching battalion party increased to 200 arranged as follows 140 in the morning + 60 in the evening all the extra men being employed on the VIERSTRAAT SWITCH Sapper Taylor wounded in the arm shrapnel.	
	6.3.17		Weather fine, Work as usual except half Pioneers bathing, heavy artillery fire on 35th Div front.	

T2134. Wt. W708–776. 500000. 4/15. Sir J. C. & S.

Instructions regarding War Diaries and Intelligence Summaries are contained in F. S. Regs., Part II. and the Staff Manual respectively. Title pages will be prepared in manuscript.

WAR DIARY
or
~~INTELLIGENCE SUMMARY~~.
(Erase heading not required.)

Army Form C. 2118.

Original ②

Vol. XVI
155th Field Coy R.E.

Place	Date	Hour	Summary of Events and Information	Remarks and references to Appendices
KEMMEL.	7.3.17		Weather fine. Work as before. CRE came late in morning to visit VIERSTRAAT Switch re new work detailed by 16th Div: G. chiefly gaps in wire for counter attacks & repairs to the old trench. CRE arranged to increase party of 1st Entrenching Battalion. AH	
	8.3.17		Ground covered with snow in the morning, clearing later with occasional snow storms. Section officer concerned shown new work required on VIERSTRAAT switch. Enemy raided trenches on Right Battalion front at about 5.45 pm & penetrated as far as PARK AVENUE. Trenches badly smashed in. MAJOR PAKENHAM-WALSH returned from RE School in evening. AH	
	9.3.17		Enemy again bombarded trenches and raided trenches of Brigade on the right at 4 am, doing further damage to trenches. In ~~to~~ the two bombardments following trenches badly damaged ASH LANE, OAK TRENCH, FIR LANE, PARK AVENUE, LEEMING LANE, and BIRDCAGE (in ROSSIGNOL). Parties working continuously got passage through OAK TRENCH & PARK STREET by MIDNIGHT. Work arranged with B.G.C in morning, and a Divl Staff Officer shewn damage in afternoon. AH	
	10.3.17		FIR LANE & ASH LANE rendered passable by 7 am. CRE went round trenches	

T2134. Wt. W708–776. 500000. 4/15. Sir J. C. & S.

Instructions regarding War Diaries and Intelligence Summaries are contained in F. S. Regs., Part II. and the Staff Manual respectively. Title pages will be prepared in manuscript.

WAR DIARY
or
~~INTELLIGENCE SUMMARY.~~
(Erase heading not required.)

(3) Original ~~Duplicate~~

Vol XVI

155 Fd Coy R.E.

Army Form C. 2118.

Place	Date	Hour	Summary of Events and Information	Remarks and references to Appendices
KEMMEL	10.3.17	(cont)	with B.G.C, and discussed formation of new line of defence	R.A.A.
— " —	11.3.17		Rest day but continuous work kept up in front area on damaged trenches. Section relief No 1 to ~~Canada Corner,~~ BALDOYLE CAMP, No 4 in Back, No 3 in middle & No 2 in front areas. Orders received that 47th Bde (on our right) will be relieved by 36th Divn on 13th, our area to be extended to KETCHEN AVENUE	R.A.A.
— " —	12.3.17		Very wet night and ground very muddy. At midday 49th Inf Bde started to wire the whole G.H.Q Line. Orders received for 157th Fd Coy RE to take over left Subsector of 48th Inf Bde Area, the 155th Coy remaining in Right subsector.	R.A.A.
— " —	13.3.17		C.R.E visited trenches to arrange about new wire near the HARINGHEBEER in connection with M.Guns. O.C & O.C. 157 Fd Coy R.E visited 48th Inf Bde H.Q to arrange about distribution of work in new area.	R.A.A.
— " —	14.3.17		O.C 157 R.E handed over work in VIERSTRAAT SWITCH in new sector to O.C. Work as usual. 2 reinforcements arrived.	R.A.A.
— " —	15.3.17		Handed over work in left Subsector ~~to~~ on VIERSTRAAT SWITCH to O.C. 157 Coy R.E. Arranged positions of M.G. Dugouts with Div & O.C. 49th M.G. Coy.	R.A.A.
— " —	16.3.17		Handed over work in remainder of left subsection to O.C 157 Coy R.E. G.O.C & B.G.C	

Instructions regarding War Diaries and Intelligence Summaries are contained in F. S. Regs., Part II. and the Staff Manual respectively. Title pages will be prepared in manuscript.

(4) Original

WAR DIARY
or
~~INTELLIGENCE SUMMARY~~.
(*Erase heading not required.*)

Vol XVI

155 Fd. Coy R.E

Army Form C. 2118.

Place	Date	Hour	Summary of Events and Information	Remarks and references to Appendices
KEMMEL	16.3.17	(cont)	48th & 49th Inf Bdes went round trenches in area preparatory to Brigades handing over. RPM	
"	17.3.17	(cont).	Stopped work in Left Subsector & took over all work in Right Subsector. CRE went round ~~all~~ trenches and pointed out various works to be carried out. RPM	
"	18.3.17		Only important trench work carried out. OC with OC 157 Fd Coy RE visited BGC 49th Inf Bde and discussed arrangements for work 48th Bde Pioneer Coy disbanded RPM	
"	19.3.17		48th Inf Bde relieved in trenches by 49th Inf Bde. Work as usual but very little labour available. RPM	
"	20.3.17		Still difficulty in obtaining working parties. Arrangements made through CRE Work as usual RPM	
"	21.3.17		BGC 49th Inf Bde visited billet for conference with OsC 155 & 157 Fd Coys. Letter of appreciation for work of company in clearing trenches after raid of 8.3.17 received from BGC 48th Inf Bde. Work as usual plenty of labour RPM	
"	22.3.17		Test of Pipe line of KEMMEL Water supply system started after completion of new filter. Alternate snow & fine weather. Work as usual RPM	
"	23.3.17		Frost during night. Changeable weather during day. OC Subsector selected points for Lewis Guns & Dugouts RPM	

T2134. Wt. W708–776. 500000. 4/15. Sir J. C. & S.

Instructions regarding War Diaries and Intelligence Summaries are contained in F. S. Regs., Part II. and the Staff Manual respectively. Title pages will be prepared in manuscript.

(5) Original

WAR DIARY
or
~~INTELLIGENCE~~ SUMMARY.
(Erase heading not required.)

Vol XVI

155 Fd Coy R.E

Army Form C. 2118.

Place	Date	Hour	Summary of Events and Information	Remarks and references to Appendices
KEMMEL ~~24-3-17~~	24.3.17		Fine weather. Work as usual	RAM
— " —	25.3.17		Only sufficient men to employ infantry working parties at work in line. One of Infantry working parties killed by Shell fire at CHINESE WALL. Snowing at intervals.	RAM
— " —	26.3.17		C.R.E called Conference of Fd Coy Commanders to arrange work for next few weeks. Work as usual	RAM
— " —	27.3.17		D.T.M.O selected site for new H.T.M Emplacement. Lieut JENNINGS ordered to CANADA CORNER to erect new Brigade H.Q. Work as usual	RAM
— " —	28.3.17		O/C R.E, with two officers of 156 Fd Coy R.E. visited area with regard to taking over. Orders received for company to move into rest on 30.3.17. Lt JENNINGS detailed for special duty erecting new Brigade H.Q	RAM
— " —	29.3.17		Two officers of 156 Fd Coy R.E visited trenches & were shewn work in progress. Work as usual but no night work. Packing up for move	RAM
— " —	30.3.17		Company marched out of Billets at 9 am and marched via LOCRE and BAILLEUL to FLETRE and moved into billets lately occupied by 156 Fd Coy R.E. Weather cold & Showery.	RAM

T2134. Wt. W708–776. 500000. 4/15. Sir J. C. & S.

Instructions regarding War Diaries and Intelligence Summaries are contained in F. S. Regs., Part II. and the Staff Manual respectively. Title pages will be prepared in manuscript.

(6) Original

WAR DIARY
or
~~INTELLIGENCE SUMMARY.~~
(Erase heading not required.)

Vol XVI
155 Fd Coy. R.E

Army Form C. 2118.

Place	Date	Hour	Summary of Events and Information	Remarks and references to Appendices
FLETRE.	31.3.17	-	Company on Squad drill. Mounted men riding drill. Whole company cleaning wagons, harness, etc. O.C visited a/C.R.E at new H.Q at CANADA CORNER re future arrangements. RPPW	
			R.P. Pakenham Walsh Major. R.E O.C. 155 Fd Coy. R.E	

T2134. Wt. W708-776. 500000. 4/15. Sir J. C. & S.

WAR DIARY FOR MONTH OF APRIL, 1917.

VOLUME:- 17

UNIT:- 155th Field Coy R.E.

Vol 17

Instructions regarding War Diaries and Intelligence Summaries are contained in F. S. Regs., Part II. and the Staff Manual respectively. Title pages will be prepared in manuscript.

WAR DIARY
or
~~INTELLIGENCE SUMMARY~~.
(*Erase heading not required.*)

Army Form C. 2118.

(1) Original

Volume XVII
155 Fd. Coy. R.E

Place	Date	Hour	Summary of Events and Information	Remarks and references to Appendices
			Company training in Squad & Company Drill & Route Marching	[illegible]
FLETRE	1.4.17			[illegible]
—"—	2.4.17		Snow on ground Training as before	[illegible]
—"—	3.4.17		Blizzard in morning. Training as before	[illegible]
—"—	4.4.17		Fine weather. Training as before Instruction in explosives	
—"—	5.4.17		Fine weather. Training as before. Instruction in explosives & Knotting. Orders received for Company to move to MONT ROUGE.	[illegible]
			Capt HUGHES went on leave	[illegible]
—"—	6.4.17		Company ~~to~~ marched to MONT ROUGE. Formed camp in old brushwood bed	
MONT ROUGE	7.4.17		No 4. Section working under C.R.E Remainder of company clearing camp site, erecting Nissen Bow hut, Kitchens, Latrines etc. IX Corps Water supply Officer visited camp relative to proposed water supply. 2/Lt JENNINGS rejoined	R. [illegible]
MONT ROUGE	8.4.17		Latrines, Kitchens etc finished. Parade Service. No work after 12 noon.	[illegible]
—"—	9.4.17		Nos 3 & 4 Sections working under C.R.E Nos 1 & 2 Sections Completing Camp	[illegible]
—"—	10.4.17		Ditto. Fall of snow.	[illegible]
—"—	11.4.17		No. 3 & 4 Sections as before No 2 Section training in morning No. 1 on Camp construction No. 1 & 2 changed over in afternoon.	[illegible]
—"—	12.4.17		Nos 3 & 4 Sections Working Nos. 1 & 2 Sections training	[illegible]

T2134. Wt. W708-776. 500000. 4/15. Sir J. C. & S.

Instructions regarding War Diaries and Intelligence Summaries are contained in F. S. Regs., Part II. and the Staff Manual respectively. Title pages will be prepared in manuscript.

(2) Original

WAR DIARY
or
INTELLIGENCE SUMMARY.
(Erase heading not required.)

Army Form C. 2118.

Volume XVII

155 Field Coy R.E

Place	Date	Hour	Summary of Events and Information	Remarks and references to Appendices
				RPM
MONT ROUGE	13.4.17		No 1 Section mobilization Test. Remainder as before	RPM
—"—	14.4.17		A son 12/4/17. One man admitted to F.A. sprained ankle	
—"—	15.4.17		Heavy rain. No 2 Section marched out to CLARE CAMP for work. Remainder Washing clothes & baths. 1 reinforcement received	RPM
—"—	16.4.17		No 1 & 3 working for C.R.E. No 4 training, but taken to unload heavy machinery at BAILLEUL	RPM
—"—	17.4.17		Orders received to move to BEAVER FARM to relieve 157 Fd Coy on 20.4.17. Arranged taking over details with O.C. 157 Fd Coy. No 1.2 & 3 Sections working. No 4 Training	RPM
—"—	18.4.17		Snow. Nos 1 2 & 3 Section working. No 4 Training.	
—"—	19.4.17		Officers went round area & work to be taken over from 157 Fd. Coy R.E. and handed over work on laundry and CLARE CAMP.	RPM
—"—	20.4.17		Company left camp and marched to BEAVER FARM. (Sheet 28 N. 15 d. 0.5). Took over left subsection (VIERSTRAAT – WYTSCHAETE Road to BOSSIGNOL ROAD both exclusive). Work commenced at 8.30 pm. No 1 & 3 Sections in new CHINESE WALL trenches. YUM-YUM and SWATOW. No 2 Section on artillery work in rear. No 4 on General work in front of YORK ROAD. Fine weather. Heavy bombardment at night owing to raid on 41st Div. & relief opposite right subsector.	RPM

T2134. Wt. W708–776. 500000. 4/15. Sir J. C. & S.

Instructions regarding War Diaries and Intelligence Summaries are contained in F. S. Regs., Part II. and the Staff Manual respectively. Title pages will be prepared in manuscript.

(3)

Original

WAR DIARY
or
INTELLIGENCE SUMMARY.
(Erase heading not required.)

Volume XVII

155 Field Coy R.E

Army Form C. 2118.

Place	Date	Hour	Summary of Events and Information	Remarks and references to Appendices
KEMMEL	21.4.17		Work in line. Enemy extraordinarily quiet. No hostile sign except for counter battery work.	RAM
—"—	22.4.17		Only sufficient men to keep Infantry employed working. Remainder resting etc. Rifles overhauled. 2/Lt H. TAYLOR left to join 2nd Army Tramway Coy R.E. Fine day	RAM
—"—	23.4.17		Fine day. C.R.E visited all trenches in subsection. VIERSTRAAT Road reached by new Trench	RAM
—"—	24.4.17		Fine day. Owing to continued shrapnel fire work on SWATOW & YUM-YUM had to be discontinued for some time in the morning. Work as usual	RAM
—"—	25.4.17		~~Some~~ Absolute quiet on whole front. Work as usual. 3 reinforcements arrived. Lieut DIXON R.E. joined unit.	RAM
—"—	26.4.17		Some shelling of YUM-YUM in early morning only temporarily stopped work	RAM
—"—	27.4.17		Battalion relief. Work as usual. New A.D.S. at the FOSSE started	RAM
—"—	28.4.17		Work as usual.	RAM
—"—	29.4.17		Work as usual. Orders received for Company to take over work in DIEPENDAL Sector from 81st & 82nd Coys R.E. 19th Div. O.C. & One Officer went round right subsector DIEPENDAL SECTOR with O.C. 82nd Field Coy R.E. Capt HUGHES returned from leave.	

T2134. Wt. W708-776. 500000. 4/15. Sir J. C. & S.

Instructions regarding War Diaries and Intelligence Summaries are contained in F. S. Regs., Part II. and the Staff Manual respectively. Title pages will be prepared in manuscript.

Original
(5)

WAR DIARY
or
INTELLIGENCE SUMMARY.
(Erase heading not required.)

Army Form C. 2118.

Volume XVII

155 Field Coy R.E.

Place	Date	Hour	Summary of Events and Information	Remarks and references to Appendices
KEMMEL	30.4.17		O.C. & 1 officer took over left Subsector DIEPENDAL Sector from O.C. 81st Fd Coy R.E. Officers of Company handed over work in VIERSTRAAT SECTOR to Officers of 156 & 157 Fd Coys R.E. Strength of Company 217	
			R P Pakenham Walsh Major R.E. O.C. 155 Field Coy R.E.	

W A R   D I A R Y :

-----------oOo----------

VOLUME:- 18

FOR MONTH OF MAY, 1917.

U N I T :- 155th Fd. Coy. Royal Engineers

Vol 18

Instructions regarding War Diaries and Intelligence Summaries are contained in F. S. Regs., Part II. and the Staff Manual respectively. Title pages will be prepared in manuscript.

WAR DIARY
or
INTELLIGENCE SUMMARY.
(Erase heading not required.)

Army Form C. 2118.

(1)

Volume XVIII

155 Field Coy. RE

Place	Date	Hour	Summary of Events and Information	Remarks and references to Appendices
KEMMEL	1.5.17	–	Nos 2 & 3 Sections moved to advanced billets in DIEPENDAAL Sector at HALLEBAST HOEK. Relieved by 2 Sections of 157 Fd. Coy. R.E. Demonstration of pipe pushing given. From 6.30 to 9.0 am battery in rear of billet heavily shelled with 15 cm & 21 cm shells. O.C. accompanied C.R.E's of 19th & 16th Divisions round DIEPENDAAL SECTOR and received instructions.	[initials]
KEMMEL	2.5.17		Conference of C.R.E., B.G.C. 49th Bde & O.C. Coy on work in Sector at 9 am. Company H.Q. & No. 4 Section moved to BALDOYLE CAMP, No. 1 Section moved to advanced billets at HALLEBAST. C.R.E. approved site for new camp at HALLEBAST. 49th Brigade took over DIEPENDAAL SECTOR	[initials]
LA CLYTTE	3.5.17		Commenced work in ~~new~~ DIEPENDAAL SECTOR. No 2 Section in Right Subsector (VIERSTRAAT – WYTSCHAETE Road to BOIS CARRE exclusive) No 3 Section in left Subsector (BOIS CARRE inclusive to P&O Trench exclusive) No. 1 Section behind reserve line of Sector. No. 4 for Workshops, & back work. Gas alarm 10 pm.	[initials]
LA CLYTTE	4.5.17		Work as before. Very hot weather. Camp at HALLEBAST practically finished	[initials]
—"—	5.5.17		Work as usual. Men in advanced billets moved into camp near HALLEBAST HOEK. R.E. FARM KEMMEL (occupied by 156 Fd. Coy RE) shelled & partly set on fire	

Instructions regarding War Diaries and Intelligence Summaries are contained in F. S. Regs., Part II. and the Staff Manual respectively. Title pages will be prepared in manuscript.

(2)

WAR DIARY
or
INTELLIGENCE SUMMARY.
(Erase heading not required.)

Army Form C. 2118.

Volume XVIII

155 Fd Coy R.E.

Place	Date	Hour	Summary of Events and Information	Remarks and references to Appendices
LA CLYTTE	5.5.17		at about 10.0 pm 156 Fd Coy accommodated in DE ZON CAMP.	[illegible]
— " —	6.5.17		Work as usual 6.30 pm O.C attended C.R.E's office for special instructions re work in company with other Coy Commanders. LA CLYTTE shelled 9.0 pm. also HALLEBAST DUMP. 2 O.R. and 2 mules wounded slightly. Both Sgt Buckwood & D? Scowcroft admitted F.A.	[illegible]
— " —	7.5.17		Work as usual. In the evening 8.45 pm & 11.0 pm the whole Army artillery fired intense bombardment for 5 mins in retaliation for shelling of back billets.	[illegible]
— " —	8.5.17		Work as usual. Orders received for 49th Bde etc to be relieved again in DIEPENDAAL SECTOR, & concentrate in VIERSTRAAT SECTOR. Site for new camp selected at sheet 28 M 23 a 88.	[illegible]
— " —	9.5.17		Work as usual to 6 pm. 1 Section preparing new camp. 11.30 am transport moved to lines at DONCASTER HUTS, LOCRE. H.Q. & 2 Sections of 156 Fd Coy accommodated in BALDOYLE CAMP. Cpl PERRIN wounded remaining at duty.	[illegible]
— " —	10.5.17		O.C handed over work in the DIEPENDAAL Sector to O.C. 81st Company. Company moved to new camp WOULDHAM CAMP near LOCRE (M.23 b.7.9) New Reserve line in DIEPENDAAL sector much damaged by hostile fire during previous night	[illegible]
LOCRE	11.5.17		Nos 1 & 4 Sections moved from HALLEBAST forward billets to R.E. FARM KEMMEL. No 2 & 3 Sections and H.Q at WOULDHAM CAMP. O.C & officers took over work in right	

T2134. Wt. W708–776. 500000. 4/15. Sir J. C. & S.

Instructions regarding War Diaries and Intelligence Summaries are contained in F. S. Regs., Part II. and the Staff Manual respectively. Title pages will be prepared in manuscript.

WAR DIARY
or
INTELLIGENCE SUMMARY.
(Erase heading not required.)

Army Form C. 2118.

(3)

Volume XVIII

155 Field Coy. RE

Place	Date	Hour	Summary of Events and Information	Remarks and references to Appendices
LOCRE	11.5.17 (cont)		Subsector, VIERSTRAAT SECTOR.	[initials]
—"—	12.5.17		Work on formation of Camp. Company bathed. 4 Officers & 100 men arrived from 48th Infantry Brigade for permanent attachment to Company.	[initials]
—"—	13.5.17		Company started work in subsector. No. 1 Section on H & M.T.M. emplacements. No 2 Section Work in back area No 3. Work in connection with Artillery No. 4 Section work in forward area. Infantry Officers shewn work to be done on Divisional and Brigade Dumps. Overland Routes etc.	[initials]
—"—	14.5.17		Work as before. Infantry started work. One reinforcement arrived	[initials]
—"—	15.5.17		Work as usual. One attached Infantryman shot himself in the leg at 11 pm	[initials]
—"—	16.5.17		Work as usual. Turned wet in the evening 1 O.R slightly wounded at duty	[initials]
—"—	17.5.17		Wet morning Work as usual.	[initials]
—"—	18.5.17		Fine day. CAPT A.E. HUGHES and LIEUT R.B. JENNINGS in list of "mentioned in despatches" dated 9.4.17 published today. Work as usual	[initials]
—"—	19.5.17		Warm day. 2 O.R of unit & 4 of a working party wounded by Shrapnel at ~~RE~~ CHINESE WALL Work as usual	[initials]
—"—	20.5.17		Hot day Work as usual.	[initials]

Instructions regarding War Diaries and Intelligence Summaries are contained in F. S. Regs., Par. II. and the Staff Manual respectively. Title pages will be prepared in manuscript.

(4)

WAR DIARY
or
INTELLIGENCE SUMMARY.
(*Erase heading not required.*)

Army Form C. 2118.

Volume XVIII

155 Field Coy. RE.

Place	Date	Hour	Summary of Events and Information	Remarks and references to Appendices
LOCRE	21.5.17		Work as usual. Front line near LARK CORNER damaged by 5.9"	[initials]
"	22.5.17		Work as usual	[initials]
"	23.5.17		Handed over work to Officers of 156 Fd Coy. RE, and took over work from them in back area. PARK AVENUE & OAK TRENCH	[initials]
"	24.5.17		Moved to URNOR CAMP, Mt VIDAIGNE. Started work on Divisional Laundry LOCRE	[initials]
"	25.5.17		No 1 Section Training. No 2 on work in YORK ROAD area, No 3 & 4 Sections Divisional Laundry	[initials]
"	26.5.17		No 1 Section Divisional H.Q. SCHERPENBERG. No 2 3 & 4 as before, party started work on CLARE CAMP	[initials]
"	27.5.17		Work as usual. 1 N.C.O. & 10 men with mobile charges accompanied large raid by 2nd R. Dublin Fusiliers at 10 pm. 3 dugouts & one machine-gun emplacements destroyed. 1 officer & 30 men taken prisoner and valuable documents captured. Casualties ~~2~~ R.E. Sapr YOUNG slightly wounded in leg, at duty. R.D.F. 2 officers & 3 O.R. missing 2 killed & 27 wounded.	[initials]
"	28.5.17		Work as usual.	[initials]

A6945 Wt. W11422/M1160 350,000 12/16 D. D. & L. Forms/C./2118/14.

Instructions regarding War Diaries and Intelligence Summaries are contained in F. S. Regs., Part II. and the Staff Manual respectively. Title pages will be prepared in manuscript.

(5)

WAR DIARY
or
INTELLIGENCE SUMMARY.
(Erase heading not required.)

Army Form C. 2118.

Volume XVIII

155th Fd. Coy. R.E

Place	Date	Hour	Summary of Events and Information	Remarks and references to Appendices
LOCRE	29.5.17	–	Work as usual. C.R.E inspected raiding party. Telegram of thanks received from G.O.C 48th Inf Brigade	RPW
"	30.5.17	–	Work as usual. Two reinforcements (Drivers) arrived	RPW
"	31.5.17	–	Divisional H.Q moved to SCHERPENBERG which was ready for their reception. Work as usual	RPW
			R P Pakenham Walsh. Maj. RE	
			1.6.17. O.C. 155 Field Coy. RE	

A6945 Wt. W11422/M1160 350,000 12/16 D. D. & L. Forms/C./2118/14.

16

WAR DIARY.

FOR MONTH OF JUNE, 1917.

VOLUME:- 19

UNIT:- 155 Field Company R.E.

Vol 19

Army Form C. 2118.

Instructions regarding War Diaries and Intelligence Summaries are contained in F. S. Regs., Part II. and the Staff Manual respectively. Title pages will be prepared in manuscript.

WAR DIARY
or
INTELLIGENCE SUMMARY.
(*Erase heading not required.*)

(1) (original) Volume XIX

155 Field Coy RE

Place	Date	Hour	Summary of Events and Information	Remarks and references to Appendices
LOCRE	1.6.17		Work as usual. Strength of Company 217. Bombardment of WYTSCHAETE ridge commenced.	RMM
—"—	2.6.17		Work as usual	RMM
—"—	3.6.17		1 & 2 sections training 3 & 4 Sections on Divisional Laundry	RMM
—"—	4.6.17		3 & 4 started training in afternoon	RMM
—"—	5.6.17		All sections training	RMM
—"—	6.6.17		CRE's operation orders No. 105 & 106 (Appendices I (a)) ~~(attached)~~ bringing in C.R.E's instructions for offensive received. 11.20 p.m. Company paraded at UPNOR CAMP	RMM
~~Locre~~ KEMMEL	7.6.17	1.30am	Company arrived in assembly positions in G.H.Q. trenches E of PIONEER FARM (Sheet 28 N.15 a 5.1). Arrival reported to C.R.E	
		2.0am	O.C. arrived at H.Q. 48th Inf Bde FOSSE Dugouts (N.16 d 70.95.	
		3.10am	Zero mines fired, bombardment & barrage opened and attack commenced	
		3.11am	LIEUT DIXON RE reported Special wiring party of 4 officers & 130 men in position at N.17 c 5.6. (Append C.1).	
		5.0am	BLUE objective as shewn in map attached to C.R.E's instruction reported captured.	

A6945 Wt. W11422/M1160 350,000 12/16 D. D. & L. Forms/C./2118/14.

Instructions regarding War Diaries and Intelligence Summaries are contained in F. S. Regs., Part II. and the Staff Manual respectively. Title pages will be prepared in manuscript.

(2) Original

WAR DIARY
or
INTELLIGENCE SUMMARY.
(Erase heading not required.)

Army Form C. 2118.

Volume XIX

155 Field Coy. R.E.

Place	Date	Hour	Summary of Events and Information	Remarks and references to Appendices
near KEMMEL in action	(cont) 7.6.17	6.50am	Verbal instructions from B.G.C. 42nd Inf Bde, approved on telephone by C.R.E., ~~to~~ received to move up sections for forward work	
		6.55am	Orders dispatched to Capt HUGHES Appendix B 1.	
		7.0am	O.C. reconnoitred from MACAW TRENCH to find barrage which was on SHANTUNG (N 17 d central)	
		7.35am	No 1 & 4 Sections and attached Infantry left Pioneer Farm. Report received (App C.2.) 7.57am.	
		7.50am ~~7.45am~~	Shell struck part of No 4 Section near N 15 d cent. Sgt WHITLOCK & 4 O.R. killed; LIEUT JOHNSON & 8 O.R. wounded.	
		8.15am	1 & 4 Sections arrived at FOSSE. Hostile Barrage had lifted to front line so at	
		8.40am	Sections were sent to SHANTUNG.	
		9.0am	O.C. moved to S.P. 13 (N 17 d central) Coy H.Q. reported (App B 2 ~~C 3~~).	
		9.45am	The BLACK LINE having been captured O.C. consulted C.R.E. relative to special wiring party moving forward. LIEUT DIXON instructed to get party with materials to SHANTUNG. (App B 3).	
		10.0am	2/LIEUT LEACH reported personally that sections 1 & 4 & infantry were ready.	

A6945 Wt. W11422/M1160 350,000 12/16 D. D. & L. Forms/C./2118/14.

Instructions regarding War Diaries and Intelligence Summaries are contained in F. S. Regs., Part II. and the Staff Manual respectively. Title pages will be prepared in manuscript.

(3)

Original

WAR DIARY
or
INTELLIGENCE SUMMARY.
(Erase heading not required.)

Army Form C. 2118.

Volume XIX

155 Field Coy R.E.

Place	Date	Hour	Summary of Events and Information	Remarks and references to Appendices
In action	7.6.17	10.20am	Telegraphic Orders for Lieut DIXONS party to move received (App A 2) &	
		1	transmitted to LIEUT DIXON (App. B 4)	
		10.50am	LIEUT DIXON'S party moved	
		11.20am	Bde Major informed O.C that 2 Battalions moving to attack to ~~BLACK~~ MAUVE	
			LINE would cross BLACK LINE at 1pm. 2/LIEUT LEACH ordered to	
			have sections ready to move by 2pm. O.C reconnoitred mule	
			route to WYTSCHAETE. Telephone message sent through C.RE for Coy	
		x	H.Q to move to the FOSSE	
		12.22pm	Arrival of Coy H.Q at the FOSSE reported by 2nd in Command. (C.3)	
		12.28pm	mules with wire ~~moved up~~ ordered up. (B.5)	
		1.30pm	The Mauve Line being reported held by 45th Bde with patrols in front	
			with approval of B.G.C 45th Inf Bde. O.C ~~led~~ led up Nos 1 & 4	
			Sections & Attached Inf + 10 mules	
		2.15pm	Report on contents of Enemy dumps received from LIEUT DIXON. (C.4)	
		2.30pm	On arrival in dip between NORTH HOUSE & the HOSPICE party was	
			halted & O.C & 2/Lt LEACH went forward. A hostile barrage	
			dropped at this moment & 2/Lt LEACH wounded but able to get away	

A6945 Wt. W11422/M1160 350,000 12/16 D. D. & L. Forms/C./2118/14.

Instructions regarding War Diaries and Intelligence Summaries are contained in F. S. Regs., Part II. and the Staff Manual respectively. Title pages will be prepared in manuscript.

(4)

Original.

WAR DIARY
or
~~INTELLIGENCE SUMMARY.~~
(Erase heading not required.)

Volume XIX

155 Field Coy R.E.

Army Form C. 2118.

Place	Date	Hour	Summary of Events and Information	Remarks and references to Appendices
In action	7.6.17		Party withdrawn behind S. BRICKSTACK, but had to be withdrawn further to replace carrying party	
		5.0pm	Sent for No 2 & 3 sections (B.6).	
		6.0pm	Started again & arrived at LEG COPSE (O.20.B). without further incident. No Garrisons of strong points found for work. Sites selected for strong points N & S of LEG COPSE, and circles wired. Battalion Commanders informed of position of strong points. {For details see report (Appendix D)}	
		9.15pm	Arrived back at Bde. H.Q. Report received from Lieut DIXON that the wiring of the BLACK LINE was complete. (C.5).	
		9.45pm	Orders received from B.G.C that no further work was required that night.	
		10.45pm	Report on days work sent to C.R.E. also report on State of German Dumps (B.6 & ~~RDD~~)	
	8.6.17	7.0	O.C. reported to G.O.C. 48th Inf Bde who informed him that no work was required till evening. Lieut DIXON went to interview Os.C. Battalions	

A6945 Wt. W11422/M1160 350,000 12/16 D. D. & L. Forms/C.2118/14.

Instructions regarding War Diaries and Intelligence Summaries are contained in F. S. Regs., Part II, and the Staff Manual respectively. Title pages will be prepared in manuscript.

(5) Original.

WAR DIARY
or
~~INTELLIGENCE SUMMARY.~~
(Erase heading not required.)

Volume XIX

155 Field Coy. RE.

Army Form C. 2118.

Place	Date	Hour	Summary of Events and Information	Remarks and references to Appendices
In the field	8.6.17	(cont)	to report on work required as O.C. Coy was instructed to await arrival of A/Adjt	
		12.55pm	Orders for work sent to Coy H.Q (Appendix B 7)	
		2pm	20 mules laden with wire & screw pickets sent to SONEN FARM	
		4pm	C.R.E met Fd. Coy Commanders at S.P. 13	
		6.10pm	Report received that mules had all returned having dumped wire at SONEN FARM	C. 6
		7.30pm	Lieut JENNINGS paraded No 2 Section & 50 Inf and proceed to S. LEG POST	
		8.30pm	Enemy counterattacked Heavy artillery fire on both sides Lieut JENNINGS & party delayed till 9.30pm	
		11.5pm	Report sent to C.R.E. ~~also report on state of [illegible] Dumps B 9.~~	B. 8 ~~B.9~~
— " —	9.6.17	4.0am	Lieut JENNINGS & party returned	
		7.45am	Lieut DIXON with No's 1 & 3 sections & 50 Infantry sent to work on S. LEG POST, FARM POST at TORREKEN FARM (O 20 d 4.3) mules prepared to take wire to SONEN FARM	
		8.30am	O.C. visited work & found that work had ceased on S. LEG COPSE under instructions from B.G.C. 48th Inf Bde through O.C. 8th Bn R.D.F, he having chosen a site which could not be worked on till nightfall O.C returned to S.P. 13 to see B.G.C & received orders	
		1.0pm ~~1.40am~~	that Coy (& Division) would be relieved in the evening by 11th Div.	A. 4.
		1.0pm	Also received note from Lieut DIXON reporting re S. LEG CORSE	C. 7

A6945 Wt. W11422/M1160 350,000 12/16 D. D. & L. Forms/C.2118/14.

Instructions regarding War Diaries and Intelligence Summaries are contained in F. S. Regs., Part II. and the Staff Manual respectively. Title pages will be prepared in manuscript.

(6)

Original

WAR DIARY
or
~~INTELLIGENCE SUMMARY~~.
(Erase heading not required.)

Volume XIX

155 Field Coy R.E.

Army Form C. 2118.

Place	Date	Hour	Summary of Events and Information	Remarks and references to Appendices
In the field	9.6.17	1.30pm	Orders sent to Coy H.Q. & Lieut DIXON	B.9410
		11.45pm	Officer of 86th Field Coy 11th Divn arrived at S.P.13 and O.C. went with him round the works returning to S.P. 13 at 4.30pm. where papers were handed over.	
		5.45pm	Reported to B.G.C. 48th Inf. Bde & then by telephone to Adjutant R.E. who in the absence of any staff of 11th Divn gave orders for withdrawal.	
		6.30pm	Arrived at Company H.Q. and gave orders to move at 7.30 pm	
		11.30pm	Company all correct at UPNOR CAMP, MONT ROUGE ~~T~~	[illegible]
MONT ROUGE	10.6.17		Company attended combined Church Parade of 16th Divn R.E. at CHATHAM CAMP.	
			Total casualties in Battle of ~~Wyt~~ WYTSCHAETE Killed 1 Sgt 4 O.R. & 1 attached Infantry. Wounded 2 officers 8 O.R. 3 attached Infantry. Report sent C.R.E.	App. D [illegible]
—"—	11.6.17		Cleaning up etc & resting.	[illegible]
—"—	12.6.17		Ditto ~~Or~~ Preliminary orders received for Company with other 16th Divn R.E. to return to consolidate WYTSCHAETE Ridge.	[illegible]
—"—	13.6.17		Company moved to camp on the R.B. YORK ROAD (N.16 d cent.) O.C. reconnoitred Ridge with O.s C. 156 & 157 Fd Coys. LIEUT SULLIVAN returned to Coy	[illegible]
KEMMEL	14.6.17		Work started on consolidation of line from O 20 a 66 to O 14 d 1.4. Work	

A5945 Wt. W11422/M1160 350,000 12/16 D. D. & L. Forms/C./2118/14.

Instructions regarding War Diaries and Intelligence Summaries are contained in F. S. Regs., Part II. and the Staff Manual respectively. Title pages will be prepared in manuscript.

(7) Original.

WAR DIARY
or
~~INTELLIGENCE SUMMARY.~~
(Erase heading not required.)

Army Form C. 2118.

Volume XIX

155 Field Coy R.E.

Place	Date	Hour	Summary of Events and Information	Remarks and references to Appendices
KEMMEL	14.6.17	(cont)	Started at 8.30. From about 10.30 am hostile shelling by 5.9" howitzers & 4.2" guns considerably impeded work till the party withdrew at 3.30 pm. No casualties.	RAH
KEMMEL	15.6.17		Work continued on Black line, not very much shelling. O.C. went on leave in the afternoon.	RAH
KEMMEL	16.6.17		Weather very hot, work as yesterday one man slightly wounded, remaining at duty C.E. IX Corps visited work with CRE	RAH
KEMMEL	17.6.17		Weather as yesterday No work Parade service for 3 Companies in the morning	RAH
KE			orders received in evening that 16th Div was relieving 19th in line. Company to move to Rd Farm & take over dumps etc. Orders cancelled about 10 pm & new orders received at 2 am next morning that Company is to move to MERRIS area, to join 48th Bde	
STRAZEELE	18.6.17		Weather very hot, heavy thunderstorm later. Company left VIERSTRAAT SWITCH at 8.30 am to pass point near LOCRE at 10 am. LIEUT. O'SULLIVAN returned to CRE early. Company reached billets in STRAZEELE at 3.30 p.m The Lorry was detailed to assist in moving surplus gear LIEUT HAUGH & LIEUT WEBSTER joined Company from Base	RAH

A6945 Wt. W11422/M1160 350,000 12/16 D. D. & L. Forms/C./2118/14.

Instructions regarding War Diaries and Intelligence Summaries are contained in F. S. Regs., Part II. and the Staff Manual respectively. Title pages will be prepared in manuscript.

(8) Original

WAR DIARY
or
~~INTELLIGENCE SUMMARY.~~
(Erase heading not required.)

Army Form C. 2118.

Volume XIX
155th Field Coy RE

Place	Date	Hour	Summary of Events and Information	Remarks and references to Appendices
STRAZEELE	19.6.17		Weather fine & hot. Company cleaning wagons etc. Lieut O'Sullivan returned & brought 14 infantry from CRE with him. The 100 attached infantry & 4 Officers returned to units at 9 a.m. Orders received to move with 48th Bde in morning.	AH
STEENVOORDE	20.6.17		Weather wet. Company paraded at 6.15 a.m. to pass starting point at 7.5 a.m. Reached billets at STEENVOORDE at 10.30 a.m. One N.C.O. left behind to hand over stores to 11th Div. Orders received that Bde is not moving tomorrow. Later orders received from CRE for Company to move to ARNEKE on 21st & to be attached to C.E. XIV Corps.	App E
ARNEKE	21.6.17		Weather cooler, wet later. Company paraded at 9.45 a.m. to march to ARNEKE. Reached billets at 3 p.m. Lieut O'Sullivan & cyclists went ahead to get billets.	App F. AH
MERCKEGHEM	22.6.17		Weather very wet. Company paraded at 11 a.m. to march to MERCKEGHEM. Lieut O'Sullivan & cyclists went ahead for billets. Company reached billets at 1.25 p.m. Lieut JENNINGS went on leave. XIV Corps School Commandant not to be found. Enquired at Area Commandant at Bollezeele with no result.	AH

A6945 Wt. W11422/M1160 350,000 12/16 D. D. & L. Forms/C./2118/14.

Instructions regarding War Diaries and Intelligence Summaries are contained in F. S. Regs., Part II. and the Staff Manual respectively. Title pages will be prepared in manuscript.

(9) Original

WAR DIARY
or
~~INTELLIGENCE SUMMARY~~.
(Erase heading not required.)

Volume XIX

155th Field Coy RE

Army Form C. 2118.

Place	Date	Hour	Summary of Events and Information	Remarks and references to Appendices
MERCKEGHEM	23.6.17		Weather fine. CRE VIII Corps Troops called re School & reinforcement camp & requested complete billeting plan & list of village. Major Adair G.S.O.2 Training XIX Corps visited village & inspected sites. Conference arranged for morning of 24th. Senior Instructor for School arrived.	AHA
MERCKEGHEM	24.6.17		Weather fine. Conference held re. Schools &c all fields visited & inspected, sites chosen for bayonet courses & rifle ranges. No details yet available as to whether camps are to be huts or tents. Company ordered to lay out camps & estimate for materials required. One platoon of 109th Labour Coy is to arrive for work. Company bathing & cleaning up billets & wagons	AHA
MERCKEGHEM	25.6.17		Weather fine. Work started on bayonet assault courses & ranges ground very difficult for work. Rough sawed material arrived no timber yet available & no details as to camps available.	AHA
MERCKEGHEM	~~25.6.17~~ 26.6.17		109th Labour Coy reported for work but have no tools. Commandant of Reinforcement Camp arrived. Work continued on ranges. no tools for Labour Coy arrived till Afternoon about 50 of them employed on odd jobs. All camps roughly	

Instructions regarding War Diaries and Intelligence Summaries are contained in F. S. Regs., Part II. and the Staff Manual respectively. Title pages will be prepared in manuscript.

(10) Original.

WAR DIARY
or
~~INTELLIGENCE SUMMARY.~~
(Erase heading not required.)

Volume XIX
155th Fd Coy R.E.

Army Form C. 2118.

Place	Date	Hour	Summary of Events and Information	Remarks and references to Appendices
	26.6.17 (cont)		laid out. CRE 16th Div arrived & inspected work	[illegible]
MERCKEGHEM	27.6.17		Work continued on ranges & courses all Labour Company employed. CRE VIIIth Corps visited billets again re stores. Asked if we could try Norton tube wells to solve water supply problem. 200 men of Middlesex Labour Coy detailed for work under us but no tools available as yet. Lieut Dixon left to join 200th Field Coy RE.	[illegible]
MERCKEGHEM	28.6.17		Work as before. All indents for material completed, very little has arrived as yet. No tools available for Middlesex labour Coy. Major Pakenham-Walsh returned from leave. School 30x Range finished	[illegible]
— " —	29.6.17		Work as before. First loads of material arriving. All Middlesex Labour company employed. Orders received for construction of Road for Chinese Labour Corps. Materials collected. CRE VIII Corps Troops visited work. Wet in afternoon.	[illegible]
— " —	30.6.17		Work as usual. Road for Chinese Labour Corps started. Lieut Webster + 12 O.R. returned to Company from detachment. Wet. Ground very heavy.	[illegible]

C. C. Pakenham Walsh.
Maj. RE
O.C. 155th Field Coy. R.E.

WAR DIARY.

FOR MONTH OF JULY, 1917.

VOLUME :- 20

UNIT :- 155th Field Coy R.E.

Instructions regarding War Diaries and Intelligence Summaries are contained in F. S. Regs., Part II. and the Staff Manual respectively. Title pages will be prepared in manuscript.

(1)

WAR DIARY
or
~~INTELLIGENCE SUMMARY.~~
(Erase heading not required.)

Army Form C. 2118.

Volume ~~2~~XX

155 Field Coy RE

Place	Date	Hour	Summary of Events and Information	Remarks and references to Appendices
MERCKEGHEM	1.7.17	—	Strength of Unit 200. Only work on Chinese Kraal. Remainder on cleaning, inspections, Church parade & rest. Work visited by A.Q.M.G. & C.E. XIX Corps. also by C.R.E. 16th Div.	
—	2.7.17		Work continued on Chinese Kraal, Bayonet fighting courses & Reinforcement Camps. Lieut O'Sullivan went on leave	ABH
	3.7.17		Work continued as yesterday stores starting to come	ABH
	4.7.17		Work as before Colonel Devey OC Reinforcement Depot left	ABH
	5.7.17		Work as before O.C left for 61st CCS Proven in evening with Mumps. Adjutant working [illegible] Chinese Kraal finished.	ABH
	6.7.17		Work as before. Message received saying that Nissen huts were arriving for School & Store tents for Reinforcement depot	ABH
	7.7.17		Nissen Huts arrived started erecting in School field. Store tents came for Reinforcement Depot. Other work as before	ABH
	8.7.17		Half day's work four hours done on all jobs. Nine Nissen huts arrived. Chinese Labour Company arrived in morning 1/4 detailed for work with us	ABH
	9.7.17		Work as before erecting huts for both camps. Lieut Jennings returned from leave	ABH

A6945 Wt. W11422/M1160 350,000 12/16 D. D. & L. Forms/C./2118/14.

Instructions regarding War Diaries and Intelligence Summaries are contained in F. S. Regs., Part II. and the Staff Manual respectively. Title pages will be prepared in manuscript.

(2)

WAR DIARY
or
~~INTELLIGENCE SUMMARY.~~
(Erase heading not required.)

Army Form C. 2118.

Volume XX
155th Field Coy R.E.

Place	Date	Hour	Summary of Events and Information	Remarks and references to Appendices
MERCKEGHEM	10.7.17		Works as before. CRE & Adjutant 18th Div visited billets & gave parchment certificates Sergt Salter Cpls Penn & Smyth L/Cpls Wellman & Wild & Driver Rees. Major Pakenham Walsh & Lieut Drum also given Parchments	AW
	11.7.17		Works as before. All huts erected & as further supplies [illegible] one Driver reinforcement came. Improvements to Chinese Kraal started	AW
	12.7.17		Work as before. C.E. visited work & agreed with use being made of rough poles instead of scantling. 9 Reinforcements came	AW
	13.7.17		Work as before. 1 driver reinforcement. 2nd Lieut LANNON reported for duty.	
	14.7.17		Work as before. Shelters for Cookhouses & floors for ablution sheds started in Chinese Kraal. Lieut Jennings att'd CRE as acting Adjutant. CRE visited billets.	AW
	15.7.17		Work as before. Reinforcement Camp started drawing rations for itself. 2 men went on leave.	
	16.7.17		Work as before. details started to arrive for Reinforcement depot.	AW
	17.7.17		Work as usual. 3 men went on leave. CRE came & gave away 3 military medals. Lieuts Jennings & Drum received Military Crosses.	AW

A6945 Wt. W11422/M1160 350,000 12/16 D. D. & L. Forms/C./2118/14.

Instructions regarding War Diaries and Intelligence Summaries are contained in F. S. Regs., Part II. and the Staff Manual respectively. Title pages will be prepared in manuscript.

(3)

WAR DIARY
or
~~INTELLIGENCE SUMMARY.~~
(Erase heading not required.)

Army Form C. 2118.

Volume XX
155th Field Coy R.E.

Place	Date	Hour	Summary of Events and Information	Remarks and references to Appendices
MERCKEGHEM	18.7.17		Work as before Reinforcement Camp completed with exception of small details	[illegible]
"	19.7.17		Work as before one bayonet assault course finished except fakers	[illegible]
"	20.7.17		Work as before 5 men left for rest Camp & 3 men went on leave. 2 reinforcements & one mule fetched from 157 Coy. part of Labour Company started work on Lewis gun range below Windmill. Lieut O'Sullivan returned from leave. 9 Parchment certificates delivered by adjutant.	[illegible]
"	21.7.17		Work as before 2 ranges completed 4 Reinforcements arrived. Work started on public latrines & incinerator in village	[illegible]
"	22.7.17		Work as before for 4 hours only.	
"	23.7.17		Major Pakenham-Walsh returned from Hospital in morning G.O.C. XIII Corps Troops visited works.	[illegible]
"	24.7.17		Work as usual	[illegible]
"	[illegible]		Work as usual	[illegible]
"	26.7.17		Work as usual Orders received for company to rejoin division. G.O.C. XIX Corps visited school and reinforcement Depot	[illegible]
"	27.7.17		Transport marched at 8.0 am. Dismounted started at 10 am horses Arrived in camp	

A6945 Wt. W11422/M1160 350,000 12/16 D. D. & L. Forms/C./2118/14.

Instructions regarding War Diaries and Intelligence Summaries are contained in F. S. Regs., Part II, and the Staff Manual respectively. Title pages will be prepared in manuscript.

Army Form C. 2118.

WAR DIARY
or
~~INTELLIGENCE~~ SUMMARY.
(Erase heading not required.)

(4)

Volume XX

155 Field Coy R.E.

Place	Date	Hour	Summary of Events and Information	Remarks and references to Appendices
MERCKEGHEM ~~27.7.17~~	27.7.17		with 48th Inf. Bde in WATOU No 1 Area. Lieut HAUGH left Co. R and over. O.C. attended	RPW
	28.7.17		C.R.E.'s conference in POPERINGHE 5 pm	RPW
POPERINGHE	28.7.17		Training 100 Inf & 3 officers arrived for attachment. O.C. visited G.O.C. 48th Inf Bde	
			at 4 pm	RPW
	29.7.17		~~Training~~ Training Very showery. LIEUT HAUGH rejoined. 2/LIEUT LANNON left to join	
			200th Fd Coy RE & LIEUT DIXON MC returned from said company. C.R.E. visited camp	RPW
	30.7.17		Training	
		5.30 pm	Company moved with Bde to combined Field Company Camp at sheet 28 G 11 d	
			1.5. Strength of Company 2/8	RPW
			(N.B. Owing to operations diary for 31.7.17 is included in Volume XXI	
			R P Pakenham Walsh	
			Maj RE	
			O.C. 155 Field Coy RE	

A6945 Wt. W11422/M1160 350,000 12/16 D. D. & L. Forms/C./2118/14.

WAR DIARY.

FOR MONTH OF AUGUST, 1917.

VOLUME.2.........

UNIT 155th Field Company R.E.

Instructions regarding War Diaries and Intelligence Summaries are contained in F. S. Regs., Part II. and the Staff Manual respectively. Title pages will be prepared in manuscript.

(1)

WAR DIARY
or
~~INTELLIGENCE~~ SUMMARY.
(*Erase heading not required.*)

Army Form C. 2118.

XXI

155 Field Coy R.E.

Place	Date	Hour	Summary of Events and Information	Remarks and references to Appendices
BRANDHOEK	31.7.17	3.30am	Company less Pontoon & G.S. Wagons paraded	Appendix A1
		3.50am	Zero of Operations	" A2
		4.0am	Company marched with 48th Inf Brigade via VLAMERTINGHE	
		7.30am	Arrived in assembly position at H 16. a 3.9 (Sheet 28)	
		8.30am	O.C. proceeded to GOLDFISH CHATEAU (H. 11 a 8 1) to join 48th Inf Bde H.Q	
		10.30am	Assembly point shelled ~~[illegible]~~ 1 O.R. Killed (No 97566 Sapr East) + 1 O.R. wounded. 3 mules wounded. Men and horses placed in scattered groups in fields	
		6.30pm	48th Inf Bde ordered to move forward to old Front Line about Sheet 28 I 5. Instructions asked for for Company.	
		7.30pm	Orders received to remain in present position	
		8.30pm	Ordered to return to camp at G 11 d 1 5	
		9.15pm	Company marched	
		10.30pm	Arrived in Camp. About Midnight started to rain heavily	R.P.H.D.
"	1.8.17.		Raining heavily. 11 am Lieut Webster sent to the Ecole YPRES ~~with~~ to reconnoitre with a view to taking over from 15th Div. His report forwarded to C.R.E. at 5.30 pm.	R.P.H.D.

A6945 Wt. W11422/M1160 350,000 12/16 D. D. & L. Forms/C./2118/14.

Instructions regarding War Diaries and Intelligence Summaries are contained in F. S. Regs., Par. II. and the Staff Manual respectively. Title pages will be prepared in manuscript.

(2)

WAR DIARY
or
~~INTELLIGENCE SUMMARY~~.
(Erase heading not required.)

Army Form C. 2118.

Volume XXI
155 Field Coy. R.E.

Place	Date	Hour	Summary of Events and Information	Remarks and references to Appendices
				Appendix A 3
BRANDHOEK	2.8.17		Still raining heavily. No movement.	RBRW
"	3.8.17		O.C. & O.C. 156 Fd Coy went to ECOLE, YPRES, to take over from 15th Divl Engineers. Saw a Subaltern of 74th Fd. Coy. On return to BRANDHOEK saw O.C. 74th Field Coy R.E.	RBRW
	"		Orders received for company to move to billets at Dump at H 7 a 5.9. the Divn relieving 15th Divn. Lieut Dixon & advanced party sent to ECOLE.	Appendix A 3/4 RBRW
"	4.8.17		O.C. with O.C. 157 Fd Coy proceeded to YPRES and ~~Bx~~ 47th Bde H.Q at MILL COTS (I 5 a 2.6) and saw G.O.C. 47th Inf Bde relative to work to be carried out. Company marched at ~~1.0 pm~~ 11.0 am to billets as ordered. LIEUT WEBSTER with Nos 1&2 Sections and 50 attached infantry marched to billets in the RAMPARTS, YPRES (I 8 B.1.1) at 3. pm.	RBRW
"	5.8.17		No's 1 & 2 Sections & Inf attached proceeded at 2 am to carry wire at pickets forward from POTIJZE DUMP (I 4 c 3.9) and came under heavy fire. 2 Sappers wounded, 2 attached Inf. Killed & 4 Wounded. Owing to continued barrage further progress impossible. O.C. with LIEUT DIXON reconnoitred proposed route by PICCADILLY forward Billets at H 7 a 5.9. Bombed by aeroplanes 1 O.R. Wounded. No. 1 Section and 25 attached Inf. paraded at 7.30 pm to carry wire & erect entang-	

A6945 Wt. W11422/M1160 35,000 12/16 D. D. & L. Forms/C./2118/14.

Instructions regarding War Diaries and Intelligence Summaries are contained in F. S. Regs., Part II, and the Staff Manual respectively. Title pages will be prepared in manuscript.

(3)

WAR DIARY
or
~~INTELLIGENCE SUMMARY.~~
(Erase heading not required.)

Army Form C. 2118.

Volume XXI
155 Field Coy. R.E

Place	Date	Hour	Summary of Events and Information	Remarks and references to Appendices
BRANDHOEK	5.8.17	(cont)	point wire at I.6.b.9.5 Position reached safely, but at 9.15 pm a very heavy barrage put down on site of work. Men collected in shell holes + remained for about 1½ hours when party was withdrawn as work was impossible. ~~All~~ Most of men slightly affected by gas poisoning.	R.P.M.
"	6.8.17	2 am	Party returned to billets. Lieut DIXON + No. 2 Section with Infantry improving	
		10 am	of new "J" Track via PICCADILLY + IBEX DRIVE. O.C. accompanied G.O.C. 48th Inf Brigade round part of positions. Decided not to make strong point but to wire FREZENBERG REDOUBT. Party who attempted this were caught near POTIJZE CHATEAU in a barrage. 2 attached Infantry ~~and~~ killed + 2 of Company + 4 attached Infantry wounded.	R.P.M.
"	7.8.17		LIEUT. J. O'SULLIVAN transferred to ~~XIX~~ Corps School + struck off strength of Company. Work continued on tracks, and another unsuccessful effort made to reach FREZENBERG REDOUBT. 2 men attached Infantry wounded	R.P.M.
"	8.8.17		No. 4 Section relieved No. 1 section at the RAMPARTS. Work as before another unsuccessful attempt at FREZENBERG REDOUBT	R.P.M.
"	9.8.17		No. 3 Section relieved No. 2 section at the RAMPARTS. ~~Z~~ The project of wiring FREZENBERG REDOUBT abandoned in favour of N. Station	

A6945 Wt. W11422/M1160 35,000 12/16 D. D. & L. Forms/C./2118/14.

Instructions regarding War Diaries and Intelligence Summaries are contained in F. S. Regs., Par. II. and the Staff Manual respectively. Title pages will be prepared in manuscript.

(4)

WAR DIARY
or
~~INTELLIGENCE SUMMARY.~~
(Erase heading not required.)

Army Form C. 2118.

Volume XXI

155 Field Coy. R.E.

Place	Date	Hour	Summary of Events and Information	Remarks and references to Appendices
BRANDHOEK	9.8.17	(cont)	Building (map 28. I 1 a.) Lieut HAUGH reached site by party under an attached Infantry officer lost their way. Work on I track and overhauling pumps of dugouts continued.	[illegible]
"	10.8.17		Work as before. A shell burst near cooks fires at Ramparts causing casualties 155 Fd. Coy. ~~Sapr~~ No 97908 Sapr Edwards Killed No. 97738 Sapr Saunders died of wounds. 4. O.R. wounded; attached Inf. 2 Killed, 1 died of wounds 3 wounded. No. 4. Section got close to N Station buildings but were prevented working owing to continued heavy shell fire.	[illegible]
"	11.8.17		Stores sent up on mule train at 1. am to NEW COT. B.G.C. Work on I & ~~X~~ X Tracks and Dugouts continued. Decided not to continue ~~of~~ attempts to wire N. Station Buildings.	[illegible]
"	~~12.8.17~~		Work ~~on~~ 40 pack mules sent up to NEW COTT with R.E. Stores at night	
"	12.8.17		Work as before 40 mules with Stores sent up to forward dump ~~[illegible]~~ W of FREZENBERG. all delivered safely.	[illegible]
"	13.8.17		Work as before. 40 mules sent up as ~~last~~ previous night, 32 reached the dump. One driver & 2 mules slightly wounded.	[illegible]
"	14.8.17.		Work as before. "X" Track completed. Dug out in German trenches at I 6. a 0. 0.	

A6945 Wt. W11422/M1160 35,000 12/16 D. D. & L. Forms/C./2118/14.

Instructions regarding War Diaries and Intelligence Summaries are contained in F. S. Regs., Part II. and the Staff Manual respectively. Title pages will be prepared in manuscript.

(5)

WAR DIARY
or
~~INTELLIGENCE SUMMARY.~~
(Erase heading not required.)

Army Form C. 2118.

Volume XXI

155 Field Coy. R.E

Place	Date	Hour	Summary of Events and Information	Remarks and references to Appendices
BRANDHOEK	14.8.17	(Cont)	reclaimed as Battalion H.Q. No. 4 Section returned to Coy H.Q at	Appendix A5
			BRANDHOEK at 5 P.M. 2/Lt BROOK R.E. joined the Company. Lieut Dixon &	
			party laid out tapes for jumping off E of FREZENBURG.	ROTD
BRANDHOEK	15.8.17		Wet day. 5 pm Company marched to Assembly position S of ASYLUM YPRES	
			arriving 6.30pm On march near ~~VERLORENH~~ VLAMERTINGHE 3 O.R. wounded.	
			Lieut DIXON M.C. R.E. + 2 O.R wounded on the way to complete laying out	
			"jumping off" tapes.	
		11.0pm	Company less No. 3 Section marched to assembly position near OSKAR	Appendix A6
			FARM in original German Front line S of VERLORENHOEK	ROTD
YPRES	16.8.17	2.15pm	O.C. reported at 48th Inf Bde H.Q at JAMES FARM and reported assembly	
			complete by wire to C.R.E.	
		4.45pm	Zero of Battle. Barrage opened & assault commenced	
		1.0pm	situation not clear. Apparently the Brigade reached final objective but	
			isolated M.Gs & Snipers hung up supporting troops. C.R.E decided no	
			action possible at present	
		5.0pm	Further discussion on telephone with C.R.E. who after consultation with	

A6945 Wt. W11422/M1160 350,000 12/16 D. D. & L. Forms/C./2118/14.

Instructions regarding War Diaries and Intelligence Summaries are contained in F. S. Regs., Part II. and the Staff Manual respectively. Title pages will be prepared in manuscript.

(6)

WAR DIARY
or
~~INTELLIGENCE SUMMARY.~~
(Erase heading not required.)

Army Form C. 2118.

Volume XXII

155 Field Coy. R.E.

Place	Date	Hour	Summary of Events and Information	Remarks and references to Appendices
YPRES.	16.8.17		Divl G.O.C. agreed with G.O.C. 48th Inf. Bde. that at present no Engineer work is possible	
		5.30pm	O.C. visited sections and gave orders for them to move to Old British Front Line. One attached infantryman wounded.	
			Orders received to hand over BRANDHOEK Billets to 73rd Fd. Coy R.E.	
			Rear Party moved stores to 157 Fd. Coy Billet.	[illegible]
— " —	17.8.17	8.0 am	Received Orders from C.R.E. for Company to return to assembly position S of ASYLUM YPRES, No 3 Section to remain at the RAMPARTS under orders of Lieut JENNINGS.	Appendix A 7
		12 noon	Sections & attached Infantry arrived at assembly position.	
		1.30pm	C.R.E. visited Company	
		4.0pm	Orders received for Companies to return to BRANDHOEK	
		5.0pm	Company moved off.	
		6.30pm	Company arrived in billets in BRANDHOEK.	
		7.0pm	C.R.E. visited Company.	[illegible]
— " —	18.8.17		O.C. 74th Field Coy. R.E. took over work in the line from O.C. 155 Fd. Coy. R.E.	

A6945 Wt. W11422/M1160 350,000 12/16 D. D. & L. Forms/C./2118/14.

Instructions regarding War Diaries and Intelligence Summaries are contained in F. S. Regs., Part II. and the Staff Manual respectively. Title pages will be prepared in manuscript.

(7)

WAR DIARY or INTELLIGENCE SUMMARY.

(Erase heading not required.)

Volume XXI

155 Field Coy R.E.

Army Form C. 2118.

Place	Date	Hour	Summary of Events and Information	Remarks and references to Appendices
YPRES.	18.8.17	4.0am	No 3 Section returned to Coy	
		3.30pm	Dismounted portion marched to VLAMERTINGHE and entrained at 4.15pm	
			for POPERINGHE Transport moved by ~~train~~ road to WATOU No 1 Area	
			Company encamped near POPERINGHE Total casualties during 18 days 3 Killed	
~~POPERINGHE~~			1 officer & 18 O.R. wounded and shell shock	RAMA
POPERINGHE	19.8.17		No work Church Parades Orders for move received at 10.30pm	RAMA
"	20.8.17	8.0am	Company marched with 48th Bde into billets at WORMHOUDT.	RAMA
WORMHOUDT	21.8.17	1.30pm	Company marched to ESQUELBEC & entrained complete. Train left at 5.20pm	RAMA
COURCELLES LE-COMTE	22.8.17	2.0am	Train arrived at BAPAUME ~~[illegible]~~ Detrained & marched at 5.0am to Camp	
			at COURCELLES-LE-COMTE arrived 8.0am	RAMA
"	23.8.17		Cleaning up wagons checking tools etc	RAMA
"	24.8.17		Training Close Order Drill Judging Distance Driving Drill etc	RAMA
"	25.8.17		O.C. & 2 officers proceeded to St LEGER and took over work from 98th Fd	Appendix A.8
			Coy R.E. in 21st Div Sector N.W. of BULLECOURT.	RAMA
"	26.8.17	11.0am	Combined Church Parade of Field Companies	
		12noon	Inspection & address by G.O.C. 16th Divn. 2/Lt GLYNN joined Company.	RAMA

A6945 Wt. W11422/M1160 350,000 12/16 D. D. & L. Forms/C./2118/14.

Instructions regarding War Diaries and Intelligence Summaries are contained in F. S. Regs., Part II. and the Staff Manual respectively. Title pages will be prepared in manuscript.

(8)

WAR DIARY
or
~~INTELLIGENCE SUMMARY.~~
(Erase heading not required.)

Volume XXI
165 Field Coy RE

Army Form C. 2118.

Place	Date	Hour	Summary of Events and Information	Remarks and references to Appendices
COURCELLES-LE COMTE	27.8.17	10.0am	Marched to New billets near BOIRY-BECQUERELLE No's 1 & 2 Sections to billets ~~in~~ W of ST LEGER in SENSÉE Valley. Officers & N.C.O's went round the line. Wet in afternoon & very wet night. 2/Lt ATOCH & 50 attached Infantry reported	[illegible]
BOIRY-BECQUERELLE	28.8.17	–	Wet day. Work started. No 1 section in Front. No. 2 Section in Rear of Right Battalion i.e. NELLY DRIVE to SENSÉE RIVER. No. 3 Section in Front. No 4 Section in rear of Left Battalion i.e. SENSÉE RIVER to line PUG AVENUE FULDNER LANE – HIND-TRENCH. Principal Work revetting trenches. O.C went round whole system with G.O.C. 48th Inf Bde.	[illegible]
– " –	29.8.17		O.C. went round line with C.R.E. visiting G.O.C 48th Inf Bde on return.	[illegible]
– " –	30.8.17		Work as usual. Lieut JENNINGS ~~went~~ returned from attachment to C.R.E's H.Q. CAPT HUGHES went on leave. Showery	[illegible]
– " –	31.8.17		Work as usual. ~~Conference of Field Company Commanders at C.R.E's H.Q. 157 Fd Coy to take over work in Right of left Bde area on 2.8.17.~~ Showery. Strength of Company 196.	[illegible]

R.P. Pakenham Walsh
Major RE
O.C. 165 Fd. Coy RE.

A6945 Wt. W11422/M1160 350,000 12/16 D. D. & L. Forms/C./2118/14.

W A R   D I A R Y .

FOR MONTH OF SEPTEMBER, 1917.

VOLUME 22

UNIT:- 155th Fd Co RE

Instructions regarding War Diaries and Intelligence Summaries are contained in F. S. Regs., Part II, and the Staff Manual respectively. Title pages will be prepared in manuscript.

(1)

WAR DIARY
or
~~INTELLIGENCE SUMMARY.~~
(Erase heading not required.)

Army Form C. 2118.

Volume XXII
155 Field Coy RE

Place	Date	Hour	Summary of Events and Information	Remarks and references to Appendices
BOIRY-BECQUERELLE	1.9.17		Conference of Field Coy Commanders at C.R.E's office. Orders for 157th Fd Coy to take over Right Battn of Left Brigade Area on 3.9.17.	RAM
"	2.9.17		Officers of company handed over work in Right Battalion to Officers of 157 Fd Coy. ½ company rested & cleaned up	RAM
"	3.9.17		Company ceased work in Right Battalion. 3 lines of supporting points reconnoitred	RAM
"	4.9.17		No 1 Section moved to HAMELINCOURT for hutting work under Adjutant RE. No 2 Section returned to H.Q. Lieut SULLIVAN RE returned to company from XIX Corps School.	RAM
"	5.9.17		C.R.E visited supporting points with O.C. Work as before.	RAM
"	6.9.17		Work as before. Reconnaissance for Water supply in Section.	RAM
"	7.9.17		Work as usual.	RAM
"	8.9.17		Work as usual ½ company rested & had baths in afternoon	RAM
"	9.9.17		Work as usual ½ company rested & had baths in afternoon. Projector Gas discharged from Brigade on night, apparently very successfully.	RAM
"	10.9.17		Battalion relief. Nos 3 & 4 section moved to billets in the Tunnel in SHAFT AVENUE. Work as usual.	RAM
"	11.9.17		Work as usual.	RAM

A6945 Wt. W11422/M1160 350,000 12/16 D. D. & L. Forms/C./2118/14.

Instructions regarding War Diaries and Intelligence Summaries are contained in F. S. Regs., Part II, and the Staff Manual respectively. Title pages will be prepared in manuscript.

(2)

WAR DIARY
or
~~INTELLIGENCE SUMMARY.~~
(Erase heading not required.)

Volume XXII
155 Field Coy R.E.

Army Form C. 2118.

Place	Date	Hour	Summary of Events and Information	Remarks and references to Appendices
BOIRY-BECQUERELLE	12.9.17		Work as usual. Capt HUGHES returned from leave	RPM
"	13.9.17		Work as usual.	RPM
"	14.9.17		Work as usual.	RPM
"	15.9.17		Work as usual. In the evening all sections returned to Coy. H.Q. for fortnightly relief. 2/Lt GLYNN left company to join 157 Fd Coy R.E. Division on our right made 2 successful raids, and a projector gas attack, the 2 sections in tunnel being withdrawn before these.	RPM
"	16.9.17		Company at H.Q. Church parade Inspections etc. Several promotions made in the company to fill vacancies. C.R.E. presented Parchment certificates to Lieut Webster, ~~Sapr~~ 2/Cpl Holmes, Sapr Addison D, Addison J, & Davies. In the evening sections proceeded to new positions. Nos 1 & 2 Sections to the Tunnel, No. 3 to hutting (attached to 157 Fd Coy RE) at HAMELINCOURT. 48th Bde relieved 49th Bde in section.	RPMD
"	17.9.17		Work as usual.	RPM
"	18.9.17		Work as usual. Lieut HAUGH went on leave.	RPM
"	19.9.17		OC accompanied G.O.C. 48th Inf Bde to select site for new Brigade O.P. Work as usual	RPM

A6945 Wt. W11422/M1160 350,000 12/16 D. D. & L. Forms/C./2118/14.

Instructions regarding War Diaries and Intelligence Summaries are contained in F. S. Regs., Part II. and the Staff Manual respectively. Title pages will be prepared in manuscript.

(3)

WAR DIARY
or
INTELLIGENCE SUMMARY.
(Erase heading not required.)

Army Form C. 2118.

Volume XXII

155 Field Coy. RE

Place	Date	Hour	Summary of Events and Information	Remarks and references to Appendices
BOIRY-BECQUERELLE	20.9.17		Work as usual. G.O.C. VI. Corps visited trenches. Reconnaissance of RIVER ROAD tunnel made	[illegible]
"	21.9.17		Work as usual. At 4.0 am enemy blew in SHAFT TRENCH in two places and HIND SUPPORT in several places. Passage cleared. Award of Military Medal to No 101552 Sgt HARRIS F.W.J. No 96409 Cpl PERRIN J. No 140244 2/cpl McALLISTER D. No 98036 Sapr CORNERA No 51406 Dr PEARL J.	[illegible]
"	22.9.17		Work as usual.	[illegible]
"	23.9.17		Work as usual. ½ Company given ½ day for washing and mending.	[illegible]
"	24.9.17		Work as usual. CRE visited billets. 12 reinforcements arrived	[illegible]
"	25.9.17		Work as usual	[illegible]
"	26.9.17		Work as usual. a/C.R.E. visited trenches in area. C.E. VI. Corps visited billets.	[illegible]
"	27.9.17		Work as usual. Major PAKENHAM-WALSH went on leave	aEH
"	28.9.17		Work as usual.	aEH
"	29.9.17		Work as usual. Sections in line & hutting section returned to Coy HQ for relief	aEH
"	30.9.17		Company washing clothes etc & kit inspections. No 3 & 4 Sections went into billets in tunnel. No 2 Section went to 157th Fd Coy for hutting. No 1 Section doing intermediate work. Lieut HAUGH returned from leave.	aEH

1.10.17. A.E. Hughes Capt RE
O.C. 155th Field Coy RE

A6945 Wt. W11422/M1160 350,000 12/16 D. D. & L. Forms/C./2118/14.

W A R   D I A R Y

FOR MONTH OF OCTOBER, 1917.

UNIT 155th Field Coy RE

VOLUME NUMBER 23

Vol 23

Army Form C. 2118.

Instructions regarding War Diaries and Intelligence Summaries are contained in F. S. Regs., Part II. and the Staff Manual respectively. Title pages will be prepared in manuscript.

(1)

WAR DIARY
or
~~INTELLIGENCE SUMMARY.~~
(Erase heading not required.)

Vol XXIII
155th Field Coy RE.

Place	Date	Hour	Summary of Events and Information	Remarks and references to Appendices
BOIRY-BECQUERELLES	1.10.17		Work as before. 1st train went to GREYSTONES Dump taking 12 push trucks.	
"	2.10.17		Work as usual. Storekeeper found for new Dump arrangements made for Battalions to draw stores from dump direct.	
"	3.10.17		Work as usual Lt WEBSTER went on leave.	
"	4.10.17		Work as usual	
"	5.10.17		Work as usual.	
"	6.10.17		Work as usual arrangements made for repairs to Battalion Cookhouse, at STALEY BRIDGE work started	
"	7.10.17		Work as usual All ~~[illegible]~~ Officers & N.C.Os & sappers to a total of 40 went to lecture at ERVILLERS on booby traps,	
"	8.10.17		Work as usual G.O.C 49th Inf Bde visited line to choose site for Gumboot Store & inspect Cookhouse	
"	9.10.17		Work as usual O/CRE visited trenches. MAJOR PAKENHAM-WALSH returned from leave	
"	10.10.17		Work as usual. Brigade Relief	
"	11.10.17		Work as usual.	

A6945 Wt. W11422/M1160 350,000 12/16 D. D. & L. Forms/C./2118/14.

Army Form C. 2118.

Instructions regarding War Diaries and Intelligence Summaries are contained in F. S. Regs., Part II. and the Staff Manual respectively. Title pages will be prepared in manuscript.

(2)

WAR DIARY
or
~~INTELLIGENCE SUMMARY.~~
(Erase heading not required.)

Volume XXIII

155 Field Coy. RE

Place	Date	Hour	Summary of Events and Information	Remarks and references to Appendices
BOIRY-BECQUERELLE	12.10.17		Work as usual.	RAMM
"	13.10.17		Work as usual. Sections returned to H.Q. in evening.	RAMM
"	14.10.17		Inspections etc. C.R.E inspected Billet with M.O. Sections returned to Work as below. No 1 & 2 Sections to Trenches, No 3 Section Coy. H.Q. No 4 Section HAMELINCOURT for hutting. Div. on left made successful large raid. Lieut WEBSTER returned from leave	RAMM
"	15.10.17		Work as usual. C.R.E. went round trenches with O.C.	RAMM
"	16.10.17		Work as usual.	RAMM
"	17.10.17		Work as usual. Lieut O'SULLIVAN went on leave	RAMM
"	18.10.17		Work as usual. SNIPERS O.P. at RIVER ROAD heavily shelled but undamaged	RAMM
"	19.10.17		Work as usual. C.E. went round Trenches with B.G.C. 48th Inf Bde. New O.P. in U¼ had loopholes filled & concrete & rail roof put on at night	RAMM
"	20.10.17		Work as usual. Rations for line sent up by train for first time.	RAMM
"	21.10.17		Corps W.S.O. visited Tunnel Water Supply with O.C. Raid at noon from LUMP LANE by 2nd R.D.F successful. Work as usual	RAMM
"	22.10.17		Work as usual. Work started on laying out full sized plan of Trenches	RAMM
"	23.10.17		Brigade relief. Work rather curtailed.	RAMM

A6945 Wt. W11422/M1160 350,000 12/16 D. D. & L. Forms/C./2118/14.

Instructions regarding War Diaries and Intelligence Summaries are contained in F. S. Regs., Part II. and the Staff Manual respectively. Title pages will be prepared in manuscript.

(3)

WAR DIARY
or
~~INTELLIGENCE SUMMARY.~~
(Erase heading not required.)

Army Form C. 2118.

Volume XXIII
155 Field Coy. R.E.

Place	Date	Hour	Summary of Events and Information	Remarks and references to Appendices
BOIRY-BECQUERELLE	24.10.17		Work as usual. Wet day.	RPPW
~~—~~	~~25.10.17~~		~~Work as usual.~~	RPPW
"	25.10.17		Work as usual. Field Company Commanders Conference at C.R.E's H.Q. Wiring Class for Officers & N.C.O's of 48th Inf Bde Started	RPPW
"	26.10.17		Work as usual. C.R.E & G.S.O.2 visited wiring class & discussed forms of wire.	RPPW
"	27.10.17		Very Wet. Work as usual. Capt Hughes & Lieut Jenning M.C went on short leave to Paris. O.C visited B.G.Cs 48 & 49 Bdes. All sections returned for relief	RPPW
"	28.10.17		Inspections etc. Battalion Relief. Sections moved to new positions as follows No.1 Hutting. No.2 Coy H.Q. No.3 & 4 In Trenches.	RPPW
"	29.10.17		O.C went round left Subsection with C.R.E. Then accompanied him round centre Subsection to reconnoitre forward dumps & ~~Fof~~ Forward communication Trenches. Successful raid by R Inniskilling Fusiliers. Work as usual.	RPPW
"	30.10.17		O.C accompanied C.R.E & B.G.C. 48th Inf. Bde to CROISILLES CAVES. Work as usual. Lieut O'SULLIVAN returned from leave.	RPPW
"	31.10.17		Special Party of 100 men of 1st Dublins had first lesson in rapid wiring. Work as usual.	

R.P. Pakenham Walsh
Maj RE
O.C. 155th FIELD COY. R.E.

A6945 Wt. W11422/M1160 350,000 12/16 D. D. & L. Forms/C./2118/14.

W A R   D I A R Y

FOR MONTH OF NOVEMBER, 1917.

VOLUME:- 24

U N I T :- 155th Field Coy RE

Vol 24

Army Form C. 2118.

Instructions regarding War Diaries and Intelligence Summaries are contained in F. S. Regs., Part II. and the Staff Manual respectively. Title pages will be prepared in manuscript.

(1)

WAR DIARY
or
~~INTELLIGENCE SUMMARY~~.
(Erase heading not required.)

Vol. XXIV

155 Field Coy. R.E.

Place	Date	Hour	Summary of Events and Information	Remarks and references to Appendices
BOIRY-BECQUERELLE	1.11.17	–	Strength of Company 213. Work as usual: Capt HUGHES & Lieut JENNINGS returned from leave. Work started on CROISILLES CAVES. Brigade Relief.	RMM
"	2.11.17	–	Work as usual. Wiring party continued training.	RMM
"	3.11.17	–	Work as usual. ~~Wir~~	RMM
"	4.11.17	–	Work as usual.	RMM
"	5.11.17	–	Work start on enlarging FACTORY DUMP. Party at CROISILLES increased to 11. Other work as usual.	RMM
"	6.11.17	–	Damp weather. Work as usual.	RMM
"	7.11.17	–	No 1 Section less 7 men returned from Hutting. Work as usual. Batt Relief.	RMM
"	8.11.17	–	No 1 Section moved to CROISILLES CAVES. O C & Lieut Webster accompanied B.G.C. 48th Inf Bde round Right subsector to visit special work to be carried out. Other work as usual	RMM
"	9.11.17	–	~~No 2 Section~~ ½ No 2 Section rested and moved in evening to CROISILLES CAVES relieving ½ No. 3. Work as usual	RMM
"	10.11.17		No 3 section returned to H.Q. Work as usual. O.C. visited Right Subsection with ~~B~~G.O.C. 48 Inf Bde. Work as usual	RMM

A6945 Wt. W11422/M1160 350,000 12/16 D. D. & L. Forms/C./2118/14.

Instructions regarding War Diaries and Intelligence Summaries are contained in F. S. Regs., Part II. and the Staff Manual respectively. Title pages will be prepared in manuscript.

(2)

WAR DIARY
or
~~INTELLIGENCE SUMMARY.~~
(Erase heading not required.)

Volume XXIV

155 Field Coy RE

Army Form C. 2118.

Place	Date	Hour	Summary of Events and Information	Remarks and references to Appendices
BOIRY-BECQUERELLE	11.11.17	—	No 3 Section & H.Q. rested. O.C. visited Right subsection with O.C. 48th Bde Signals to select site off FACTORY AVENUE for Visual Signal Station otherwise work as usual. O.C.R.E. & M.O. ½ inspected billet.	[illegible]
	12.11.17		Work as usual. Arrangements for dumping & carrying up of wire made with G.O.C. Bde & O.C. Wiring Coy. Relief	[illegible]
	13.11.17		Work as usual	[illegible]
"	14.11.17		Work as usual. Experiments in blowing trenches with explosives made	[illegible]
"			No 3 section relieved No 4 Section in Shaft Trench, the latter returning to Coy H.Q.	[illegible]
"	15.11.17		Representatives of the Company cooperated with 48th Inf Bde in practice of offensive. Demonstration of blowing trenches with explosives. Work as usual.	[illegible]
"	16.11.17		Work as usual.	[illegible]
"	17.11.17		Representatives of Company again practised offensive with 48th Inf Bde. Beds for Trench Mortars put in in front Line (BURG TRENCH). Work as usual	[illegible]

A6945 Wt. W11422/M1160 350,000 12/16 D. D. & L. Forms/C./2118/14.

Instructions regarding War Diaries and Intelligence Summaries are contained in F. S. Regs., Part II. and the Staff Manual respectively. Title pages will be prepared in manuscript.

(3)

WAR DIARY
or
~~INTELLIGENCE SUMMARY.~~
(Erase heading not required.)

Army Form C. 2118.

Volume XXIV

155 Field Coy. R.E.

Place	Date	Hour	Summary of Events and Information	Remarks and references to Appendices
BOIRY-BECQUERELLE	18.11.17		48 & 49 Inf Bde H.Q moved into CROISILLES CAVES Work as usual	R.A.M.
"	19.11.17		O.C moved his H.Q to CROISILLES CAVES. Attached Infantry moved to billets in T.17.a.5.0. 5 pm Working parties paraded. No 1. Section erected bridges over Front Line (3) Lincoln Support (1) & HUMP Support (1) also erected O.P at Left Battalion H.Q ~~No 2 Sectn~~ Attached Infantry carried up Bangalore Torpedos to Mebu in BEAUMAN'S LOOP. also exploder etc	R.A.M.
"	20.11.17	12.30am	Working parties returned to Section H.Qs	
		4.0am	Parties paraded and moved to assembly positions. No 1 Section to STRAY SUPPORT, Lieut WEBSTER to Rt. Battn H.Q. ½ No 2 Section & Attached Infantry in STRAY SUPPORT. 2/Lieut BROOK to Left Battn H.Q 2/Lt ATOCK (2nd Bn R.D.F attached) to Right Bn. H.Q	
		6.20am	Zero. Attack launched.	
		6.25am	Lieut Webster & 2/Lt Atock sent back for their parties and proceeded as follows. Lieut Webster and No. 1. Section to BEAUMANS LOOP from which they blew a communication trench average depth 4 feet using 23 Torpedos in 3 series 2/Lt Atock & 8 OR. of No. 2 Section proceeded	

A6945 Wt. W11422/M1160 350,000 12/16 D. D. & L. Forms/C./2118/14.

Instructions regarding War Diaries and Intelligence Summaries are contained in F. S. Regs., Part II. and the Staff Manual respectively. Title pages will be prepared in manuscript.

(4)

WAR DIARY
or
~~INTELLIGENCE SUMMARY.~~
(Erase heading not required.)

Army Form C. 2118.

Volume XXIV
155 Field Coy R.E.

Place	Date	Hour	Summary of Events and Information	Remarks and references to Appendices
BOIRY-BECQUERELLE	20.11.17	(cont)	to MINERVA MEBU to consolidate a Lewis Gun strong point	
		6.~~25~~am	2/Lt BROOK sent back for party to consolidate similar post at MEBU JUNO.	
			Both these parties later brought up attached Infantry for Wiring	
		8.30am	"X" Coy 1st Bn R.D.F. trained & organized by 155 Fd Coy RE completed wiring the whole Bde front, 800 yards with two rows of concertina wire	
		9.0am	Lieut Webster reported MINERVA LANE blown as far through as was safe with surrounding troops i.e all but 20x at near end.	
		9.45am	All No 1 Section reported returned No casualties.	
			2nd Reliefs for No 2 Section ~~complete~~ started out.	
		10.30pm	~~P~~ Report of progress from 2/Lt ATOCK at MINERVA all progressing favourably Progress reported verbally to C.R.E by telephone	
		11.30pm	All 1st Reliefs from No 2 Section in	
		12 noon	C.R.E arrived at CROISILLES CAVES.	
		4.0pm	Enemy barrage put down heavily on BURG TRENCH, FACTORY AVENUE, and	

A6945 Wt. W11422/M1160 350,000 12/16 D. D. & L. Forms/C./2118/14.

Instructions regarding War Diaries and Intelligence Summaries are contained in F. S. Regs., Part II. and the Staff Manual respectively. Title pages will be prepared in manuscript.

(5)

WAR DIARY
or
~~INTELLIGENCE SUMMARY.~~
(Erase heading not required.)

Volume XXIV
155 Fd Coy RE

Army Form C. 2118.

Place	Date	Hour	Summary of Events and Information	Remarks and references to Appendices
BOIRY-BECQUERELLE	20.11.17	(cont)	Mebus MINERVA & JUNO	
		5.0pm	2nd reliefs from Mebus returned. A trench about 16' deep and a small chamber under the Mebu completed. Working parties stopped till	
		7.30pm	When all being quiet 3rd reliefs & carrying parties went up till 11.0 pm	RAM
	21.11.17		Parties sent to clear out MINERVA LANE & revet backs of dugouts at Mebus. Total casualties for 2 days No154100 Sapper BREMNER A. Killed. 3 O.R. wounded	
		noon	Orders received from Divn for R.E work to cease where possible and the men to be rested in case of further advance.	RAM
	22.11.17		Sections employed in making pegs to mark overland routes. Scheme of work discussed by G.O.C 48th Inf Bde	RAM
	23.11.17		No. 1 & 2 Section relieved by No. 3. Work continued on Mebus and improving accommodation in CROISILLES CAVES. No 3 Section reconnoitred line & O.C. discussed work with C.O. Bn in the line (1st R.D.F)	RAM
	24.11.17		No 4 Section arrived and accommodated with Infantry in Sunken Road T.23.d. Work of improving line started. O.C. accompanied Bde Major round the trenches, later he returned to Coy H.Q at BOIRY-BECQUERELLE	RAM

Instructions regarding War Diaries and Intelligence Summaries are contained in F. S. Regs., Part II. and the Staff Manual respectively. Title pages will be prepared in manuscript.

(6)

WAR DIARY
or
~~INTELLIGENCE SUMMARY.~~
(Erase heading not required.)

Army Form C. 2118.

Volume XXIV

155 Field Coy RE

Place	Date	Hour	Summary of Events and Information	Remarks and references to Appendices
BOIRY-BECQUERELLE	25.11.17		Work continued in line. Very quiet. Strong drying wind from N.W. Heavy rain at night. One reinforcement arrived.	[illegible]
"	26.11.17		Damp day. Trenches hopelessly full of mud. Work as usual.	[illegible]
"	27.11.17		Trenches still very bad, difficult to make any progress. Corps Commander visited Trenches. Drying wind.	[illegible]
"	28.11.17		Much progress made in new trenches. Work as usual.	[illegible]
"	29.11.17		Trench much better. Good progress in revetting & trenchboarding. Work as usual. 2/Lt BROOK went on leave.	[illegible]
"	30.11.17		Very heavy bombardment of trenches from 6 am to 2 pm. Damage insignificant considering intensity. Chief damage to FACTORY AV^UE on left & TOP LANE on right. All trenches cleared with passage through in the evening. Strength of Company 207. 3 reinforcements arrived.	[illegible]

R.P. Pakenham Walsh
Maj. RE
O.C. 155 Fd. Coy. RE

A6945 Wt. W11422/M1160 350,000 12/16 D. D. & L. Forms/C./2118/14.

WAR DIARY

FOR MONTH OF DECEMBER, 1917.

VOLUME :- 25

UNIT :- 155th Field Coy R.E.

Vol 25

Instructions regarding War Diaries and Intelligence Summaries are contained in F. S. Regs., Part II. and the Staff Manual respectively. Title pages will be prepared in manuscript.

(1)

WAR DIARY
or
~~INTELLIGENCE SUMMARY.~~
(Erase heading not required.)

Army Form C. 2118.

Volume XXV

155 Field Coy. R.E.

Place	Date	Hour	Summary of Events and Information	Remarks and references to Appendices
BOIRY-BECQUERELLE	1.12.17	–	Fine day. Quiet after early morning. Work as usual. Attached Inf returned to Coy H.Q.	~~[illegible]~~
	2.12.17		Sections working as usual. Att'd Infantry returned to their battalions	alH
	3.12.17		O.C 224th Field Company came to take over line. The 40th Division having relieved the 16th in the line. Two sections in CROISILLES caves returned to H.Q. Orders received to proceed tomorrow by lorry to RUYAULCOURT & thence to HAVRINCOURT	alH
ROCQUIGNY	4.12.17		Very cold. Company embussed at BOYELLES at 9 a.m. Transport left for HAVRINCOURT at same time. These orders changed on the road. Company billeted the night at ROCQUIGNY. MAJOR Pakenham-Walsh left for R.E. School of Instruction. Billets consisted of tents & Nissen Huts.	alH
COURCELLES	5.12.17		Fine & cold. Orders received to march with 49th Bde Group to TINCOURT area. Arrived in billets at COURCELLES at 7.30 p.m. (Nissen huts)	Appendices A + B alH
RONSSOY	6.12.17		O.C & one subaltern sent to RONSSOY to take over work from 419th Field Coy RE 55th Div. Company moving also. Horse lines at VILLERS FAUCON. Dismounted in dugouts at RONSSOY. Arrived billets at midnight.	Appendix C alH
	7.12.17		Took over billets from 423rd Field Coy. Work started. 1 & 2 Sections front line. No 3 LEMPIRE defences. No 4 general work. 48th Bde holding the whole front	alH

A6945 Wt. W11422/M1160 350,000 12/16 D. D. & L. Forms/C. 2118/14.

Instructions regarding War Diaries and Intelligence Summaries are contained in F. S. Regs., Part II. and the Staff Manual respectively. Title pages will be prepared in manuscript.

(2)

WAR DIARY
or
~~INTELLIGENCE SUMMARY.~~
(Erase heading not required.)

Army Form C. 2118.

Volume XXV
155th Field Coy RE

Place	Date	Hour	Summary of Events and Information	Remarks and references to Appendices
RONSSOY	8.12.17		Sections starting work No 1 with left Battalion Nos 2 & 4 with Right No 3 LEMPIRE defences left sector now belongs to 49th Bde. Work consists chiefly of clearing & revetting after the Thaw.	[illegible]
"	9.12.17		Work as before everything fairly quiet Trenches in very bad state.	[illegible]
"	~~[illegible]~~		C.R.E. visited billets 2 sections & H.Q. to be relieved tomorrow. ~~Work as usual~~	[illegible]
VILLERS FAUCON	10.12.17		Coy H.Q. & Nos 3 & 4 Sections returned to VILLERS FAUCON in the evening being relieved by 2 sections of 157th Fd Coy in billets, leaving No 1 with left Battalion & No 2 with Right Battalion 7 men of No 3 & Lt O'Sullivan attached to ~~[illegible]~~ Bde for building a new H.Q. MAJOR E.I. SCOTT took command of the Company 2 reinforcements arrived.	[illegible]
	11-12-17		Dull day. No 1 & 2 sections remain in RONSSOY working in front line. No 3 section working on new Bde HQ & Aid post. No 4 Section working in camp & RE dump.	[illegible]
"	12-12-17		Bright day, aircraft active. work as for 11-12-17. 98249 Cpl Chubb severely wounded by shellfire.	[illegible]
	13-12-17		Cloudy. work as above for 1 2 & 3 sections. No 4 section commence erecting new battalion camp in St EMILIE.	[illegible]
	14-12-17		Cloudy overcast. work as for 13-12-17.	[illegible]

A6945 Wt. W11422/M1160 350,000 12/16 D. D. & L. Forms/C./2118/14.

Instructions regarding War Diaries and Intelligence Summaries are contained in F. S. Regs., Part II. and the Staff Manual respectively. Title pages will be prepared in manuscript.

(3)

WAR DIARY
or
~~INTELLIGENCE SUMMARY.~~
(*Erase heading not required.*)

Army Form C. 2118.

Volume XXV
155 Field Coy RE

Place	Date	Hour	Summary of Events and Information	Remarks and references to Appendices
VILLERS FAUCON	15-12-17		Fine & clear day. Sections employed as for 14-12-17. No 2 section under 2Lt Atock also commence work on support line strong points at QUEUCHETTES WOOD. Z copse. SART FARM SART FARM EAST. DOLEFUL POST. LEMPIRE EAST POST.	SIS
"	16-12-17		Fine day. work as for 15-12-17. VILLERS FAUCON shelled about 9.p.m. by heavies.	SIS
"	17-12-17		Snowing. work as for 16-12-17. one reinforcement arrived in exchange for Cpl Northgate	SIS
"	18-12-17		Fine day. No 3 & 4 Sections relieved No 1 & 2 in Forward billets RONSSOY. Lt O'Sullivan & 4 sappers under 1 NCO attached to RFA for RARE work.	SIS
	19-12-17		Fine day. No 3 & 4 sections working on front line & strong Points. No 2 section Bde Hqrs. Lt Webster & 6 men on hutting in charge of Divl hutting Coy at TINCOURT. 140594 Cpl J Holmes awarded M.M. for gallantry to date from 24-9-17	SIS
	20-12-17		misty. work as for 19-12-17. 6 reinforcements arrived	SIS
	21-12-17		misty. owing to hard state of ground work concentrated on strong points instead of front line	SIS
	22-12-17		frost & snow. work as for 21-12-17	SIS
	23-12-17		do work as usual. Brigade relief.	SIS
	24-12-17		do work as usual	SIS
	25-12-17		do Xmas dinner. no work in progress	SIS
	26-12-17		do work as usual for 2.3 & 4 Sections. No 1 Section take over work on RONSSOY-LEMPIRE defences	SIS

A6945 Wt. W11422/M1160 350,000 12/16 D. D. & L. Forms/C./2118/14.

Instructions regarding War Diaries and Intelligence Summaries are contained in F. S. Regs., Part II. and the Staff Manual respectively. Title pages will be prepared in manuscript.

(4)

WAR DIARY
or
~~INTELLIGENCE SUMMARY.~~
(Erase heading not required.)

Army Form C. 2118.

Volume XXV
155 Field Coy RE

Place	Date	Hour	Summary of Events and Information	Remarks and references to Appendices
VILLERS FAUCON	27-12-17		Fine day frosty. work as usual.	EHS
	28-12-17		do work as usual CRE visited Bde sector with GOC 49th Bde. 3 reinforcements arrived.	EHS
	29-12-17		do work as usual OC handed over RONSSOY defences to Major Whitall DSO 157 Fld Co RE. 139661 Cpl Black. 18635 2 Cpl McLean 85850 Sapper Crouch awarded MM for services during capture of TUNNEL TRENCH. Battalion relief.	EHS
	30-12-17		Fine day frosty. work as usual. Parade for presentation of MM ribbons & Parchment certificates at 2pm by CRE. MMs presented to Sergt Holmes. Corpl Black. 2Cpl McLean. (Sapper Crouch in hospital) Parchment certificates presented to Sergt Holmes. 2nd Cpl McAlister. 2nd Cpl Corner. Driver Pearl. (Sgt Harris & Cpl Perrin awarded but in hospital)	EHS
	31-12-17		Fine day frosty. work until midday as usual. In the afternoon No 1 & 2 Sections under Lt Webster & 2Lt Brook relieve Nos 3 & 4 Sections. No 1 Section take over Left Battn sector No 2 right battn. No 1 & 2 Sections in forward billets RONSSOY No 3 & 4 at Coy hqrs VILLERS FAUCON. CRE held conference of Field Coy commanders. Strength of Company 208.	EHS

E. Scott Major
OC. 155 Field Coy RE

W A R   D I A R Y,

FOR MONTH OF JANUARY, 1918.

VOLUME :- 26.

U N I T :- 155th Fd. Coy. R.E.

6

Army Form C. 2118.

Instructions regarding War Diaries and Intelligence Summaries are contained in F. S. Regs., Part II. and the Staff Manual respectively. Title pages will be prepared in manuscript.

(1)

WAR DIARY
or
~~INTELLIGENCE SUMMARY.~~
(Erase heading not required.)

volume XXVI
155 Field Coy RE

Place	Date	Hour	Summary of Events and Information	Remarks and references to Appendices
VILLERS FAUCON	1-1-18		Fine day. No 1 & 2 sections working in Right Bde Sector No 3 on marking tracks & in camp No 4 Bde Hqrs St EMILIE.	GS
	2-1-18		Cloudy. work as usual Lt Haugh proceeded on 14 days leave to England 97103 Spr Wyatt P. wounded by shell fire	GS
	3-1-18		Fine day work as usual Priority of work settled by GOC 48th & OC for work in line	GS
	4-1-18		Fine day work as usual 48th Bde relieved 49th Bde in Right sector.	GS
	5-1-18		do work as usual deep dugout at GOSUCHRISTS WOOD commenced by No 2 section.	GS
	6-1-18		do do	GS
	7-1-18		Wet day. work as usual GOC 48th Bde. CRE & OC plan out new battle line in front of RONSSOY	GS
	8-1-18		Snowing do OC sited & taped out new battle line RONSSOY	GS
	9-1-18		Thawing. work as usual.	GS
	10-1-18		Thawing work as usual. inter battalion relief in 48th Bde	GS
	11-1-18		do work as usual SHAMROCK TRENCH & THISTLE TRENCH excavation commenced	GS
	12-1-16		do work as usual.	GS
	13-1-18		Frost. do remainder of battle line to ORCHARD Post taped out by OC	GS
	14-1-18		Frost do No 3 Section relieved No 2 in forward billets	GS

Instructions regarding War Diaries and Intelligence Summaries are contained in F. S. Regs., Part II. and the Staff Manual respectively. Title pages will be prepared in manuscript.

(2)

WAR DIARY
or
INTELLIGENCE SUMMARY.
(Erase heading not required.)

Army Form C. 2118.

Volume XXVI
155 Field Co R.E.

Place	Date	Hour	Summary of Events and Information	Remarks and references to Appendices
VILLERS FAUCON.	15-1-18		Raining. work as usual. 25 miners under Lt Maitland RDF attached for dug out work. rationed by Support Batt. RONSSOY.	SJS
do	16-1-18		Raining. work as usual. trenches almost impassable. Batt. relief. 1st & 2nd Batt: RDF go into line.	SJS
do	17-1-18		Wet day. work as usual. trenches almost impassable	SJS
	18-1-18		Showery. work as usual. OC took a/CRE round the line	SJS
	19-1-18		Wet day work as usual infantry working parties concentrated on opening up trenches. DUNCAN AVENUE & CAUSEWAY LANE. SHAMROCK trench completed to 2' deep	SJS
	20-1-18		Fine day - warm. work as usual OC took over Brown line & switches from OC 156 Fld Co RE.	SJS
	21-1-18		Wet day. work as usual. OC handed over front line work to OC 156 Fld C.	SJS
	22-1-18		Fine day. 156 Fld Coy relieve this unit on line work & take over RONSSOY billets. All sections accomodated in reserve at VILLERS FAUCON	SJS
	23.1.18		~~Fine~~ Showery Day. The Company resting on account of Bde relief. O.C presented Parchment certificates	
	24.1.18		Fine day. Major Scott left for 14 days leave to U.K. No 2 section working on RONSSOY defences No 3 started work on Brown Line switches, No 1 on Old D.H.Q.	

A6945 Wt. W11422/M1160 350,000 12/16 D. D. & L. Forms/C./2118/14.

Instructions regarding War Diaries and Intelligence Summaries are contained in F. S. Regs., Part II. and the Staff Manual respectively. Title pages will be prepared in manuscript.

(3)

WAR DIARY
or
~~INTELLIGENCE SUMMARY.~~
(Erase heading not required.)

Army Form C. 2118.

Volume XXVI
155th Field Company RE

Place	Date	Hour	Summary of Events and Information	Remarks and references to Appendices
VILLERS FAUCON			reerecting huts & bunking a/CRE visited Switches & laid out S.Ps	AHH
"	25.1.18		Fine day. Work as yesterday. No 3 Sect started work on Shelter for YMCA. St Emilie.	AHH
"	26.1.18		Very foggy Work as before	AHH
	27.1.18		Very foggy Company resting with the exception of ½ No 3 who were working on Brown Line switches & No 1 on D.H.Q.	AHH
"	28.1.18		Fine day a/party Work as for 26.1.18. No 1 section completed their work. No parties for No 3 Sect. Lt Haugh returned from leave 5 days extension	AHH
"	29.1.18		Fine day No 1 Section clearing up remains of work, Other Sections as before CRE visited billets. False Gas alarm at 8.0 p.m. E.A active at night.	AHH
"	30.1.18		Fine day No 1 Sect: resting Other work as before	AHH
"	31.1.18		Very foggy Nos 2 & 3 Sects working as before Strength of Company 210	AHH
			1.2.18	

AHHughes Capt RE
O/C 155th Field Coy RE

A6945 Wt. W11422/M1160 350,000 12/16 D. D. & L. Forms/C./2118/14.

Vol 27

W A R   D I A R Y .

FOR MONTH OF FEBRUARY, 1918.

VOLUME:- 24

UNIT:- 155th Field Compy R.E.

Instructions regarding War Diaries and Intelligence Summaries are contained in F. S. Regs., Part II. and the Staff Manual respectively. Title pages will be prepared in manuscript.

(1)

WAR DIARY
or
~~INTELLIGENCE SUMMARY.~~
(Erase heading not required.)

Army Form C. 2118.

Volume XXVII
155th Field Company RE

Place	Date	Hour	Summary of Events and Information	Remarks and references to Appendices
VILLERS-FAUCON	1.2.18		Fine day Work as for last month No 2 Sect on Ronssoy Defences No 3 on Brown Line Switches	
			Nos 1 & 4 Camp & general work Working parties 285 men CRE had conference of Fld Coy Commanders	AH
	2.2.18		Fine day very clear Lts Haugh & Atork went up to take over work in Left Bde Sector from Lts	
			Osmond & Black 157th Field Company Work as usual One man went on leave	AH
	3.2.18		Fine Day Sect officers handing over reserve work to 157th Fld Coy. O.C. went round line	
			with O.C 157th Field Coy RE to take over work Ronssoy defences taken over by 11th Hants (Pioneers)	
			O.C B Coy 11th Hants handed over work on Room & Ockenden Trenches to us	AH
	4.2.18		Fine day Nos 3 & 4 Sects went up to billets in Ronssoy Work started on new area	
			No 1 Sect on Red Line (Ridge Reserve) No 2 Sect Workshops & Bde H.Q. No 3 Sect on	
			Left Battalion Sector No 4 on Right Battn sector Work chiefly revetting. Lt Webster	
			went on leave in the evening 2nd Lt Brook looking after both intermediate Sects.	AH
	5.2.18		Fine day work as yesterday. Raining towards evening	AH
	6.2.18		Fine day CRE inspected whole line with O.C & gave details of Ridge Reserve	
			support. CRE visited Bde H.Q. & told G.O.C that infantry must dig the trenches	
			large without sapper assistance Templates made & distributed to Battalions.	AH
	7.2.18		Fine day Ridge support taped out complete work started with 125 men Other work as before	AH

A6945 Wt. W11422/M1160 350,000 12/16 D. D. & L. Forms/C./2118/14.

Instructions regarding War Diaries and Intelligence Summaries are contained in F. S. Regs., Part II, and the Staff Manual respectively. Title pages will be prepared in manuscript.

(2)

WAR DIARY
or
INTELLIGENCE SUMMARY.
(Erase heading not required.)

Army Form C. 2118.

Volume XXVII
155th Field Coy RE

Place	Date	Hour	Summary of Events and Information	Remarks and references to Appendices
VILLERS FAUCON	7.2.18		Two reinforcements arrived	ACH
	8.2.18		Wet day G.O.C + Bde Major took O.C. round Reserve lines & inspected work. Work as before. An Officer appointed from Bde Bde in charge of all working parties.	ACH
	9.2.18		Fine day Work as before OC returned from Leave.	ACH
	10-2-18		Fine day work as before.	SHS
	11-2-18		Fine day work as usual.	SHS
	12-2-18		Fine day No 2 section relieved No 3 in RONSSOY billets & took over work in left batn sector. No 3 section employed on RIDGE RESERVE & MALASSISE Farm	SHS
	13-2-18		Wet day work as usual.	SHS
	14-2-18		Fine day work as usual CRE went round left sector with OC. 2 reinforcements (arrived)	SHS
	15-2-18		Fine day work as usual	SHS
	16-2-18		Fine day party work as usual antitank line commenced in front of OCKENDEN TRENCH	SHS
	17-2-18		Fine day. party work as usual. wiring party in front of OCKENDEN TR encountered enemy patrol which was driven off.	SHS
	18-2-18		Fine day. party work as usual. trenches greatly improved & revetment proceeding fast. Lewis Gun added to establishment of the unit. In action about 6.45 p.m. on Gotha bombing machine flying over VILLERS FAUCON.	SHS

A6945 Wt. W11422/M1160 350,000 12/16 D. D. & L. Forms/C./2118/14.

Army Form C. 2118.

WAR DIARY
or
INTELLIGENCE SUMMARY.
(Erase heading not required.)

Instructions regarding War Diaries and Intelligence Summaries are contained in F. S. Regs., Part II. and the Staff Manual respectively. Title pages will be prepared in manuscript.

Volume XXVII
155 Field Coy RE

Place	Date	Hour	Summary of Events and Information	Remarks and references to Appendices
VILLERS	19-2-18		Fine day. [illegible] work as usual. One reinforcement arrived.	ES
FAUCON	20-2-18		Cloudy. raining after midday. No 1 section relieved No 4 section in Right batt. sector	ES
	21-2-18		Showery. work as usual	ES
	22-2-18		Wet day. work as usual. line very muddy. Lt Webster returned from leave. Capt O'Sullivan RE went on leave	ES
	23-2-18		Fine day work as usual. Lcpl Muller mounted section. Sapr. Woodcock killed and Sap Palmer wounded both No 1 Section on LEMPIRE Rd whilst with transport. Shelling slightly above normal.	ES
	24-2-18		Fine day work as usual. 2 men killed on 23-2-18 buried in VILLERS FAUCON	ES
	25-2-18		Fine day work as usual. O.C. 126 Fld Co called to discuss relief of this coy.	ES
	26-2-18		Fine day work as usual. O.C. went to CRE TINCOURT Divl hqrs to discuss the relief of 16th Divl RE by 21st Divl RE	ES
	27-2-18		Dull day work as usual. O.C. took O.C. 126 Fld Coy round the Brigade sector preparatory to handing over. Marked improvement in progress of work in BIRD TRENCH, MULE TRENCH, OCKENDEN trench & ROOM trench	ES
	28-2-18		Fine day work as usual. CRE's conference of O.C. companies. Relief by 21st Divl cancelled. 48th Bde remain in line sector between EPEHY & LEMPIRE. Strength of Coy 206.	

G I Scott Major
O.C. 155 Field Coy RE

A6945 Wt. W11422/M1160 350,000 12/16 D. D. & L. Forms/C./2118/14.

16th Divisional Engineers

155th FIELD COMPANY R. E.

MARCH 1918

13

16

Army Form C. 2118.

Instructions regarding War Diaries and Intelligence Summaries are contained in F. S. Regs., Part II. and the Staff Manual respectively. Title pages will be prepared in manuscript.

WAR DIARY
or
~~INTELLIGENCE SUMMARY.~~
(Erase heading not required.)

155th Field Coy RE
Volume XXVIII

WO 28

Place	Date	Hour	Summary of Events and Information	Remarks and references to Appendices
VILLERS FAUCON.	1-3-18		Fair day hailstorm. Divl relief by 21st Divn being postponed, 48th Bde remain in Left sector from EPEHY to LEMPIRE exclusive of the villages. No 1 section employed on front line from ROOM trench to GRAFTON Trench & live in billets RONSSOY. No 2 section in reserve No 3. Yellow line & support Red line. No 4 Section Red front line & wire. 3 reinforcements arrived. Lt Atock went on leave.	S/S
	2-3-18		Snowing. work as above. CRE visited sector with O.C.	S/S
	3-3-18		Fine day. work as above	S/S
	4-3-18		Fine day work as usual No 2 section relieve No 4 on RED LINE & No 4 come into reserve	S/S
	5-3-18		Fine day work as usual. 2 Lieut Gornell RE arrived as reinforcement	S/S
	6-3-18		Fine day work as usual 2Lt Gornell transferred to 157 Fld Co RE	S/S
	7-3-18		Fine day work as usual No 4 Section relieve No 1 section in forward billets RONSSOY & work on front line, concrete dugout being constructed at No 12 copse. Lt F J King R.I.R. is attached for instruction with view to transfer to RE	S/S
	8-3-18		Fine day work as usual CRE goes round sector	S/S
	9-3-18		Fine day work as usual	S/S
	10-3-18		Fine day work as usual	S/S

Instructions regarding War Diaries and Intelligence Summaries are contained in F. S. Regs., Part II. and the Staff Manual respectively. Title pages will be prepared in manuscript.

WAR DIARY
or
~~INTELLIGENCE SUMMARY.~~
(Erase heading not required.)

Army Form C. 2118.

158 Fd Coy RE
Volume XXVIII

Place	Date	Hour	Summary of Events and Information	Remarks and references to Appendices
VILLERS FAUCON	11-3-18		Fine day. Work as usual orders for 64th Bde to relieve 48th Bde issued & cancelled	
			one reinforcement arrived	S/S
	12-3-18		Fine day work as usual. Capt O'Sullivan returned from leave	S/S
	13-3-18		Fine day work as usual Capt O'Sullivan departs to report to 222 Fld Co RE. 2 Lieut	
			Barnes joined the Coy and posted to No 1 Section. Lt Webster is attached to	
			CRE as assistant adjutant. 2nd RMF raided KILDARE Post & took 4 prisoners	S/S
	14-3-18		Fine day. work as usual. Enemy attack expected at dawn of 15th or 16th	S/S
	15-3-18		stand to 3 am to 7 am. work as usual. on Yellow line behind EPEHY.	S/S
	16-3-18		stand to 5 am to 7 am do	S/S
	17-3-18		No 1, 2 & 3 sections rest day & washing day combined RE service C of E at 11 am	S/S
	18-3-18		Quiet day work as usual on Yellow line & Ridge Reserve North.	S/S
	19-3-18		No 3 section under Lt King (attached infantry officer from R I R) relieve No 4.	S/S
	20-3-18		stand to 5 am to 7 a.m. work as usual. 2/Lt Atock returned from leave midnight	S/S
	21-3-18	am. 4:30	Heavy shell fire & gas shell fire commenced on front line extending to VILLERS FAUCON	
			billets heavily shelled & several direct hits. Company stands to in cellars with	
			patrols out in front on VILLERS FAUCON towards St EMILIE	S/S

A6945 Wt. W11422/M1160 350,000 12/16 D. D. & L. Forms/C./2118/14.

Instructions regarding War Diaries and Intelligence Summaries are contained in F. S. Regs., Part II. and the Staff Manual respectively. Title pages will be prepared in manuscript.

WAR DIARY
or
~~INTELLIGENCE SUMMARY.~~
(*Erase heading not required.*)

Army Form C. 2118.

153 Field Coy RE
Volume XXVIII

Place	Date	Hour	Summary of Events and Information	Remarks and references to Appendices
VILLERS FAUCON	21-3-18	am 5.15	Stables cleared of all horses except six which were badly gassed, assembling on the VILLERS FAUCON – MARQUAIX Rd. Heavy shelling continued until midday when the Company was turned out & manned VILLERS FAUCON Ridge facing St EMILIE & dug & wired in.	
		1 pm	Stragglers from No 3 section in RONSSOY returned with Lt King. RONSSOY reported captured by enemy. several men wounded & missing.	
		7 pm	All wagons cleared out of village by this hour except two destroyed by shell fire. Double journey done by horses owing to several sets of harness being destroyed by shellfire. officers saddlery also destroyed. direct hits on the camp destroyed three section huts, QM stores, officers cookhouse & batmens quarters & partially destroyed the office & officers mess. calibre of shells from 5.9 to 14 inch.	
		pm 11.25	Company ordered to retire to Green line in front of TINCOURT. CSM remained behind to salve office papers when shelling abated. Casualties light	SKS
TINCOURT. GREEN line	22-3-18	5 am	position taken up in Green line in front of TINCOURT wood. along with Hants Entrenching Battn. 1 Bde 39th Divn on left. Corps cyclists & 157 Fld Coy on right	
		2 pm	enemy attacked without success.	
		6.30 pm	Coy withdrawn to TINCOURT – BUSSU Rd. Transport in BUSSU under Capt Hughes	

A6945 Wt. W11422/M1160 350,000 12/16 D. D. & L. Forms/C./2118/14.

Army Form C. 2118.

Instructions regarding War Diaries and Intelligence Summaries are contained in F. S. Regs., Part II. and the Staff Manual respectively. Title pages will be prepared in manuscript.

WAR DIARY
or
~~INTELLIGENCE SUMMARY.~~
(Erase heading not required.)

155 Fld Co RE
Volume XXVIII

Place	Date	Hour	Summary of Events and Information	Remarks and references to Appendices
TINCOURT - BUSSU Rd	22-3-18	pm 10.30	Ordered to proceed to COURCELLES, with dismounted company.	Sheet 62D S/S
COURCELLES	23-3-18	am 12.30	arrived at COURCELLES. joined by transport at 4 am.	
BIACHES		7 am	marched to BIACHES via PERONNE arriving midday. 4 hours rest, & foot inspection made.	
			Enemy reported to be approaching PERONNE. Toolcarts left at BUSSU owing to shortage of harness.	
HERBECOURT		pm 6.30	marched to HERBECOURT standing to for orders until 10 pm. line in front of BIACHES being held.	
		10 pm	marched to road entrance to CAPPY village. halted until midnight	S/S
CAPPY.	24-3-18	am 12.30	crossed canal. bivouaced in wood behind village. together with remaining transport	
		4 pm	Sappers marched to FROISSY to prepare bridge for demolition. Mounted section under Capt	L.28.c.
			Hughes withdrawn to PONT NOYELLES & then to LAMOTTE. accompanied by CAPT MILLEN C of E chaplain.	S/S
FROISSY.	25-3-18	4 am	FROISSY bridge ready for demolition 160 lbs guncotton used. 2 Lt Baines - 4 men No 1 section	
			left behind under orders 48 Bde for ~~blowing~~ firing charge.	
BRAY		6 am	Coy in reserve in billets southern outskirts of BRAY SUR SOMME	L.21.b.
		3 pm	remainder of No 1 section join 2Lt Baines attached to 48 Bde.	
PROYART.		3.30 pm	rest of Company move to PROYART. & rest night in billets	S/S
	26-3-18	11 am	OC Fld Coys conference with GOC 16th Div & CRE. work commenced preparing defensive line	
MERICOURT			FROISSY - PROYART. 3.30 pm Coys withdrawn to defensive position in front of MERICOURT	R.21.15/a.b.4
MORCOURT		8 pm	Coy withdrawn to MORCOURT to defend south side of village on left on main AMIENS Rd.	S/S

A6945 Wt. W11422/M1160 350,000 12/16 D. D. & L. Forms/C./2118/14.

Army Form C. 2118.

Instructions regarding War Diaries and Intelligence Summaries are contained in F. S. Regs., Part II. and the Staff Manual respectively. Title pages will be prepared in manuscript.

WAR DIARY
or
~~INTELLIGENCE SUMMARY.~~
(Erase heading not required.)

1st Fld Co RE
Volume XXVIII

Place	Date	Hour	Summary of Events and Information	Remarks and references to Appendices
MORCOURT line	27.3.18	2 am	Coy sent up to MERICOURT to reinforce 49 & 48 Bdes & defend village. O.12.a.	Sheet 62D
		6 am	manning positions of MERICOURT – BRAY ARI road. covering infantry retirement on the left	Q.12.a.
			enemy broke through along the SOMME N of MERICOURT. retired to MORCOURT.	Q.16.d.
		9 am.	Sunken road from MORCOURT to AMIENS main road manned & infantry reorganised	Q.22 central Q.27 do
LAMOTTE.		3 pm.	retirement to LAMOTTE ordered. infantry harassed by enemy MG on left from direction of CERISY. Coy extended & covered retirement with rapid rifle fire	
		5 pm	position taken up in front of LAMOTTE. noone on the flanks of Company.	Q.20 a&b.
			O.C. instructed personally by XIX Corps commander to advance & meet approaching	P30.a&c.
		6 pm	enemy. Company advanced in extended order. enemy in large numbers – probably 2 battalions. heavy firing. No 3 section under 2Lt Atock surprise MG of enemy at 50 yds & kill gunners. Owing to pressure OC orders retirement to sunken road in front of LAMOTTE. still no troops on either flanks	Q.20 a&b.
		7.30 pm	heavily attacked by enemy in large numbers. line held for one hour against great odds & all ammunition almost spent. LG fired 300 rounds. rifles 60 rounds per man.	P30 a&c
		8.30 pm	OC ordered Coy to fall back through village. 2Lt Atock remained behind with a few men to cover retirement. Excellent village fighting & sniping done.	
		9 pm	Coy hard pressed & almost surrounded fell back on trenches behind LAMOTTE on the VILLERS BRETONNEUX road. The whole company fought bravely. casualties fairly light. all wounded saved.	P33 b&d

Instructions regarding War Diaries and Intelligence Summaries are contained in F. S. Regs., Part II. and the Staff Manual respectively. Title pages will be prepared in manuscript.

WAR DIARY
or
~~INTELLIGENCE SUMMARY.~~
(Erase heading not required.)

Army Form C. 2118.

15th Fld Co RE
volume XXVIII

Place	Date	Hour	Summary of Events and Information	Remarks and references to Appendices
Trenches behind LAMOTTE	27-3-18	pm 9.30	Coy allotted portion of line on right of VILLERS BRETTONEUX road. P.33.b&d	RS Sheet 62 D Ed.1
		4.30	Mounted under Capt Hughes moved to PETIT BLANGY via FUILLOY.	
	28-3-18	3am	Coy relieved & withdrawn to HAMEL. rested for 3 hours	
HAMEL		7am	orders received to occupy sunken road in front of HAMEL facing CERISY. Coy in reserve.	P10 a & c
		2pm	to 4pm HAMEL & sunken road heavily shelled. quiet night	
		4pm	50 men under 2Lt Brook sent up to reinforce front line & remain in support	
		5am	Bosch attacked & driven off.	RS
	29-3-18		Same location in reserve. very cold & raining intermittent shelling during the day	
		8pm	2Lt Brook reinforce support line in front of HAMEL P10.b.&d.	
	30-3-18	am 5.30	Stand to at dawn. Lt Haugh relieved 2Lt Brook at 8 am	RS
		7.30	heavy shelling of HAMEL.	
		10 am	heavy barrage on front & support trenches. several casualties	
		12.	Enemy attacked & entered trenches but driven out. party of REs counter attacked	
		4pm	Sunken road heavily shelled & evacuated temporarily to position higher up road.	RS
		8pm	2Lt Atock relieved Lieut Haugh in support line	
	31-3-18	5.30 am	stand to. support line still held by 2Lt Atock & 40 men.	
AUBIGNY		11.30.	Coy relieved & withdrawn to AUBIGNY - joined by transport under Capt Hughes 2Lt Atock remained behind in support trenches & relieved at 9.30 pm. returning to AUBIGNY at 11.30 pm. Capt Hughes prepared BOUZENCOURT bridge for demolition	
			Total casualties from March 21 - 31st inclusive 2 Killed. 25 wounded 1 gassed.	
			Strength of company now 6 officers & 1 attached. 101 sappers 46 drivers	

E Scott Major
OC 15th Fld Co RE

(A7092). Wt. W12839/M1293. 750,000. 1/17. D. D. & L., Ltd. Forms/C.2118/14.

Confidential

Original

War Diary

of

155 Field Coy R.E.

from 1-4-18 to 30-4-18.

(Volume XXIX)

7

Vol 29

WAR DIARY
or
INTELLIGENCE SUMMARY.
(Erase heading not required.)

Army Form C. 2118.

Instructions regarding War Diaries and Intelligence Summaries are contained in F. S. Regs., Part II. and the Staff Manual respectively. Title pages will be prepared in manuscript.

155 Field Coy RE
Volume XXIX

Place	Date	Hour	Summary of Events and Information	Remarks and references to Appendices
AUBIGNY	1-4-18	10 am	Company in Reserve. Cleaning up parade & check parade.	SLS
—	2-4-18	10 am	Coy parade in fighting order. Inspection of equipment. List of deficiencies made out	SLS
	3-4-18	10 am	Inspection parade.	
		2pm	Mtd Section under Capt Hughes moved to SALEUX.	
SALEUX.		4pm.	Company march to crossroads south of BLANGY TRONVILLE & embus for SALEUX at 6.30pm billetted in SALEUX for the night	SLS
	4-4-18	6 am	Mounted march to ALLERY.	
		4pm.	Company entrain at SALEUX for BLANGY. & arrive at 11.30 pm.	
GREBAULT MESNIL.	5-4-18	3 am	Coy arrive at GREBAULT MESNIL after a 12 Kilom. march from BLANGY.	
		11 am	Mounted Section arrive under Capt Hughes.	SLS
—	6-4-18.	11 am	GOC 16th Div: Major General Sir P Hull KCB visited Company & expressed his thanks for the good work of the Company. Company resting & cleaning up	
	7-4-18		Company resting & cleaning up. re-equipping etc.	SLS.
	8-4-18		do	SLS.
DARGNIES.	9-4-18	11.30 am	march from GREBAULT-MESNIL to DARGNIES arriving 4.30 pm. 2Lt Brook goes in advance to billet at DARGNIES. 2Lt Alcock entrains at EU to St OMER to billet at BOUT de la VILLE.	SLS
	10-4-18	4pm	Coy entrained at WOINCOURT for WISERNES. 10 hours train journey.	SLS
Bout de la Ville	11-4-18.	2 am	arrived at WISERNES. marched to BOUT de la VILLE & billetted in HAVERRES chateau.	
do	12-4-18		Coy cleaning up & washing. O.C. met CRE 9 am. & went round Brigade areas selecting sites for rifle ranges in preparation for American army.	SLS.
	13-4-18		Coy at an hour's notice. standing to for a move.	SLS

(A7092). Wt. W12839/M1293. 750,000. 1/17. D. D. & L., Ltd. Forms/C.2118/14.

Instructions regarding War Diaries and Intelligence Summaries are contained in F. S. Regs., Part II. and the Staff Manual respectively. Title pages will be prepared in manuscript.

WAR DIARY
or
INTELLIGENCE SUMMARY.
(Erase heading not required.)

Army Form C. 2118.

155th Fld Coy RE
Volume XXIX

Place	Date	Hour	Summary of Events and Information	Remarks and references to Appendices
BOUT de la VILLE	14-4-18	9 am	No 2 section move to MOLINGHEM to work on GHQ line from MOLINGHEM – CANAL de la LYS. No 3 & 4 " to BOESEGHEM do from CANAL de la LYS to STEENBECQUE Station.	
		2 pm	remainder of Coy move to ENGUINEGATTE arriving 5 pm & billet for night. 5 officers & 110 NCOs & sappers & drivers arrived from BASE as reinforcement, under Capt Clarke	
LA ROUPIE.	15-4-18	10 am	Coy & HQ marched to LA ROUPIE & billet for night. OC went round GHQ reserve line with CRE. Taping out commenced line runs from O.9.c.5.0. to CHAPEL – O.3.b6.0. – Pont d'ISBERGUES – I 33 b.8.5. – in front of HOULERON village to FERRY at I 28 d 2.5. – lock at I 22 c 2.2.	SHEET 36A N.W.
THIENNES	16-4-18		Coy HQ moved to THIENNES I 22 c 1.2. Capt Clark 2 officers & 100 men of new reinforcement move to ISBERGUES to work under Lt Col Falcon RE who is in charge of line from MOLINGHEM to CANAL de la LYS as shown in 15-4-18. OC appointed CRE North of line from lock at CANAL de la LYS I 22 c.2.2. – in front of THIENNES station – I 16 Central – PLAINE HAUT I 10 d 1.5. – I 11 a 1.9. – school at STEENBECQUE – X crossroads I 15 d 8.5. – I 6.a 5.2. to STEENBECQUE station inclusive. OC now CRE North went round sector with GOC 48th Composite Bde. line taped out by Lt Atock & Lt Haugh by 1 pm. work commenced by 4 composite battalions in composite Bde of 16th Divn.	SH
	17-4-18		work continued on above line, under 2/Lt Atock. Lieut Haugh. 2 Lieut BOYCE a new RE officer reinforcement & Lieut King R.I.R. attchd RE assisting them.	SH
	18-4-18		work continued as above. OC went round with CRE 16th Divn & GOC Composite Bde selecting MG sites. tactical trenches. LG position at STEENBECQUE station & LE BAS.	SH
	19-4-18		work as usual. 2/Lt Brook & No 2 section returned & commenced work on STEENBECQUE station & LE BAS defended localities.	SH
	20-4-18		Lt Haugh & No 4 section & Lt King R.I.R. & No 1 section moved to billets in STEENBECQUE work as usual on GHQ line.	

(A7092). Wt. W12839/M1293. 750,000. 1/17. D. D. & L., Ltd. Forms/C.2118/14.

Instructions regarding War Diaries and Intelligence Summaries are contained in F. S. Regs., Part II. and the Staff Manual respectively. Title pages will be prepared in manuscript.

WAR DIARY
or
INTELLIGENCE SUMMARY.
(Erase heading not required.)

Army Form C. 2118.

155 Fd Co RE
Volume XXIX

Place	Date	Hour	Summary of Events and Information	Remarks and references to Appendices
STEENBECQUE	21-4-18		Coy HQ + No 2 section moved to new billets in STEENBECQUE. No 3 section + 2Lt Atock + 2Lt Boyes remained in billets at THIENNES station. work as usual on GHQ line. 2nd R.M.F. left the 16th Div. + found no working parties	Sheet 36A S.H.
	22-4-18		work as usual on GHQ line.	S.H.
	23-4-18		work as usual – 2nd RIR + 2nd Leinsters leave 16th Div. labour provided by 22nd Portuguese Batt + 2 Coys Portuguese Pioneers	S.H.
	24-4-18		work as usual. reserve line to GHQ line sited by OC with CRE 16th Div.	S.H.
	25-4-18		work as usual. 2nd RDF leave the 16th Div. all labour now found by 22nd Portuguese Batt + 2 Pioneer Coys.	
	26-4-18		work as usual – Reserve GHQ line from LE HAUT C30c56 – SW of THIENNES I21 central taped out by OC.	S.H.
	27-4-18		Distribution of work as follows. 2 Coys Portuguese Pioneers with No 2 Section under Lt Brook on defences of STEENBECQUE station + LE BAS. 2 Coys 22nd Portuguese Batt under No 1 section + Lt King + No 3 section + 2Lt Atock on Red line from STEENBECQUE station to THIENNES level crossing. 2 Coys under No 4 section + Lt Haugh commence Reserve GHQ line from LE HAUT working South.	S.H.
	28-4-18		work as usual 2 Groups Portuguese H.A. arrive + work on GHQ line.	S.H.
	29-4-18		work as usual.	
	30-4-18		work as usual. 156 + 157 Fd Coys arrive in this area + take over line from STEENBECQUE – LE BAS to the south. Strength of Company 7 officers 184 OR.	S.H.

G Wetherall? Major
OC 155 Fd Co RE

(A7092). Wt. W12839/M1293 750,000. 1/17. D. D. & L., Ltd. Forms/C.2118/14.

Confidential

Original

War Diary

of

155 Field Coy R.E.

from 1-5-18 to 31-5-18

(Volume XXX)

Vol 30

Army Form C. 2118.

WAR DIARY
or
INTELLIGENCE SUMMARY.
(Erase heading not required.)

Instructions regarding War Diaries and Intelligence Summaries are contained in F. S. Regs., Part II. and the Staff Manual respectively. Title pages will be prepared in manuscript.

Volume XXX.
155 Field Co R.E.

Place	Date	Hour	Summary of Events and Information	Remarks and references to Appendices
STEENBECQUE	1-5-18		Coy employed on GHQ line from STEENBECQUE station D25.d to LEBAS I6.d. & the switch line from LEBAS to Steenbecque in C24. Labour found by 28th Portuguese Batn. 2 Group Portuguese H.A. & 2 Coys Irish troops 49th Bde. Specially defended localities being made at STEENBECQUE station & LE HAUT.	36A NW S.S. S.S.
	2-5-18		work as above	S.S.
	3-5-18		work as above	
	4-5-18		work as above	S.S.
	5-5-18		work as above	
	6-5-18		work as above	S.S.
	7-5-18		work as above. much damage done to trenches by the heavy rainstorm	S.S.
	8-5-18		work as above.	S.S.
	9-5-18		work as above. Support line to Red Line taped out.	S.S.
	10-5-18		work as above	S.S.
	11-5-18		work as above	S.S.
	12-5-18		work as above. 9.30-12-30 pm only. church service at 8.15 am before work	S.S.
	13-5-18		do. Support line & RED LINE commenced from I6 a 3.5. northwards	S.S.
	14-5-18		work as above do CRE went round sector	
	15-5-18		unit ordered to proceed to DESVRES to prepare for arrival of American troops work on GHQ lines handed over to OC 156 Fld Coy RE. Dismounted Coy proceed by lorries to DESVRES. Mtd Section proceed by road. Halt for night at DOHEN Lt F J King RIR attd RE returns to unit	S.S.

(A7092). Wt. W12839/M1293. 750,000. 1/17. D. D. & L., Ltd. Forms/C.2118/14.

Army Form C. 2118.

Instructions regarding War Diaries and Intelligence Summaries are contained in F. S. Regs., Part II. and the Staff Manual respectively. Title pages will be prepared in manuscript.

WAR DIARY
or
INTELLIGENCE SUMMARY.
(*Erase heading not required.*)

Volume XXX.
155 Fld Co R.E.

Place	Date	Hour	Summary of Events and Information	Remarks and references to Appendices
DESVRES	16-5-18		Coy training. Carpenters employed making camp cookhouses latrines etc	S.S.
	17-5-18		Coy training. No 3 section move to SAMER to make railhead camp for American division	
	18-5-18		Coy training	
	19-5-18		Billets vacated at factory in DESVRES & others found in the town to make room for American battn	S.S
	20-5-18		No 2 section proceed to PARENTY. 47 Bde area - No 4 to FRENCQ 49th Bde.	
			No 1 remain in DESVRES 48 Bde area - No 3 in SAMER 16th Div. Area. & work on cookhouses latrines & general billet arrangements	S.S
	21-5-18		work as above. on RE services in SAMER area.	
	22-5-18		work as above. gas school constructed at DESVRES	S.S
	23-5-18		work as above. American Eng: officer attached for work. gas school at DESVRES erected	S.S
	24-5-18		work as above. 1 Coy American Eng: ~~attached~~ arrive at DESVRES 4th Regt	
	25-5-18		work as above. Each section working with a company of 4th Regt American Eng:	
	26-5-18		work as above	
	27-5-18		work as usual in DESVRES area. 3 L.G. ranges & 2-100yds rifle ranges commenced by American Eng: Coy.	S.S.
	28-5-18		work as above	
	29-5-18		work as above.	
	30-5-18		work as above.	S.S
	31-5-18		work as above Strength of Company 6 officers 185 O.R.	

E I Scott Major RE
OC 155 Fld Co R.E.

(A7092). Wt. W12839/M1293. 750,000. 1/17. D. D. & L., Ltd. Forms/C.2118/14.

Original
War Diary
of
155 Field Co. R.E.
from 1-6-18 to 30-6-18
(Volume XXXI

11

Vol 31

Instructions regarding War Diaries and Intelligence Summaries are contained in F. S. Regs., Part II. and the Staff Manual respectively. Title pages will be prepared in manuscript.

WAR DIARY
or
INTELLIGENCE SUMMARY.
(Erase heading not required.)

Army Form C. 2118.

Volume XXXI
155 Field Coy R.E.

Place	Date	Hour	Summary of Events and Information	Remarks and references to Appendices
DESVRES.	1-6-18.		Coy employed on R E Services. HQ & No 1 section DESVRES area East } 48th Bde. No 2 section PARENTY. 47 Brigade. No 3 section DESVRES area West } No 4 section HALINGHEM 49 Brigade. One American Eng Coy 4th Regt working & training with each section.	CALAIS Sheet 13 SCS
	2-6-18		work as above	
	3-6-18		work as above. 2Lt Worsley reported from RE BD. & takes over No 1 section.	SCS
	4-6-18		work as above.	
	5-6-18		Coy of Amer: Eng: 4th Regt receive orders to move to WIDEHEM. No 1 section remain with Coy HQ at DESVRES & carry on work as above.	SCS
	6-6-18		work as above.	SCS
	7-6-18		work as above. 3 - 100 yds range & 3 - 25x L.G. ranges completed	
	8-6-18		work as above	
	9-6-18		work as above. 4th American Div: leave the area.	SCS
	10-6-18		work as above. 80th American Div: move into area.	
	11-6-18		No 4 Section return to Coy hqrs DESVRES for work in the DESVRES area. No 2 Section join No 3 Section in DESVRES area (West) at CARLY. 157 Field Coy take over work from No 2 & 4 Sections.	SCS
	12-6-18		DESVRES area 48th Bde now worked by this unit complete for RE Services	SCS
	13-6-18.		work as usual in DESVRES area on R E Services.	
	14-6-18		work as above	SCS
	15-6-18		work as above.	SCS

(A7092). Wt. W12839/M1293. 750,000. 1/17. D. D. & L., Ltd. Forms/C.2118/14.

Army Form C. 2118.

Instructions regarding War Diaries and Intelligence Summaries are contained in F. S. Regs., Part II. and the Staff Manual respectively. Title pages will be prepared in manuscript.

WAR DIARY
or
INTELLIGENCE SUMMARY.
(Erase heading not required.)

Volume XXXI
155 Field Coy R.E.

Place	Date	Hour	Summary of Events and Information	Remarks and references to Appendices
VEYRES.	16.6.18		Church Service 11 30 a.m. no work for day afterwards.	
	17.6.18		Work as usual on RE Services 2 Lt Brook proceeded on leave	S/S.
	18.6.18		Work as usual.	
	19.6.18		Work as usual Site selected at HOURQUET for an RE school for American Engineers	S/S.
	20.6.18		Work as usual.	S/S
	21.6.18		Work as usual	
	22.6.18		Work as usual. 3 NCO's & 8 men sent to HOURQUET for RE school. Work commencing on Monday 24-6-18	S/S
	23.6.18		Major S.H. left for RE School Church service in morning 500 yds range completed	ACH
	24.6.18		Work started & completed 330 yds range [illegible] selected other work as usual	ACH
	25.6.18		4th 30 yds range completed work as before	ACH
	26.6.18		CRE visited billets [illegible] [illegible] of all firing points on 500 yds range work started	ACH
	27.6.18		½ B Coy 305 U.S. Eng Regt left for [illegible] HQ work as before	
	28.6.18		Work as usual	
	29.6.18		Work as before [illegible] shelter commenced	ACH
	30.6.18		No work inspection [illegible] in morning	ACH
				ACH

S H [illegible] Major RE
OC 155 Field Coy RE

(A7092). Wt. W12839/M1293 75,000. 1/17. D. D. & L., Ltd. Forms/C.2118/14.

CONFIDENTIAL
****

ORIGINAL WAR DIARY

OF

155th Field Company.R.E.

from 1st JULY.1918. to 31st JULY.1918.

(Volume xxxll)

Instructions regarding War Diaries and Intelligence Summaries are contained in F. S. Regs., Part II. and the Staff Manual respectively. Title pages will be prepared in manuscript.

(1)

WAR DIARY
or
~~INTELLIGENCE SUMMARY.~~
(Erase heading not required.)

Army Form C. 2118.

Volume XXXII

155th Field Company RE

Place	Date	Hour	Summary of Events and Information	Remarks and references to Appendices
DESVRES	1.7.18		Company strength 6 Officers & 182 OR Coy working as before on administrative services Major Scott went to CRE as acting CRE	[illegible]
	2.7.18		Work as before 2nd Lt Brook returned from leave Sgt Smyth returned to unit from Base dept (Instruct)	[illegible]
	3.7.18		Work as before Epidemic amongst Drivers only 4 men left Lt Haugh attached CRE	[illegible]
	4.7.18		Work as before All map shelters completed	[illegible]
	5.7.18		Work as before Lieut C. Baines joined unit from 156th Coy	[illegible]
	6.7.18		No work All company att for competition fired a course on the 500 yds range	[illegible]
	7.7.18		No work inspections etc	[illegible]
	8.7.18		Lt Haugh returned from CRE work as before	
	9.7.18		Work started on Baths on all assault courses No working parties available	[illegible]
	10.7.18		Work as before	
	11.7.18		Work as before	
	12.7.18		Fourteen reinforcements arrived work as before	
	13.7.18		Work as before reinforcements employed on bombing ground at DESVRES	
	14.7.18		Work as before	[illegible]
	15.7.18		Work as before Major Scott returned from CRE	[illegible]

(A7092). Wt. W12839/M1293 750,000. 1/17. D. D. & L., Ltd. Forms/C.2118/14.

Instructions regarding War Diaries and Intelligence Summaries are contained in F. S. Regs., Part II. and the Staff Manual respectively. Title pages will be prepared in manuscript.

WAR DIARY
or
INTELLIGENCE SUMMARY.
(Erase heading not required.)

Army Form C. 2118.

Place	Date	Hour	Summary of Events and Information	Remarks and references to Appendices
DESVRES	16.7.18		work as usual	S/S
	17.7.18		work as usual	
	18.7.18		~~work as usual~~. The Coy is inspected by & marched past Major Genl Heath RE. E-in-C of British Army. Parade held at LA WATINE. Calais sheet 13. 5-D.	CALAIS Sheet 13
	19.7.18		work as usual.	
	20.7.18		work as usual	S/S
	21.7.18		church parade at 9 am CRE's farewell party at SAMER in afternoon	S/S
	22.7.18		work as usual. instruction in demolitions on afternoon parade	S/S
	23.7.18		work as usual	
	24.7.18		work as usual. Packing wagons in the afternoon	
HARDELOT	25.7.18		Coy proceeded to HARDELOT for 3 days pontooning on the Lake - under canvas on the sand dunes.	S/S
	26.7.18		Pontooning drill. raining all day.	S/S
	27.7.18		Pontoon & trestle bridging raining all day.	
	28.7.18		Pontooning & rowing drill - inter section boat race won by No 1 section	S/S
	29.7.18		Coy return to DESVRES. No 3 section remain at CARLY	
	30.7.18		work as usual on RE services in DESVRES. HENNEVILLE & COURSET & SAC RIQUIER No 3 section return to DESVRES.	S/S.
			No 2 section proceed to DOUDEAUVILLE to put up water supply for 47th Bde.	S/S.
	31.7.18		work as above.	
			Strength of Coy 7 officers 203 O.R.	S/S

E. I. Scott Major RE
O.C. [illegible] Fld Coy RE

(A7092). Wt. W12839/M1293. 750,000. 1/17. D. D. & L., Ltd. Forms/C.2118/14.

CONFIDENTIAL.

ORIGINAL WAR DIARY OF

155th Field Company.R.E.

from 1-8-18&   to 31-8-18.

(Volume XXX111)

9/32 33

Army Form C. 2118.

WAR DIARY
or
INTELLIGENCE SUMMARY.
(*Erase heading not required.*)

Instructions regarding War Diaries and Intelligence Summaries are contained in F. S. Regs., Part II. and the Staff Manual respectively. Title pages will be prepared in manuscript.

volume XXXIII
153rd Fld Co RE

Place	Date	Hour	Summary of Events and Information	Remarks and references to Appendices
DESVRES.	1-8-18		Whole Coy billetted in DESVRES. Employed on RE services & training strength of Coy 7 officers 203 O.R	SLS
	2-8-18.		work as usual. 16th DW: return from England to SAMER area 48th Brigade in DESVRES.	SLS.
	3-8-18.		work as usual.	
	4-8-18.		Church parade.	SLS.
	5-8-18.		work as usual	
	6-8-18		work as usual inspection of transport by CRE	SLS
	7-8-18.		work as usual	SLS
	8-8-18		work as usual - inspection of dismounted Coy by CRE	SLS
	9-8-18		Coy training musketry. inoculation commenced	
	10-8-18		Coy training - musketry - use of prismatic compass etc	SLS
	11-8-18		Inspection & Church parade	
	12-8-18		Coy training - drill & organised recreation	SLS
	13-8-18		Coy training drill musketry & lectures - Night work with compass	
	14-8-18		Coy training Bayonet fighting. taping trenches etc	SLS.
	15-8-18		Coy drill - trestle bridging	SLS.
	16-8-18		Coy drill - gas drill. lecture on instruments etc	SLS.
	17-8-18		Wiring drill. Warning orders to move received	SLS

(A7092). Wt. W12839/M1293. 750,000. 1/17. D. D. & L., Ltd. Forms/C.2118/14.

Instructions regarding War Diaries and Intelligence Summaries are contained in F. S. Regs., Part II. and the Staff Manual respectively. Title pages will be prepared in manuscript.

WAR DIARY
or
INTELLIGENCE SUMMARY.
(Erase heading not required.)

Army Form C. 2118.

Volume XXXIII
155th Field Coy RE

Place	Date	Hour	Summary of Events and Information	Remarks and references to Appendices
DESVRES	18-8-18.		Church parade + inspection. wagons packed.	S/S.
	19-8-18.		Orders received to relieve 23rd Field Coy RE. 1st Divn. Divl HQ commence moving to BARLIN.	See App: I - II.
	20-8-18		2Lt Alcock RE proceeds with 1 O.R. as advance party to take over billets etc at SAILLY LA BOURSE. from 23rd Fld Co RE. 2Lt N.N. Gallagher RE joins company.	LENS. 11. S/S
	21-8-18		Coy packing wagons + cleaning up preparatory to move.	S/S
	[illegible]	4 pm	Coy's transport proceeds by road to RUITZ le MAISNIL - 3 days march	S/S
	22-8-18	8 am	Dismounted company embus on BOULOGNE - DESVRES road for BARLIN with 118th Brigade to relieve the 1st Divn in the 1st Corps.	
SAILLY LA-BOURSE		3 pm	arrive at BARLIN + march to SAILLY LABOURSE taking over billets from 23rd Field Coy RE. accomodation in houses + cellars. Coy in reserve + garrison troops for SAILLY defences. 1 O.R. wounded.	LENS 11 S/S
	23-8-18		Coy employed in cleaning billets, making gas curtains. Officers go over work to be done. Coy hqrs at L 3 a 2. 8 Reserve Field Coy billets	GORRE sheet
		9 pm	Transport under Capt Haigh + 2Lt Gallagher with cyclists arrive at RUITZ le MAISNIL. A. 1. c. 4 LENS 11.	S/S
	24-8-18		No 1 section on billets dump anti aircraft defences etc No 2 section on 2 shifts artillery deep dugout F. 23. c. No 3 section defences of SAILLY LA BOURSE No 4 section do	GORRE Sheet S/S.
	25-8-18		Coy employed as above for 24-8-18.	S/S

(A7092). Wt. W12839/M1293. 750,000. 1/17. D. D. & L., Ltd. Forms/C.2118/14.

Instructions regarding War Diaries and Intelligence Summaries are contained in F. S. Regs., Part II. and the Staff Manual respectively. Title pages will be prepared in manuscript.

WAR DIARY
or
INTELLIGENCE SUMMARY.
(Erase heading not required.)

Army Form C. 2118.

155 Field Coy RE
Volume XXXIII.

Place	Date	Hour	Summary of Events and Information	Remarks and references to Appendices
SAILLY LA BOURSE	26-8-18		Company in reserve - work as for 25-8-18. 2Lt Gallagher attached to 157 Fd Co	G.S.
	27-8-18		do No 1 Section at workshop. No 2. artillery mined dugout	GORRE sheet (special)
			No 3 Section repair work at Battalion camps & horse lines NOEUX-les-MINES	
			No 4 Section Divl Reception camp repairs & SAILLY defences -	G.S.
	28-8-18		work as above. Transport moved to NOEUX-les-MINES K18 b 7.7.	G.S.
	29-8-18		work as above No 3 Section moved to work & live at Transport lines	G.S.
			2 Lieut Rlock RE wounded by shell fire in NOEUX les MINES.	
	30-8-18		work as above -	
			Coy under orders to relieve 156 Field Coy in Right Bde Sector - HOHENZOLLERN.	See App III
	31-8-18		OC took over work from OC 156 Fd Coy. Officers of 156 went round	
			Reserve work in SAILLY LA BOURSE area. Road reconnaissance of forward	
			roads in CAMBRIN & HOHENZOLLERN Sectors commenced -	G.S.
			STRENGTH of Coy. 7 officers 199 O.R.	

G. S. [illegible] Major RE
O.C. 155 Field Coy RE

D. D. & L., London, E.C.
(A8001) Wt. W1771/M2031 750,000 5/17 Sch. 52 Forms C2118/14

CONFIDENTIAL.
==*=*=*=*=*=*=*=*=*=*=*=*=*=*

Original
WAR DIARY OF

155th Field Company.R.E.

from 1-9-18. to 30-9-18.

(Volume.XXXIV)

VR

Instructions regarding War Diaries and Intelligence Summaries are contained in F. S. Regs., Part II. and the Staff Manual respectively. Title pages will be prepared in manuscript.

WAR DIARY
or
INTELLIGENCE SUMMARY.
(Erase heading not required.)

Army Form C. 2118.

155 Field Coy RE.
Volume XXXIV
34

Place	Date	Hour	Summary of Events and Information	Remarks and references to Appendices
ANNEQUIN NORTH & HOHENZOLLERN Sector	1-9-18.		Coy relieved 156 Field Coy in Right Bde Sector HOHENZOLLERN sector. accomodated in cellars at F23 d 9.2. ANNEQUIN North. Horse lines remain at NOEUX les Mines.	Gorre sheet.
			No 1 section working on ANNEQUIN defences.	
			No 2. section workshop & dump section	
			No 3 do Left battn sector. working on deep dugout & general trench repair work in LEWIS ALLEY. RAILWAY Alley. MUNSTER Parade. also laying water pipe line along RESERVE line	A26 & 27. c & d. & G.3. a & b.
			No 4 section Right battn Sector work on deep dugout for RAP, Barts alley. & general trench repair work in BARTS ALLEY. FOSSES ALLEY. LEFT BOYAU.	G3 & 4 c & d
	2-9-18		work as above. 2 Lt Altock RE returned from hospital 2 Lt Gallagher RE do from 157 Fd Co. RE.	G9. a & b. SS.
	3-9-18		work as above.	
	4-9-18		work as above.	
	5-9-18		work as above for 3 & 4 sections. No 1 & 2 Sections under Lt Barnes & 2 Lt Gallagher on night work building 4 bridges across trenches on VERMELLES – AUCHY road. preparatory to an intended advance. Heavily shelled by HE gas shells. 3 men wounded. Lt Barnes & 5 OR. gassed. Bridges were completed before dawn in spite of 3 hours gas shelling & casualties.	SS
	6-9-18		No 1 & 2 sections resting. remainder employed as before.	SS.
	7-9-18		work as for 1-9-18. 20 men excused duty suffering from yellow cross gas effects	
	8-9-18.		No 1. Section on ANNEQUIN defences & repairing water supply for line supply. No 2. workshops & marking out VERMELLES-AUCHY Rd with white posts at night No 3. trench repair work & deep dugout LEWIS ALLEY. also night work preparing road approaches to bridges erected on 5-9-18. No 4. work as previously	SS

D. D. & L., London, E.C. (A8001) Wt. W1771/M2031 750,000 5/17 Sch. 52 Forms C2118/14

Instructions regarding War Diaries and Intelligence Summaries are contained in F. S. Regs., Part II. and the Staff Manual respectively. Title pages will be prepared in manuscript.

WAR DIARY
or
INTELLIGENCE SUMMARY.
(Erase heading not required.)

Army Form C. 2118.

155 Fld Co RE

Volume XXXIV

Place	Date	Hour	Summary of Events and Information	Remarks and references to Appendices
ANNEQUIN North	9-9-18		work as for 8-9-18. billets shelled with light shells for ½ hour about 6.30 p.m	map GORRE special sheet
	10-9-18		work as above.	
	11-9-18		work as above.	
& HOHENZOLLERN Sector	12-9-18		work as above. No 1 Section under 2Lt Gallagher working on repairing bridges on tracks in the Brigade area.	SIS
	13-9-18		No 1 Section on bridge repair work across trenches No 2 Section do & taking out explosives from bridges prepared for demolition No 3 Section working on dugouts & trenches in Left Battn Sector No 4 do — Right do. about 5 pm whilst reconnoitring the VERMELLES-AUCHY Rd 2Lt AG Alcock MC RE was killed by a booby trap & Sergt Wild wounded.	SIS
	14-9-18		No 1 Section working on VERMELLES-AUCHY Rd forward of reserve line No 2 Section on road from railway G3a.15.70 through A27 central No 3 Section on advanced Bde hqrs in A25d & on RAP dugout. No 4 Section on roads on tracks & roads from KING'S CROSS G10a.9.9. towards FOSSE 8. in G5.c. The enemy are now reported to be clear of AUCHY & FOSSE 8 & our patrols in front of AUCHY.	SIS.
	15-9-18		No 1 & 2 Sections on VERMELLES-AUCHY Rd. No 3 as above No 4 as above. 2Lt TS Bowie RE reported for duty a Party from Coy attended funeral of 2Lt Lt Alcock MC RE buried at HOUCHIN.	SIS
	16-9-18		work as above OC with Brigade Major 47th Bde & 2Lt Gallagher reconnoitred area round Fosse 8. for S.P.s 2Lt McKeen RE reported for duty. Capt Haigh went on leave	SIS
	17-9-18		No 1 Section digging SP at MADAGASCAR Point. No 2 on VERMELLES AUCHY Road No 3 work at battalion hqrs - work shops etc No 4 tracks to FOSSE 8.	AUCHY special sheet No 5.

Instructions regarding War Diaries and Intelligence Summaries are contained in F. S. Regs., Part II. and the Staff Manual respectively. Title pages will be prepared in manuscript.

WAR DIARY
or
INTELLIGENCE SUMMARY.
(Erase heading not required.)

Army Form C. 2118.

155 FLD COY R.E. SEPT 1918

Place	Date	Hour	Summary of Events and Information	Remarks and references to Appendices
ANNEQUIN NORTH	18-9-18		No 2 + 3 sections as for 17-9-18	
			No 1 + 4 on night work making S.Ps in FOSSE 8. locality	Sig 10CR / 5. special trench map
			S.Ps made at G5.b.5.6 and A29d 25.60.	
	19-9-18		work as for 18-9-18. Two more S.Ps commenced by No 1 & 4 Sections at A29d.2.0	
			and A29c 80.50. No 2 section opening up GRUB ALLEY through A28d & A29c.	
			No 3 section general R.E. work + workshop	
	20-9-18		No 2 & 3 sections employed as for 19-9-18	
			No 1 & 4 sections on night work.	
	21-9-18		S.P. at A29 c+d handed over to 15th Div. work as on 20th	
	22-9-18		No 1+4 Sects employed on opening up overland tracks, making bridges etc. No 2 Sect continued on GRUB ALLEY. No 3 Sect as for 20th	
	23-9-18		work as for 22nd	
	24-9-18		work as for 22nd. Reconnaissance of forward posts made with a view to consolidation of material for forward posts brought up	
	25-9-18		No 1+4 Sections continued work on tracks. No 2 Sect with 1 Coy Inf. began work on consolidation of outposts in A23 c+d, putting in shelters, firestepping etc. No 3 Sect began work on opening up TRAIN ALLEY as a main C.T.	
	26-9-18		work as for 25th. Further reconnaissance of outpost line made	
	27-9-18		work as for 25th	
	28-9-18		work as for 25th for Nos 1, 2 + 4 Sections. No 3 Sect formed dump of R.E. material in AUCHY VILLAGE. 12 G.S. wagon loads of material brought into AUCHY + dump formed at 10 pm	
	29-9-18		48th Inf Bde. advanced + established posts in A24c A30a and A30c. No 3 Section with	

D. D. & L., London, E.C. (A8001) Wt. W1771/M2031 750,000 5/17 Sch. 52 Forms C2118/14

Instructions regarding War Diaries and Intelligence Summaries are contained in F. S. Regs., Part II. and the Staff Manual respectively. Title pages will be prepared in manuscript.

WAR DIARY
or
~~INTELLIGENCE SUMMARY.~~
(Erase heading not required.)

155 FLD COY RE — SEPT 1918

Army Form C. 2118.

Place	Date	Hour	Summary of Events and Information	Remarks and references to Appendices
ANNEQUIN	29th		with 50 Infy. moved up after dark to consolidate these posts. Heavy rains + the darkness of the night made work difficult. The parties were caught in an enemy barrage but succeeded in reaching their posts. One post was wired + in one post the party had to stand-to till 12-30 a m as enemy was attempting to raid. The parties later assisted Infantry to carry up bombs to forward dumps as these were urgently required. No 4 Section worked on a forward Reg. Aid post. No 2 Sect worked on consolidation of support posts. No 1 Section worked on Overland Routes.	AUCHY SH. 5.
"	30th		No 3 Sect with 5 Platoon Inf worked again on consolidation of outposts. 4 Posts were completely wired and extra wiring material dumped in each post. Trench blocks were made in each post. Half of No 2 Sect + 2 Platoons Inf. worked on one post of outpost line. The post was wired and a defensive flank of wire formed. Trench blocks were formed and firesteps made. Remainder of No 2 Sect rested. No 4 Sect worked on R.A.P. erecting shelters etc. No 1 Sect worked on overland route No 5.	"

J Kelly Capt
for O.C. 155 FLD COY R.E.

D. D. & L., London, E.C. (A8001) Wt. W1771/M2031 750,000 5/17 Sch. 52 Forms C2118/14

CONFIDENTIAL.

****

ORIGINAL WAR DIARY OF

155th Field Company.R.E.

from 1-10-18. to 31-10-18.

(Volume XXXlV)

Instructions regarding War Diaries and Intelligence Summaries are contained in F. S. Regs., Part II. and the Staff Manual respectively. Title pages will be prepared in manuscript.

SPB/

WAR DIARY
or
INTELLIGENCE SUMMARY.
(Erase heading not required.)

Army Form C. 2118.

155 FIELD COY R.E. OCTOBER 1918

Volume XXXV

Place	Date	Hour	Summary of Events and Information	Remarks and references to Appendices
ANNEQUIN	1st		No 1 Section worked on Overland Route No 5. Nos 2 + 3 Sections rested. No 4 Section worked on forward RAP. JB	
do	2nd		Nos 1 + 4 Sects worked as on 1st. OC + 1 Sect Officer set out to reconnoitre roads thro AUCHY with a view to clearing obstructions. At 10-30 am	
		10.30 am	it was found that infantry patrols were moving forward as enemy had retired. The Road from AUCHY to HAISNES was reconnoitred as far as E. edge of HAISNES. Infantry patrols entered HAISNES soon after. No enemy seen. Road found to be in good order except for two large obstructions, one AUCHY & one in HAISNES. JB	
		1.30 pm	2 Sections proceed to AUCHY HAISNES Road to remove obstructions & to clear road for transport. JB	
		22.00	AUCHY HAINES Road cleared & all obstruction blown away, 1st Line Transport using the road & guns were moved forward. JPH	
Do	3rd	17.00	Further small obstruction along AUCHY-HAINES road removed & a reconnaissance of the forward area made with a view constructing the necessary bridges, footbridges should enemy withdraw further. JPH	
Do	4	04.00	Obstruction along the DOUVRIN - LA BASSEÉ Rd blown up & further obstruction along the DOUVRIN - BILLY BERCLAU road cleared.	
		17.00	R.E. Dumps moved forward to DOUVRIN. Nos 3 + 4 Sections moved forward to AUCHY.	
		19.00	Sapper Chambers W.W. (No 519817) wounded. JPH	

D. D. & L., London, E.C. (A8001) Wt. W1771/M2031 750,000 5/17 Sch. 52 Forms C2118/14

Army Form C. 2118.

Instructions regarding War Diaries and Intelligence Summaries are contained in F. S. Regs., Part II. and the Staff Manual respectively. Title pages will be prepared in manuscript.

WAR DIARY
or
INTELLIGENCE SUMMARY.
(Erase heading not required.)

Place	Date	Hour	Summary of Events and Information	Remarks and references to Appendices
ANNEQUIN	5-10-18	01.00	Lieut Gallagher instructed to make reconnaissance of canal ANGLE at B.18d-2-4 to the DAM at C.13c.5.9 after dark.	
		09.30	Lieut Gallagher returned with valuable information sheet was sent to C.R.E.	
AUCHY		11.00	Coy moved to billets at AUCHY transport lines remained at ANNEQUIN	
		18.00	No 3 section proceed to erect bridge over canal JPH	
	6-10-18	05.00	No 3 section returned after having successfully constructed a foot bridge over canal at B.12.c.0.0.	
		09.00	Remainder of Coy cleaning camp site & filling shell holes – Summer time changed to correct winter time on 5th 6th at 23.59	
			No 4 section gas proofing dug out re-erecting shelter for G.O.C. 48 Bde. JPH	
AUCHY	7-10-18	11.00	Coy relieved by 157 Field Co RE. JPH No 2 section proceeded forward on divisional H.Q's at SAILLY LABOURSE	
ANNEQUIN		12.15	Coy arrived at Reserve Field Coy's billets to ANNEQUIN remainder of day spent in fixing up billets JPH	
	8-10-18	08.00 to 17.00	No 1 & 3 section held in Reserve for Pontooning undergoing refresher course of Pontoon & trestle drill. No 4 section erecting "GAS ALERT" notices on LA BASSE Rd & searching dug outs for Delay Action fuzes. No 2 " working on Divl H.Q's – 2/Lieut WORSLEY reported for duty with C.R.E. JPH	
ANNEQUIN	9-10-18	00.01	Order received from C.R.E to construct two light rafts & deliver same Line Batt. before dawn. Section 1 & 3 made 3 tarpaulin rafts & 1 petrol tin raft	
		00.30	Rafts completed, loaded up & transport moved off under 2/Lieut GALLAGHER.	
		08.00 17.00	Section 2 working on Divl H.Q, section 4 erecting armstrong huts at ANNEQUIN FOSSE for 48 Bde. JPH	
ANNEQUIN	10-10-18	09.00 17.00	Sect 1 & 3 undergoing special training in pontooning. Sect 4 erecting Armstrong Huts at ANNEQUIN Fosse, Repairs to R.I.F. Batt: H.Q. Sect 2 working at Divl H.Q JPH	
"	11-10-18	09.00 to 17.00	Sect 1 & 3 special training as above Sect 2. working on Divl H.Q. Sect 4 repairs to R.I.F Batt. H.Q billets at HOUCHIN for I Corps Claims Officer under order from C.R.E. Special repairs at billets in BARLIN for 16th Div: Claims Officer JPH	
"	12-10-18	09.00 to 17.00	Sect 1 & 3 special training as above. Sect 2 working on Divl H.Q Sect 4 erecting horse troughs at ANNEQUIN – repairs to R.I.F Batt. H.Q – assistance lent to Div: RE Dump JPH	
"	13-10-18	09.00 to 17.00	as above for 12/10/18 JPH	

D. D. & L., London, E.C.
(A7001) Wt. W1771/M2031 750,000 5/17 Sch. 52 Forms/C2118/14

Instructions regarding War Diaries and Intelligence Summaries are contained in F. S. Regs., Part II. and the Staff Manual respectively. Title pages will be prepared in manuscript.

WAR DIARY
or
INTELLIGENCE SUMMARY.

(Erase heading not required.)

Army Form C. 2118.

Place	Date	Hour	Summary of Events and Information	Remarks and references to Appendices
ANNEQUIN	14-10-18	09.00 to 17.00	Sect No 1 + No 3 sections making 4 light timber canvas boats which were transported to Lere Batt. Remainder of sections training. No 2 Sect working at Divnl H.Q. No 4 Section erecting water troughs at ANNEQUIN FOSSE, repairs to Bde H.Q. Cleaning up new billets & doing minor repairs. C.R.E.'s conference of Field Coy Commanders held at Coy H.Q. 10.00 to 11.30 detailing details of pending bridging operations. JPH	
ANNEQUIN	15-10-18	11.00 to 23.59	Coy standing ~~by~~ in the morning until 11.00 hrs when orders were received from C.R.E. to establish a forward Coy bridging H.Q. No 1, 2 + 3 Sections moved forward in parties of 20 men. 17.30 hrs news received that patrols had crossed canal without opposition. 13.30 Pontoons ordered forward & bridging sections ordered to construct pontoon bridge. No 3 Pontoon Bridge completed at 17.00 hrs & field guns crossed. No 1 Pontoon Bridge completed at 19.15 hrs. Sections returned to Coy H.Q. at 23.59 hrs. JPH	
ANNEQUIN	16-10-18	02.30 12.30 17.30	Coy ordered to move forward with transport to AUCHY – move completed at 10.45 hrs. Inspected No 3 Pontoon Bridge with C.R.E., orders received to prepare to alter position of Bridge – bridge over two trenches on loop road. Sections 1, 3 + 4 arrived at Bridge at 13.15 – trenches bridged over at 16.00 hrs. Orders received from C.R.E. for Pontoon Bridge to be moved to new position ~~at~~ between 05.30 + 06.00 hrs on the 17th inst. JPH	
AUCHY	17-10-18	05.30 09.00 to 14.00	Pontoon Bridge moved to new position & traffic passing over in 11 minutes. Sects 1 & 3. Sections 2 + 4 making ~~[illegible]~~ section of canal & selecting timber for new Lorry Bridge. Sect 2 + 4 moved into advanced billets at BERCLAW. JPH	
AUCHY	18-10-18	09.00	~~Sect 2 + 4 making trestles for lorry bridge across canal. Sect 1 + 3 [illegible]~~	
BERCLAW	19-10-18	05.30 09.00 to 23.59	Sect 3 + 4, H.Q. & transport moved to billets in BERCLAW. Sects 2 + 4 working on trestle bridge with 156 Coy RE & relieved at intervals of 6 hrs work. Sects 1 + 3 Pontoon Bridge maintenance. JPH	
CAMPHIN	19-10-18	06.00 12.30	Sects 2 + 4 moved off to repair roads from ANNOELIN to CAMPHIN inclusive. Sect 1 + 3, H.Q. & transport moved to billets in CAMPHIN, move complete at 15.30 hrs. JPH	
CAMPHIN	20-10-18	06.30 to 14.00	Sects 1, 3 + 4 working on craters between ANNOELIN, CARNIN & CAMPHIN. Sect 2 loading up pontoons under Lieut Hickson R.E. 156 Coy RE. JPH	

D. D. & L., London, E.C.
(A8001) Wt. W1771/M2031 750,000 5/17 Sch. 52 Forms/C2118/14

Army Form C. 2118.

WAR DIARY
or
INTELLIGENCE SUMMARY.
(Erase heading not required.)

Instructions regarding War Diaries and Intelligence Summaries are contained in F. S. Regs., Part II. and the Staff Manual respectively. Title pages will be prepared in manuscript.

Place	Date	Hour	Summary of Events and Information	Remarks and references to Appendices
CAMPHIN PONT-A-MARCQ	21-10-18	06.00	Coy moved to billets in PONT-A-MARCQ move completed at 11.30hrs JPH	
PONT-A-MARCQ FLORENT	22-10-18	06.30	Coy moved to billets in FLORENT move completed at 15.45hrs JPH	
FLORENT	23-10-18	06.30	Secs 2 & 4 repairing crater at RUMES – road fit for lorry traffic at noon, remainder of Coy resting JPH	
do	24-10-18	08.00 14.00	Sect 2+4 repairing roads at RUMES Sect 1+3 repairing maintaining FLORENT–TAINTIGNIES – GUIGNIES – WEZ VELVAIN – ST MAUR roads JPH	
"	25-10-18	08.00 14.00	as above JPH	
"	26-10-18	08.00 14.00	as above JPH	
	27-10-18		Sect 4 working on RUMES roads – Sect 2+3 repairing Florent–TAINTIGNIES – GUINIES Rd Sect 1 in reserve JPH	
"	28/10/18	07.30 14.00	Sect 4 working on RUMES roads – Sect 1+2 as for 27th FLORENT – TAINTIGNIES Rd Sect 3 in reserve JPH Major Scott M.C. R.E. returned from leave	
"	29/10/18	07.30 14.00	Sect 4 working on RUMES roads – Sect 1+3 working on FLORENT – TAINTIGNIES road, Sect 2 in reserve training JPH	
"	30/10/18	07.30 14.00	Sect 4 in reserve Sect 2 working on RUMES – SARTINE roads Sects 1+3 as for 24th and JPH	
"	31/10/18	07.30 14.00	Sect 1 in reserve Sect 4 working on RUMES – SARTINE road Sect 2 & 3 on TAINTIGNIES road JPH	
			Strength of Coy Officers 7 O.R. 215	

James P Haugh Capt RE
for O.C. 55 Field Coy RE

D. D. & L., London, E.C. (A5004) Wt. W1771/M2031 750,000 5/17 Sch. 52 Forms/C2118/14

C O N F I D E N T I A L .
****

WAR DIARY
of
155th Field Company.R.E.

from 1-11-18. to 30-11-18.
(Volume XXXV1)

Instructions regarding War Diaries and Intelligence Summaries are contained in F. S. Regs., Part II. and the Staff Manual respectively. Title pages will be prepared in manuscript.

WAR DIARY
or
~~INTELLIGENCE SUMMARY.~~
(Erase heading not required.)

Army Form C. 2118.

NOVEMBER 1918 PAGE 1

Ref Sheet 37 & 44 1/40,000 Belgium & France

Volume XXXVI

Place	Date	Hour	Summary of Events and Information	Remarks and references to Appendices
TAINTIGNIES FERME FLORENT	1-11-18		Coy employed on roads RUMES - BACHY - TAINTIGNIES & forward. Labour found by infantry & civilians. S.S. 2Lt Brook went to hospital	
	2-11-18.		Coy relieved 157 Field Coy in the line. road work handed over to 156 Field Coy. No 1 & 4 sections employed on constructing new battle line zone round LONGUE SAULTE. No 2 section on forward outposts in front of St MAUR & MERLIN. No 3 section preparing bridge sections for canal bridges. SS	
"	3-11-18.		work as for 2-11-18. SS	
	4-11-18		No 1 & 4 sections work on battle zone from U29 central - LONGUE SAULT - Farm at U16C55. - MONT AU GRIS. No 2 section outpost line V19C - V19 central - Mont de la JUSTICE - V12C90.00 East of St MAUR. No 3 section preparing girder bridge sections. SS.	
"	5-11-18.		work as for 4-11-18 SS.	
	6-11-18	11-00	Major E.I. SCOTT having been detailed to proceed to ROUEN to be chief Instructor at the R.E. School of Instruction hands over 155 FIELD COY. and War Diary to MAJOR H. HOLBROW R.E. late 476 S.M. FIELD COY. R.E. 61st Div. who assumes command AUTHORITY AG 55/5571 (5th Army). Work as for the 5/11/18. Weekly Work Report to Nov. 6th forwarded to CRE. HH	
"		1800	Received CRE Instruction No 4 6/11/18 with reference to the division crossing the ESCAUT Canal. Be prepared detailed instructions for officers	HH
	7/11/18	0920	Received B.M. 33/20 Working Party Table from 4th Brigade	HH

D. D. & L., London, E.C. (A5004) Wt. W1771/M2031 750,000 5/17 Sch. 52 Forms C2118/14

Instructions regarding War Diaries and Intelligence Summaries are contained in F. S. Regs., Part II. and the Staff Manual respectively. Title pages will be prepared in manuscript.

WAR DIARY or INTELLIGENCE SUMMARY.

(Erase heading not required.)

Army Form C. 2118.

NOVEMBER 1918

PAGE 2

REF. SHEET 37 + 44 1/40,000
36 + 44a BELGIUM + FRANCE

Place	Date	Hour	Summary of Events and Information	Remarks and references to Appendices
TAINTIGNIES FERME FLORENT.	7th	09.20	Work now as follows – LT GALLAGHER with No 1 + 4 Sections 155 Field Coy and 1½ Companies of SCOTTISH RIFLES and 2 Companies 22 North. FUSILIERS rendezvous at LONGUE SAUTE Fm. 16.30 hrs and work on MAIN LINE of RESISTANCE. 2LT BOWES with No 2 Section and one Company 18th SCOTTISH RIFLES work on Outpost LINE of RESISTANCE. 4 G.S. LIMBERS from 48th Brigade used for carting Wiring Stores. LT MCKEEN + No 3 Section preparing material for Bridges over the ESCOUT.	HED
"	"	13.00	Conference of Commanding Officers + C/O 11th Army Pioneers with CRE at FLORENT Fm. 155 Field Coy. HQ. to discuss operations for crossing the ESCOUT. Infantry to cross the Canal in small boats made by the Field Companies. Floating footbridges to be erected after the first wave have crossed.	
"		16.30	OC sees B.M. 48th Brigade and arranges Working Parties for 8/11/18.	
"		22.00	Brigade cancell all working Parties as arranged above.	
"	8th	08.00	Received CRE wire 797 + arranges to accomodate R.E. HQ at 155 Coy billets.	HED
"		09.45	Received CRE wire 580 Bridging Parties detailed in CRE Instructions No 4 to proceed to FLORENT and TAINTIGNIES at once. Sappers + Pioneers to stop ordinary work.	
"	"	10.20	Received CRE wire 582 – 2LT BOWES detailed to carry out a reconnaissance of forward roads West of Canal ESCOUT in the event of an enemy retirement.	
"	"	11.30	Received 48th Infty Bde. Order No 42 re attack of the enemy lines by the 18th SCOTTISH RIFLES.	HED

D. D. & L., London, E.C. (A8001) Wt. W1771/M2031 750,000 5/17 Sch. 52 Forms C2118/14

Instructions regarding War Diaries and Intelligence Summaries are contained in F. S. Regs., Part II. and the Staff Manual respectively. Title pages will be prepared in manuscript.

WAR DIARY
~~or~~
~~INTELLIGENCE~~ SUMMARY.
(Erase heading not required.)

Army Form C. 2118.

PAGE 3.

NOVEMBER 1918

Place	Date	Hour	Summary of Events and Information Ref. Sheets. 37 + 44 1/40,000 36, 44a BELGIUM + FRANCE	Remarks and references to Appendices
TAINTIGNIES FERME FLORENT	8th	11-30	Received 48th Infty Bde Order No 43 details of inter Battalion relief.	
	"	"	Received B.M. S/72 48th I.B. Warning Instructions, previous instructions No B.M. S/68 cancelled. A crossing of the River ESCAUT to be forced by the ~~8th~~, 15th, 16th and 55 Divisions at a time to be notified later. Preparation to be made so that the attack can be delivered at 48 hours notice from 0700 hrs on 7th. Detailed instructions for above are given in CRE Instructions No 4 6/11/18 for work to be carried out by the DIV. R.E.	[initials]
	"	11.45	Nos 1 and 4 Sections 155 Field Coy under Lt McKEEN and Nos 2 + 3 Sections under 2Lt GALLEGHAR dispatched in trestle wagons to BRUYELLE Dump in accordance with instructions received from 48th Bde over the telephone. Reported arrived at BRUYELLE and stand by for orders to go forward with Bridging Stores for crossing the ESCAUT.	
		"	Received CRE wire 586 detailing above Sections to proceed to BRUYELLE + get into touch with the forward Battalion Commander.	
		12.00	OC sees GOC 48th Brigade, parties unable to proceed with Bridging operations owing to being held up by enemy MG fire, an attempt to be made under cover of darkness.	
		14.00	OC + Brigade Major visit Battalion HQ LONGUE SAUTE FM. OC visits Sections at BRUYELLE Dump	[initials] [initials]

Instructions regarding War Diaries and Intelligence Summaries are contained in F. S. Regs., Part II. and the Staff Manual respectively. Title pages will be prepared in manuscript.

WAR DIARY
or
INTELLIGENCE SUMMARY.
(*Erase heading not required.*)

Army Form C. 2118.

PAGE 4.

NOVEMBER 1918

Ref. Sheet 37 & 44 1/40,000
36-44 BELGIUM + FRANCE

Place	Date	Hour	Summary of Events and Information	Remarks and references to Appendices
TAINTIGNIES FERME FLORENT	8th	1600	and arranges for meal to be sent down for men. One Company of Infantry to assist carrying boats and one Coy - "C" of 11th Hants Pioneers to assist R.E Sections with floating Bridges, rendezvous & arrange details of work at BRUYELLE Dump with Lt McKEEN & 2Lt GALLEGHAR 155th Fd. Coy, RE.	
"		1720	OC visits 48th Brigade HQ and reports all details of work by 155th Field Coy. R.E arranged & parties ready to go forward	H.G.
	9th	0030	2Lt GALLEGHER with NOs 2 & 3 SECTIONS 155 Field Coy. and 2 Platoons "C" Coy. 11th Hants Pioneers and 2 Platoons 15th SCOTTISH RIFLES started off with boats for ferrying across the ESCAUT followed by Lt McKEEN & Nos 1 and 4 SECTION 155th Field Coy. R.E and one Platoon "C" Coy. 11th Hants Pioneers with two Floating Bridges.	
		0230	Bridges completed & Infantry passed over & reported to 48th Brigade and CRE.	
"		05.00	Lt McKEEN. R.E makes reconnaissance of four crossings over the ESCAUT at ANTOING, report sent to CRE.	
		10.00	Sections return to billets except for R.E. Guard left on Bridges.	
"		1200	2Lt BOWES completes reconnaissance of roads in accordance with CRE S/82 7/11/18, ~~and~~ detailed report forwarded to CRE.	
		18.00	Weekly Report forwarded to CRE for week ending 6pm 9-11-18.	H.G.

D. D. & L., London, E.C. (A5091) Wt. W1771/M2031 750,000 5/17 Sch. 52 Forms C2118/14

Instructions regarding War Diaries and Intelligence Summaries are contained in F. S. Regs., Part II. and the Staff Manual respectively. Title pages will be prepared in manuscript.

Army Form C. 2118.

WAR DIARY
or
~~INTELLIGENCE SUMMARY.~~
(Erase heading not required.)

PAGE 4.

NOVEMBER 1918

Place	Date	Hour	Ref Sheets 37 + 44 - 37 + 44a 1/40000 BELGIUM + FRANCE — Summary of Events and Information	Remarks and references to Appendices
TAINTIGNIES FERME	9th	2220	Receive B.M. 96 - 48th Brigade Group less Artillery will concentrate in ANTOING on 10/11/18.	[illegible]
FLORENT	10th	0600	Nos 1-2-3 + 4 Sections with Lt McKEEN + 2Lt GALLEGHER and Section transport move to ANTOING and commence construction of two heavy Bridges over ~~the~~ ESCAUT.	
"	"	0700	2Lt BOWES with 1 LORRIES and 2 Trestle Wagons increased during the day to 2 LORRIES and 4 Trailers transporting bridging stores to ANTOING.	
"	"	0930	O.C. Captain & remainder of Company join 48th Brigade Group and march to billets at ANTOING. 2 Platoons "C" Coy. 11th Hants assist R.E. on construction of approaches to Bridges at ANTOING.	
BILLETS ANTOING	"	1200	155 Field Company moves into billets at ANTOING	
"	"	1400	Work continued until dusk on bridges.	[illegible]
	11th	0600	155 Field Coy. and 3 Platoons "C" Coy. 11th Hants Pioneers and 2 Sections 157 Field Coy. R.E. work on four bridges at ANTOING	
		1800	Progress Report to CRE.	
"	12th	0600	Work as above with 4 Platoons Pioneers instead of 3.	
"	"	1800	Progress report to CRE.	[illegible]

D. D. & L., London, E.C. (A8001) Wt. W1771/M2031 750,000 5/17 Sch. 52 Forms/C2118/14

Instructions regarding War Diaries and Intelligence Summaries are contained in F. S. Regs., Part II. and the Staff Manual respectively. Title pages will be prepared in manuscript.

WAR DIARY
or
INTELLIGENCE SUMMARY. PAGE 5.

NOVEMBER 1918 (*Erase heading not required.*)

Army Form C. 2118.

Place	Date	Hour	Summary of Events and Information	Remarks and references to Appendices
			Ref Sheets 1/40,000 37 + 44-44236 BELGIUM + FRANCE	
ANTOING	13th	0600	Work on heavy bridges at V15 d 0.2 and V15 d 3-2 continued with three platoons 11th Hants Pioneers on approaches and loading stones.	
"		1700	Bridge at V15 d 0.2 completed.	
		1800	Progress report to CRE.	
"	14th	0600	Work continued on Bridge at V15 d 3-2, 2 Platoons "C" Coy. 11th Hants complete approaches. Bridge completed 16-30 hrs. Receive 48th I B. warning order of probable move tomorrow to TAINTIGNIES Area also CRE wire R.E. 135 re move.	H.H.
"		1800	Progress Report to CRE.	
"		2330	Received 48 I.B. order No 44 re move of 16 DIV. Westwards on 15/11/18 and march table with 48 I B. letter Q59/201 re lorries for spare kit.	
"	15th	0700	Receive CRE wire RE 139. Company to remain at ANTOING and complete two bridges under construction by 157 Field Coy. R.E.	H.H.
"		0800	Receive 48 Bde. wire B.M.10 cancelling move of 155th Field Coy. today, orders for move to come from CRE. later.	
"		"	Company parade for work on Bridges above.	
"		1300	Receive CRE wire S 6, Company to move to BACHY tomorrow.	
"		1630	Bridges completed and reported to CRE, 16 DIV. HQ and C.E. 1st Corps in accordance with CRE wire S7 received at 1400 hrs.	
"		1630	Receive CRE wire RE 145 15/11/18 orders for Company to move to come from 48 I. Bde.	H.H.

D. D. & L., London, E.C. (A8001) Wt. W1771/M2031 750,000 5/17 Sch. 52 Forms C2118/14

Instructions regarding War Diaries and Intelligence Summaries are contained in F. S. Regs., Part II. and the Staff Manual respectively. Title pages will be prepared in manuscript.

WAR DIARY ~~or~~ INTELLIGENCE ~~SUMMARY.~~

(Erase heading not required.)

Army Form C. 2118.

PAGE 6.

NOVEMBER 1918

Place	Date	Hour	Summary of Events and Information (Ref. Sheet 37 + 44 1/40,000 Belgium + France)	Remarks and references to Appendices
ANTOING	16th	0700	Receive 48th I. Bde order No 45 re move of 16th DIV. to TEMPLEUVE area and march table attached	
"		1015	155 Field Company move by road to PLACE COMTE	
"		1630	Move completed, Company billet in houses.	
PLACE COMTE	17th	0130	Receive 48 I.B. order No 46 and march table attached	H.A.
"		0745	Company and Transport move to MONCHEAUX and billet in huts in accordance with 48 I.B.O. No. 46	
MONCHEAUX.	"	1400	Move completed.	
	18	0930	Company Parade for inspection, work–repairs to PUBLIC BATHS cleaning and improving billets.	H.A.
"	19th	10.00	Company Parade for address by CRE.	
	"	11-30	Remainder of day repairs to Baths & improvements to billets.	H.A.
"	20	9-00	Company Parade for inspection by OC.	
		9.30	Remainder of day spent in Baths & cleaning equipment and transport. GOC 16 DIV. inspects the Camp.	H.A.
"	21	9-0	Company Parade, work in camp & training.	
"	22	9-0	" " " " " "	H.A.

D. D. & L., London, E.C. (A8004) Wt. W1771/M2031 750,000 5/17 Sch. 52 Forms C2118/14

Instructions regarding War Diaries and Intelligence Summaries are contained in F. S. Regs., Part II. and the Staff Manual respectively. Title pages will be prepared in manuscript.

WAR DIARY
or
INTELLIGENCE SUMMARY.
(Erase heading not required.)

Army Form C. 2118.

PAGE 7.

NOVEMBER 1918

Ref. Sheet 37 + 44 1/40,000

Place	Date	Hour	Summary of Events and Information	Remarks and references to Appendices
MONCHEAUX billets & huts	23	8-0	In accordance with CRE letter C6/21 of 22/11/18 Lt McKEEN and No 1 Section, 2Lt GALLEGHER and No 3 Section move complete with Section transport to PONT-A-MARCQ to be rationed & billeted by 47 I. Bde. and work on improvement of accomodation and recreational facilities for 47 Bde. and Divisional Theatre for 16 DIV. Troupe.	
			OC saw GOC 47th Bde. and A/Adjutant to CRE re above work	
"		9-0	Remainder of Company Parade for inspection, training & work in camp and taking down enemy notice boards.	H.H.
"	24	9-30	" " " "	
"		15-00	Church Parade.	
			Nos 1 + 3 Sections as for 23rd.	H.H.
	24	2300	Receive CRE wire R.E. 194 re move to WACHEMY.	
	25	1100	Headquarters and Nos 2 and 4 Sections with Transport move to billets in FACTORY at X28b5-9 in accordance with CRE wire 194 above. Move completed 1700 hrs.	
BILLETS IN FACTORY AT X28b5-9 near FRETIN	26	9-30	Company employed in clearing billets and bunking	H.H.
		1500	OC saw Sections at PONT-A-MARCQ re work	
2 SECTIONS PONT-A-MARCQ	"	1700	OC saw GOC 48th I. Bde. re work to be done at TEMPLEUVE and arranges for two Sections to start work tomorrow.	H.H.

D. D. & L., London, E.C. (A5001) Wt. W1771/M2031 750,000 5/17 Sch. 52 Forms C2118/14

WAR DIARY
or
~~INTELLIGENCE SUMMARY.~~
(Erase heading not required.)

Army Form C. 2118.

Instructions regarding War Diaries and Intelligence Summaries are contained in F. S. Regs., Part II. and the Staff Manual respectively. Title pages will be prepared in manuscript.

NOVEMBER 1918

PAGE 8

Place	Date	Hour	Summary of Events and Information	Remarks and references to Appendices
			Ref. Sheet 37+44 1/40,000 Belgium + France	
BILLETS IN FACTORY AT X28b5-9 NEAR FRETIN 2 SECTIONS AT PONT-A-MARCQ.	27th	8.00	Work now divided as follows — Nos 1+3 Section at PONT-A-MARCQ on repairs to DIV. THEATRE, improvements to billets, recreation rooms and education rooms for 47th Brigade. Nos 2+4 Sections repairs to Horse Lines for 48th Bde HQ and improvements to billets recreation rooms etc for 48th Bde. at TEMPLEUVE.	
"	"	1000	OC visits work + sees CO 18 Scottish Rifles at CAPPELLE re supply of materials.	HH
"	"	1530	GOC 48th Bde visits Company billets at Factory X28b5-9.	
"	"	"	Received CRE wire S 14 - Sections at PONT-A-MARCQ to work on Crater at F24 d7-4.	HH
"			Received CRE order No 93 re move of 157 Fd. Coy. to ATTICHES.	
	28th	8.00	Works Parade.	
		8-30	Receive BM 3/76 48th I.B. re move of D.H.Q less RA+RE HQ to AVELIN.	HH
"	29th	8-0	Works Parade. OC visits work at TEMPLEUVE.	
"	"	11-0	Court of enquiry held at Coy HQ re fire of rick at FLORENT. OC arranges with CRE for one section to move to ATTICHES tomorrow and issues orders for move of No 1 Section under 2Lt GALLEGHAR to take place. Sections in future to rest Wednesday + Saturday afternoons and Sunday free for Church Parade.	HH
"	30th	8-00	Works Parade	HH

Instructions regarding War Diaries and Intelligence Summaries are contained in F. S. Regs., Part II. and the Staff Manual respectively. Title pages will be prepared in manuscript. NOVEMBER 1918

WAR DIARY
or
INTELLIGENCE SUMMARY.
(Erase heading not required.)

PAGE 9.

Army Form C. 2118.

Place	Date	Hour	Summary of Events and Information	Remarks and references to Appendices
			Ref. Sheets 37 & 44 1/40,000 Belgium & France.	
BILLETS IN FACTORY AT X28 b 5-9 S of FRETIN. 1 Section at PONT-A-MARCQ & 1 Section at ATTICHES.	30th	1400	No 1 Section under 2 LT GALLEGAR move with transport complete to billets at ATTICHES for work under orders of CRE.	AH
			Strength of Company 6 Officers. 196. OR.	
			H Holbrow Major OC 155 Field Coy. R.E.	

D. D. & L., London, E.C. (A8001) Wt. W1771/M2031 750,000 5/17 Sch. 52 Forms/C2118/14

Confidential

War Diary

of

155 Field Co R.E.

from 1-12-18 to 31-12-18.

WAR DIARY
or
INTELLIGENCE SUMMARY. PAGE
(Erase heading not required.)

Army Form C. 2118.

Instructions regarding War Diaries and Intelligence Summaries are contained in F. S. Regs., Part II. and the Staff Manual respectively. Title pages will be prepared in manuscript. DECEMBER 1918

Place	Date	Hour	Summary of Events and Information	Remarks and references to Appendices
			Ref. Sheets 36 + 44a 1/40,000 Belgium + France + N.W. EUROPE 1/250,000	
Company Headquarters + Nos 2 + 4 Section in Factory at X28b 5-9 No 3 Section PONT-A-MARCQ No 1 Section ATTICHES	1st	8.30	Sunday Rest Day no work. Baths at TEMPLEUVE for Coy. HQ + 2 Sections. 2Lt GALLAGHER. R.E. makes a reconnaissance of demolished bridge at COURRIERES	HH
	2nd	8.00	Works Parade – work now as follows:— 2Lt WORSLEY with No 4 Section on Recreation Rooms & R.E. Services for 48th Infty Bde at TEMPLEUVE. 2Lt ROWES + No 2 Section work at FRETIN for Black Watch 44 Infty Bde and 48th Bde. HQ TEMPLEUVE. Lt MCKEEN. RE and No 3 Section R.E. Services for 44th Infty Bde at PONT-A-MARCQ and 18th Scottish Rifles 48th Bde at CAPPELLE. 2Lt GALLEGHER and No 1 Section R.E. Services under CRE at ATTICHES.	
	"	10.00	CRE with Major H. HOLBECW and 2Lt GALLEGHER visit COURRIERES + inspect demolished crossing of HOUTE DOULE CANAL & ascertain what bridging materials there are available at CARVIN Dump and LIBERCOURT Dump.	
	"		Work as for 2/12/18. 4 OR proceed on leave to U.K.	HH
"	3rd	8.00	Work continued as for 2/12/18.	
"	4th	8.00	" " Half holiday. 4 OR proceeded on 14 days leave to U.K.	HH
"	5th	8.00	Work continued as for the 2nd.	
"	6th	8.00	" " " " " " OC arranges for work to be commenced for Div. Salvage Officer at PONT-A-MARCQ. 2 Sappers wounded by accidental explosion of German Rifle Grenade at 1500 hrs	HH

D. D. & L., London, E.C. (A8004) Wt. W1771/M1031 750,000 5/17 Sch. 52 Forms C2118/14

Army Form C. 2118.

WAR DIARY
or
~~INTELLIGENCE SUMMARY.~~
(Erase heading not required.)

PAGE

Instructions regarding War Diaries and Intelligence Summaries are contained in F. S. Regs., Part II. and the Staff Manual respectively. Title pages will be prepared in manuscript.

DECEMBER 1918

Place	Date	Hour	Summary of Events and Information	Remarks and references to Appendices
			Ref Sheet 36 & 44a 1/40,000 Belgium & France N.W. EUROPE 1/250,000	
Coy HQ Nos 2-3 & 4 Sections in FACTORY at X28b5.9	7th	8.00	Work parade as for 6th sheet, resume at 1300 hrs for half holiday. No 3 Section under Lt McKEEN moves complete with transport to Coy. HQ move completed 11-30 hrs. Lt GALLAGHER takes section of gaps of Canal at COURRIERES	HH
	8th		Sunday Rest Day	
		1800	Church parade in Factory. CRE calls to see OC re work	HH
No 1 SECTION ATTICHES	9th		CRE takes over the duties of A/CE 1st Corps. Major Shelly OC 157th Coy RE assumes duties of CRE. A/CE & Col. Simmons MC visit Major Hollins proceed to ATTICHES & arrange for proposed bridging work for 155 Fd. Coy at COURRIERES. Work now as follows:— No 3 Section billets repairs etc for 47th Infy Bde. No 2 & 4 Sections ditto for 48 Infty Bde. No 3 Section at ATTICHES under CRE's orders. OC receives First Army letter No 989/565 A. 4-12-18 re Lt C V BROOK 155 Field Coy R.E. to be struck off strength of this unit with effect from 2/12/18 Authority (A.G. 55/6021 (O) of 3/12/18	HH HH
do	10th	800	Work as before.	HH
	11th	800	Ditto. Half holiday; 2Lt MONTIETH RE and 11 OR reinforcements join the Coy for duty.	
do	12th 13th	800	Work as for 9th	HH

D. D. & L., London, E.C. (A8001) Wt. W1771/M2031 750,000 5/17 Sch. 52 Forms/C2118/14

Instructions regarding War Diaries and Intelligence Summaries are contained in F. S. Regs., Part II. and the Staff Manual respectively. Title pages will be prepared in manuscript.

Army Form C. 2118.

WAR DIARY
~~or~~
~~INTELLIGENCE SUMMARY.~~
(Erase heading not required.)

DECEMBER 1918 PAGE

Place	Date	Hour	Summary of Events and Information	Remarks and references to Appendices
			Ref. Sheets 36. 44a Belgium & France 1/40,000	
COY. HQ Nos 2-3 + 4 SECTIONS IN FACTORY X28 b 5-9	14th	8.00	Work now as follows — 2Lt GALLAGHER RE and No 1 Section at ATTICHES on construction of 2 Heavy Bridges at COURRIERES over the HAUTE DEULE Canal for CRE with 25 OR HANTS Pioneers and 2 motor lorries. Nos 2 + 3 Sections under Lt McNEEN +	
No 1 SECTION at ATTICHES	"		2Lt MONTIETH RE work for 47th Bde and Camp Improvement. No 4 Section + 2Lt WORSLEY work for 46th Bde and 16 Div Salvage Officer PONT-A-MARCQ. Nos 2-3 + 4 Sections work all day to complete billets	HH
	15th	8.30	Bath Parade for Coy.	
	"	1800	Church Parade.	
	16th	8.00	In accordance with arrangements made with CRE a Brigade Workshops is opened at X28 b 5-9 for 47 + 48 Inf. Bdes and work started with Capt HAVOM RE in charge. The running of Officers Billets, messes + Recreation Rooms at TEMPLEUVE continued with ready for the E + M Coy to connect the lighting set.	HH
	17th	800	Work continued as above	HH
	18th	"	" " " " Half day holiday	HH
	19th	"	" " " "	
	20th	"	" " " "	HH
	21st	"	" " " " " " "	

D. D. & L., London, E.C.
(A8001) Wt. W1771/M2031 750,000 5/17 Sch. 52 Forms C2118/14

Instructions regarding War Diaries and Intelligence Summaries are contained in F. S. Regs., Part II. and the Staff Manual respectively. Title pages will be prepared in manuscript.

WAR DIARY
or
~~INTELLIGENCE~~ SUMMARY.
(Erase heading not required.)

Army Form C. 2118.

PAGE

DECEMBER 1918

Place	Date	Hour	Ref. Sheet 36 + 44a 1/40,000 Belgium + France — Summary of Events and Information	Remarks and references to Appendices
COY HQ, Nos 2-3 + 4 SECTIONS in FACTORY AT X28 b5.9 No 1 SECTION at ATTICHES	23	8.00	Work now as follows:- No 1 Section under 2Lt GALLAGHER R.E with 25 OR of 11th HANTS "P" on construction of two heavy bridges at COURRIERES. Material drawn from 5th Army Dump at SECLIN + trestles made there and taken to site by 1 motor lorry. Sappers + Pioneers leave ATTICHES daily for work at site of bridges in 1 motor lorry which returns with men after work.	
"			Nos 2 + 3 SECTIONS under Lt McKEEN + 2Lt MONTIETH engaged on billet repairs for 14? INF. Bde. all stores etc being made at Coy. HQ in the workshop. Steam engine + saw mill, also dynamo now in working order at Coy. HQ.	
"			No 4 SECTION work on billet repairs for 48th I Bde. and workshops in Camp. Train of R.E. materials (31 trucks) was unloaded at 12.30 hrs yesterday and is being issued to units in the DIVISION today. 2Lt GALLAGHER + No 1 SECTION RE move to Coy. HQ for Xmas.	HH
FACTORY X28 b5.9	24th	9.00	Work as for 23rd except No 1 Section employed on billet repairs in Camp.	
"	25th	9.00	Company Parade for inspection.	
		10.00 12.00	Sports - inter Section Football Competition	HH
		17.30	Company Xmas Dinner followed by Concert.	
"	26	9.00 12.30	Company Parade + Sports	HH
"	27	8.00	47 + 48 Bde School reassembles at Coy HQ under Capt. HAUGH.	

(A8001) Wt. W1771/M2031 750,000 5/17 D. D. & L. London, E.C. Sch. 52 Forms C2118/14

Instructions regarding War Diaries and Intelligence Summaries are contained in F. S. Regs., Part II. and the Staff Manual respectively. Title pages will be prepared in manuscript.

WAR DIARY
or
~~INTELLIGENCE SUMMARY.~~

(Erase heading not required.)

Army Form C. 2118.

PAGE

DECEMBER 1918

Place	Date	Hour	Summary of Events and Information	Remarks and references to Appendices
			Ref Sheet 36 + 44a 1/40,000 France	
Coy HQ with Nos 1-2 & 3 Sections [illegible] No 4 Section in billets at ATTICHES	27	9-00	No 4 Section under 2LT WORSLEY relieves No 1 Section under 2LT GALLAGHER on the construction of 2 heavy timber & girder bridges at COURRIERES and proceeds to ATTICHES for billets. 2LT MONTIETH RE proceeds with No 4 Section to act as Officer i/c of supply of material for Bridges. No 1 Section take over work for 46th Infty Bde & DIV. SALVAGE Officer PONT-A-MARCQ. Remainder of Sections work as before described.	HH
"	28th	9-00	Work Parade as for 27th. Saturday half day holiday for sports. Very wet day & ground around billets flooded	
"	29th	9-30	Sunday. Parade for Baths.	HH
"	30th	9-00	Works parade, Engineer Services as before.	
	31st	9-00	OC & Staff Capt 46th Bde visit Battalion billets in TEMPLEUVE and arrange for further work to be carried out. Total Reinforcements during month December 1918 1 Officer 11 OR. Total strength of Company now 7 Officers & 197 OR 50 Infantry attached for work in Brigade School	HH HH

A Hollerow Major
O.C. 465th FIELD COY. R.E.

D. D. & L., London, E.C. (A8004) Wt. W1771/M2031 750,000 5/17 Sch. 52 Forms/C2118/14

16
98 38

— War Diary. —

— Confidential War Diary of —

— 155th Field Company, R.E. —

— From 1-1-19 to 31-1-19. —

— Volume 1. 1919. —

Instructions regarding War Diaries and Intelligence Summaries are contained in F. S. Regs., Part II. and the Staff Manual respectively. Title pages will be prepared in manuscript.

WAR DIARY or ~~INTELLIGENCE SUMMARY.~~

(Erase heading not required.)

Army Form C. 2118.

VOL. I

PAGE 1

JANUARY 1919

Place	Date	Hour	Summary of Events and Information	Remarks and references to Appendices
			Ref Sheet 36c + 37 FRANCE 1/40,000	
COY HQ. + Nos 1-2 + 3 SECTIONS + TRANSPORT IN FACTORY X28 b 5-9. No 4 SECTION BILLETS at ATTICHES	1st	9-00	Company work Parade - Distribution of work as follows:- 2Lt GALLAGHER RE with No 1 Section on RE services for 48th Infty Bde at TEMPLEUVE + CAPELLE. 2Lt McKEEN, RE with Nos 2 + 4 SECTIONS erection of huts for DIV SALVAGE OFFICER PONT-A-MARCQ, R.E SERVICES for 47th INFTY BDE. and running 155 Fd. Coy R.E workshops at X28 b 5-9. 2Lt MONTIETH. RE at ATTICHES in charge of supply of bridging material for Bridges at COURRIERES with 2 motor lorries from CRE. 2Lt WORSLEY R.E. with No 4 Section construction of Heavy Timber + Girder Bridges at COURRIERES and billeted at ATTICHES. 25 OR 11 HANTS P. detailed as working party for the above, both parties proceed to work in lorry daily + return. MATERIALS drawn from TEMPLEUVE, ATTICHES + SECLIN RE Dumps. CAPT. HAUGH R.E i/c of 47 + 48 INF. BDE. workshops at Coy HQ. X28 b 5-9 with 20 INFTY. attached for Instruction. 6 OR from 22 N.F. Battn. attached for Instruction to Coy workshops. CSM ARGYLE RE. and 6 OR 155 FIELD COY. R.E. attached to 48 INF BDE. for rations + billets at TEMPLEUVE working on ELECTRIC LIGHT INSTALLATION for 48 Infty Bde.	HH
			Half Day Holiday	
	2nd	9-0	Works Parade for work as above. Cease work 1630 hrs. Major H HOLBROW RE. visits 48th Bde + Battn. TEMPLEUVE + CAPELLE re work in hand. CRE calls at Coy HQ. also A/Brigade Commander.	HH
	3rd	9.00	Works Parade as above for 1st. CAPT. HAUGH, RE + 2Lt MONTIETH hold a Court of Inquiry at ATTICHES on the loss of 1 Bicycle of 157 Field Coy. RE	HH

D. D. & L., London, E.C. (A5004) Wt. W1771/M2031 750,000 5/17 Sch. 52 Forms C2118/14

Instructions regarding War Diaries and Intelligence Summaries are contained in F. S. Regs., Part II. and the Staff Manual respectively. Title pages will be prepared in manuscript.

WAR DIARY
~~or~~
~~INTELLIGENCE SUMMARY.~~
(Erase heading not required.)

Army Form C. 2118.

VOL. I
PAGE 2

JANUARY 1919

Place	Date	Hour	Summary of Events and Information (Ref. Sheets 36 + 37 FRANCE 1/40,000)	Remarks and references to Appendices
Coy HQ + 1-2 + 3 Sections + Transport in Factory X28b5-9 Non Sect Billets at Attiches.	4th	9-0	Work as for 3rd Saturday Half holiday. II Lt BOWES reports for duty having returned from 14 days leave + 7 days duty to U.K. 4 OR Reinforcements.	
	5th	9-30	Sunday Baths for Coy. at TEMPLEUVE. Major Kelburn + 2Lt BOWES RE meet CRE at SALVAGE Dump PONT A MARCQ + arrange for No 2 Section to work on erection of Sheds + Baths for 47 Bde.	HH
	6th	9-0	Work as above. AFZ 16 filled in for the Coy.	HH
	7th	9-0	Work Parade as for 6th. GOC 16 Div. inspects the Coy. HQ + workshops. OC visits 48th Inf. Bde HQ + work at TEMPLEUVE.	HH
	8th	9-0	Work Parade as for 7th. Col. Rennie AA+QMG 16 Div + CRE visit Coy. HQ + workshops. 26 OR proceed to LILLE on leave in motor lorry provided by 48 Bde. Half day holiday for recreation.	HH
"	9th	9-0	Work Parade. ~~No 2 Section on ...~~ No 3 Section in Coy. workshops. No 2 Section takes over all work for 47th Inf Bde. Lt McKeown RE detailed to take over duties of Demobilization + Recreation hands over No 3 Section to Lt MONTIETH RE.	HH
"	10th	9-0	OC rides to ATTICHES and visits Bridge at COURRIERES + returns at 6pm. Work parade as for 9th. OC visits 48 Bde HQ. + Battalions in TEMPLEUVE.	
"	11th	9-0	II Lt GALLAGHER R.E. proceeded to LILLE for 14 days to U.K. on 12/1/19. Coy Work parade for work as usual.	HH
				HH

D. D. & L., London, E.C. (A6001) Wt. W1771/M2031 750,000 5/17 Sch. 52 Forms C2118/14

Instructions regarding War Diaries and Intelligence Summaries are contained in F. S. Regs., Part II. and the Staff Manual respectively. Title pages will be prepared in manuscript.

WAR DIARY
or
~~INTELLIGENCE SUMMARY.~~
(Erase heading not required.)

JANUARY 1919

VOL I

PAGE 3

Army Form C. 2118.

Place	Date	Hour	Summary of Events and Information	Remarks and references to Appendices
			Ref Sheets 36 + 37 FRANCE 1/40,000.	
COY. HQ + 1-2 + 3 SECTS at X 28 b S.A. FACTORY	12S	9-30	Coy Bath Parade for Baths. Sunday Church Parade 1800 hrs. OC meets CRE at PONT-A-MARCQ & arranges for erection of Baths for 47 Bde	HH
No 4 SECT. ON DETACHMENT ATTICHES	13	9-0	Works Parade for work as before described. OC visits 48 I. Bde HQ at TEMPLEUVE and work at PONT-A-MARCQ. No 2 Section commence work on Baths for 47th Infty Bde	HH
	14S	9-0	Works Parade for work as usual. OC attends conference of	
		11-0	COs at CRE HQ ATTICHES and afterwards visits the bridge at COURRIERES with CRE.	HH
"	15S	9-0	Works Parade. OC sees 48 Inf Bde re work in hand. Half holiday. Football match V 18 Scottish Rifles at CAPELLE. Very wet day. No 4 SECTION having completed the bridge rejoin COY HQ.	HH
COY. HQ No 4 SECTION	16S	9-0	Works Parade. No 3 SECTION relieves No 2 SECTION and takes over work for 47 Bde + DIV SALVAGE OFFICER PONT-A-MARCQ. Lt McKEEN RE proceeds to U.K. on 14 days leave. All work cancelled for 16/1/19 & Coy employed on stock taking of mobilization stores.	HH
"	17S	9-0	Works Parade. Checking of mob. stores continued. OC visits 48 Bde HQ re work & inspects work in hand at PONT-A-MARCQ.	HH
"	18S	9-0	Works Parade. OC with 2Lt MONTIETH & CSM meet CRE + GOC 47 Bde at PONT-A-MARCQ & arranges for site of electric light set and installation of wiring. Half holiday.	HH
"	"	2-0	Football match V 156 Field Coy RE.	

D. D. & L., London, E.C. (A8004) Wt. W1771/M2031 750,000 5/17 Sch. 52 Forms C2118/14

Army Form C. 2118.

Instructions regarding War Diaries and Intelligence Summaries are contained in F. S. Regs., Part II. and the Staff Manual respectively. Title pages will be prepared in manuscript.

WAR DIARY
or
~~INTELLIGENCE SUMMARY.~~
(Erase heading not required.)

VOL. 1

JANUARY 1919

PAGE 4.

Place	Date	Hour AM	Summary of Events and Information	Remarks and references to Appendices
			Ref. Sheets 36 + 37 FRANCE 1/40,000	
COY. HQ 1-2-3+4 SECTIONS +TRANSPORT IN FACTORY BILLETS X28 b-5-9	19th	9-30	Coy Parade for Baths.	
	"	1200	Coy. Parade for address by CRE on DEMOBILIZATION - CANTEEN - LEAVE + RATIONS.	HH
		1800	Church Parade in Coy. Dining Hall	
	20th	9-0	Coy Parade for work now as follows:— No 2 SECTION under 2LT BOWES i/c workshops, No 1 Section work for R.T.O FRETIN. No 3 Section construction of Baths & Electric Light for 47 Bde. erection of huts for Salvage officer PONT-A-MARCQ. No 4 Section erection of hut 60' x 16' for Royal Irish Rifles TEMPLEUVE.	HH
"	21st	9-0	Work as above.	HH
"	22nd	9-0	" " " Half holiday.	HH
"	23rd	8-0	Billet Cleaning Parade	
		9-0	Work Parade as above	HH
"	24th	9-0	"	HH
		10-15	1st Corps Commander, GOC 16 Div + CRE inspect Coy HQ + workshops.	HH
"	25th	9-0	Work Parade for work as above. II Lt RAVEGE & MONTEITH RE proceeds on Chemical Survey Course near CALAIS.	HH
"	26th	9-30	Sunday Baths Parade.	HH

Instructions regarding War Diaries and Intelligence Summaries are contained in F. S. Regs., Part II. and the Staff Manual respectively. Title pages will be prepared in manuscript.

WAR DIARY
or
~~INTELLIGENCE SUMMARY.~~
(Erase heading not required.)

JANUARY 1919

VOL 1

PAGE 5

Army Form C. 2118.

Place	Date	Hour	Summary of Events and Information	Remarks and references to Appendices
			Ref. sheets 36 + 37 FRANCE 1/40,000	
Coy. H.Q.	27th	8-0	No 3 Indian works parade for work at PONT-A-MARCQ.	HH
and		9-0	Coy. works Parade	
		4-30pm	work at PONT-A-MARCQ completed	
TRANSPORT	28th	8-0		
		9-0	do do do	HH
IN BILLETS	29th	8-0	do do do	
AT FACTORY		9-0	17 OR including CSM ARGYLE demobilized making the total to date 47. II LT H. GALLAGHER returns from 14 days leave to U.K.	HH
X28 b 5-9			Half Holiday for Sports	
FRETIN.	30th	9-30a	Parade for Baths	
		11-0	Work carried on as for 29th CRE visited Coy. HQ	HH
			OC saw B.M. 168th Bde	
	31st	9-0	Company Parade for work	HH
			Ration Strength of Company 4 Officers + 130 OR	
			" " men attached " 18 OR	
			On leave to U.K. 2 " 14 OR	
			On Detachment 1 " 12 OR	
			Total strength of Coy. excluding attached Infty. 7 " 156 OR	HH
			31-1-19	
			H Holbrow Major OC 155th Field Coy. R.E.	

D. D. & L., London, E.C. (A8004) Wt. W1771/M2031 750,000 5/17 Sch. 52 Forms C2118/14

Confidential

War Diary

of

155 Field Coy RE

from 1-2-19 to 28-2-19.

(Volume II)

Instructions regarding War Diaries and Intelligence Summaries are contained in F. S. Regs., Part II. and the Staff Manual respectively. Title pages will be prepared in manuscript.

WAR DIARY
or
~~INTELLIGENCE SUMMARY.~~
(Erase heading not required.)

VOL. II

Army Form C. 2118.

FEBRUARY 1919

PAGE 1.

Place	Date	Hour	Summary of Events and Information	Remarks and references to Appendices
			Ref. Sheets FRANCE 36+37 1/40,000	
HQ, SECTIONS + TRANSPORT IN BILLETS AT FACTORY X28.b.5.9 near FRETIN	1st	9-0	Coy Parade for work now as follows – Under II LT GALLAGHER No1 Section on Camp details, No3 Section 48 Bde Hut at TEMPLEUVE, No4 Section Chicory Factory FRETIN billet for troops. II LT BOWES with No2 Section i/c of Workshops and Infty School. Major H Hollow having been detailed to act as Draft Conducting Officer to U.K. hands over the War Diary to II LT P. WORSLEY RE. Half Holiday for Sports	HH
	2nd	9.00	Work as above	
	3rd	9.00	Work as above	
	4th	9.00	Work as above	
	5th	9.00	Work as above	
	6th	9.30	Paraded for baths and proceed from baths & work as above	
	7th	9.00	~~Forty four~~ ~~Seven~~ O.R.s left unit for demobilisation, remainder of Coy work as above. Cpl Hensman W.G. promoted acting Sergeant. from 30-1-19	
	8th	9.00	Half holiday for sports	
	9th		Eight other ranks left unit for demobilisation	
	10th	9.00	Company employed on work in camp, Capt. McPhee returned from leave Six O.Rs. left unit for demobilisation	

D. D. & L., London, E.C. (A8001) Wt. W1771/M2031 750,000 5/17 Sch. 52 Forms/C2118/14

Instructions regarding War Diaries and Intelligence Summaries are contained in F. S. Regs., Part II. and the Staff Manual respectively. Title pages will be prepared in manuscript.

WAR DIARY
or
INTELLIGENCE SUMMARY.
(Erase heading not required.)

Army Form C. 2118.

FEBRUAR 1919 VOL II PAGE 2

Place	Date	Hour	Summary of Events and Information (Ref 36 + 37 FRANCE 40000)	Remarks and references to Appendices
FACTORY near FRETIN X.28.b.5.9	11th	9.00	Works in camp	[illegible]
	12th	9.00	Work in Camp and wings erected in Mairie TEMPLEUVE	[illegible]
	13th	9.00	Work in camp	[illegible]
	14th	9.00	2 O.Rs left unit for demobilization, 14 "X" horses, in care of L/Cpl Stock and four drivers left unit for base. 26 O.R. proceeded to LILLE in lorry. T. H. Worsley proceeded to UK on leave	[illegible]
	15th	9.00	Half holiday. 1 O.R. left unit for demobilization	
	16th	9.00	Sections amalgamated for billeting to save fuel.	[illegible]
	17th	9.00	Baths at PONT A MARCQ put in order and TEMPLEUVE baths reported on	[illegible]
	18th	9.00	Work in Camp	
	19th	9.00	As above, Capt J P HAVAGH returned from leave	[illegible]
	20th	9.00	Work as above	[illegible]
	21st	9.00	Work as above	[illegible]
	22nd	9.00	Work as above half holiday.	[illegible]
	23rd		No work	[illegible]
	24th	9.00	Work in Camp	
	25th	8.45	10 men at work on Divl Race Course BERSEE, remainder employed in Camp. L/Cpl Stock and four drivers returned to unit from conducting duty	[illegible]
	26th	8.45	Work as above	[illegible]
	27th	8.45	Work as above	
	28th	8.45	Work as above	[illegible]

[illegible] Capt RE
for OC 155 Fd Coy RE

D. D. & L., London, E.C. (A8001) Wt. W1771/M2031 750,000 5/17 Sch. 52 Forms C2118/14

Confidential

War Diary

of

155 Field Coy RE

from 1-3-19 to 31-3-19.

(Volume III.)

5

Instructions regarding War Diaries and Intelligence Summaries are contained in F. S. Regs., Part II. and the Staff Manual respectively. Title pages will be prepared in manuscript.

WAR DIARY
or
INTELLIGENCE SUMMARY.
(*Erase heading not required.*)

Army Form C. 2118.

MARCH 1919 — VOL 3 PAGE I

Place	Date	Hour	Summary of Events and Information (Ref. Sheet 36 1/40,000 France)	Remarks and references to Appendices
Company in Billets	1st	07-00	Company Parade for work in Camp & Stable Routine	HH
in Billets	2nd	"	" " "	HH
at X28a5.9	3rd	"	" " "	
FACTORY		16.30	Major H Hollbrow R.E. having returned from leave to U.K. assumes Command of the Company.	HH
Nr FRETIN	4th	09.00	Company parade for work in Camp & stable routine	
		15.00	CRE Calls with reference to reduction of Coy. to Cadre "A".	HH
"	5th	09.00	Company parade for work in Camp & stable routine OC & Captain proceed to CRE's office for Conference re Demobilization & army of occupation. 1 OR proceeds on leave to U.K.	
"	6th	09.00	Company parade for work in Camp & stable routine Strength now 90 all ranks. Weather very wet & billets surrounded by water. The following men have been awarded Divisional parchments in respect of consistent good work during the period October to December 1918:- CPL. CHALKLEY, SAP. JOHNSON, DRIVER DARWIN, S.& C.S. MULLETT, DRIVER GOOD, DRIVER HIGGS, PION. RICHARDS and L/C BURFORD & L/C ROBERTS for Gallant Conduct in the Field.	HH
"	7th	07.00	Company Parade for work	HH
"	8th	09.00	" " " Half holiday	HH
"	9th	"	Sunday. OC sees CRE at ATTICHES re Div. Sales Conference	HH

155th FIELD COY., R.E.
No. ....
Date ....

D. D. & L., London, E.C. (A8001) Wt. W1771/M2031 750,000 5/17 Sch. 52 Forms C2118/14

Instructions regarding War Diaries and Intelligence Summaries are contained in F. S. Regs., Part II. and the Staff Manual respectively. Title pages will be prepared in manuscript.

Army Form C. 2118.

WAR DIARY
or
~~INTELLIGENCE SUMMARY.~~
(Erase heading not required.)

MARCH 1919 Vol. 3 PAGE 11.

Place	Date	Hour	Summary of Events and Information (Ref Sheet 36 1/40,000 France)	Remarks and references to Appendices
Company in Billets at FACTORY X 28 b 5.9	10th	09.00	Company parade for work in Camp & repairs to TEMPLEUVE siding	H.H.
		09.30	Capt. McKeen R.E. proceeds to CRE HQ ATTICHES to be attached whilst acting as Div. Sales Officer. OC meets C.R.E. at TEMPLEUVE-T. to arrange for repairs to Railway siding & Parking ground for Div R.E. Transport.	
FRETIN	11th	09.00	Company parade for work at TEMPLEUVE siding. Working party of 11 OR from 4 B. J. Bde. employed.	H.H. / H.H.
"	12th	09.00	Company parade for work as above. OC sees CRE at ATTICHES & visits bridges at COURRIERES.	
			1 Horse + 3 mules transferred to WATTIGNIES 108 Army Bde. R.F.A. auth. C.R.E. No 19/6.	H.H.
"	13th	07.30	8 OR dispatched for demobilization.	
		09.00	Company parade for work as above. OC forms Company Cadre A.	
		11.00	13 OR transferred to 157 Field Coy. for Army of Occupation auth. C.R.E. 18/7	
			22 OR " " 155 " " from 157 Field Coy. " "	
			10 Horses dispatched to BOULOUGNE auth. C.R.E. letter 19/5.	
			6 " " " MONS EN PEVELE for sale auth. C.R.E. letter 19/7	H.H.
			2 " " " 108 Army Bde. R.F.A. at WATTIGNIES auth. CRE wire 279.	
	14th	08.45	Company parade for work at TEMPLEUVE siding & dismantling electric light fittings.	
			6 OR transferred to 157 Field Coy. R.E. for Army of Occupation duty. RE letter 18/7 dated 13/3/19.	H.H.
	15th	14.00	Sunday. 2 lorries from CRE report & take men to hear the R.E. Band Concert at ATTICHES.	H.H.

155th FIELD COY., R.E.
No. ....
Date ....

D. D. & L., London, E.C. (A8001) Wt. W1771/M2031 750,000 5/17 Sch. 52 Forms C2118/14

Instructions regarding War Diaries and Intelligence Summaries are contained in F. S. Regs., Part II. and the Staff Manual respectively. Title pages will be prepared in manuscript.

Army Form C. 2118.

WAR DIARY
or
~~INTELLIGENCE SUMMARY.~~
(*Erase heading not required.*)

MARCH 1919 VOL. 3 PAGE 3

Place	Date	Hour	Summary of Events and Information	Remarks and references to Appendices
			Ref. Sheet 36 1/40,000 FRANCE	
Company in Billets at FACTORY K28b5.9. FRETIN	16th	08.45	11 OR to TOURNAI for Demobilization. Company parade for work at TEMPLEUVE ST. erecting Ramp & repairs to huts for Div. Store.	[illegible]
	17th	08.45	Coy. parade for work as above. Ramp completed at TEMPLEUVE ST.	
	18th	08.45	" " " " " to be extended.	[illegible]
		11.00	Coy. transport moves to TEMPLEUVE & is parked near station for entraining. 3 wagons returned for Coy. work. All Coy. stores checked in billets before move & G1098 amended.	[illegible]
"	19th	08.45	Coy. parade for work as above.	
"		11.00	20 2 mules dispatched to TOURNAI for entraining to ROUEN	
			7 OR " " " " mules & return next day.	
			OC sees CRE at ATTICHES. Coy. transport parked at TEMPLEUVE completed.	[illegible]
"	20th	08.45	Coy. parade for work at TEMPLEUVE STN.	
"		11.00	1 OR reported from 157 Field Coy. & taken on strength of Coy.	
			OC sees CRE at ATTICHES.	[illegible]
"	21st	08.45	Work as above.	
	"	11.00	7 L.D. Mules to TOURNAI for dispatch to BOULOGNE	
			2 L.D. Horses " " "	[illegible]
	22nd	08.45	Work as above. OC with Capt. H.E. McKeen & 2/Lt N.W. Gallagher report to RE HQ for instructions. 4 L.D. Mules attached to this Coy. from 157 Fd. Coy. less harness. Siding at TEMPLEUVE STN. completed.	[illegible]
	23rd	08.45	Sunday. Capt. J.P. Hamp & 3 OR ordered for Demobilization & cancelled by CRE wire R.E. 336 & 1st Corps. 438 D.	[illegible]

155th FIELD COY, R.E.
No. ......
Date ......

D. D. & L., London, E.C.
(A8004) Wt. W1771/M2031 750,000 5/17 Sch. 52 Forms/C2118/14

Army Form C. 2118.

Instructions regarding War Diaries and Intelligence Summaries are contained in F. S. Regs., Part II. and the Staff Manual respectively. Title pages will be prepared in manuscript.

WAR DIARY
or
INTELLIGENCE SUMMARY.
(Erase heading not required.)

MARCH 1919. Vol. 3 PAGE 4

Place	Date	Hour	Ref. Sheet 36 FRANCE 1/40,000 — Summary of Events and Information	Remarks and references to Appendices
H.Q & COY. IN BILLETS AT FACTORY X28b5-9 FRETIN TRANSPORT PARKED AT TEMPLEUVE	24	08.45	Company parade for work at TEMPLEUVE & cleaning billets. 1 OR returned from leave to U.K. Order received from CRE to resume demobilization of 1 Off. & 5 OR.	HH
	25th	08.45	Work parade as above. OC meets D.A.A.G. 16 DIV. at TEMPLEUVE St. and arranges for more work to be done & confirms this over telephone to CRE. Capt. J. P. HAUGH. R.E. & 5 OR sent to Concentration Camp TOURNAI for demobilization	HH
	26th	08.45	Work as above.	HH
"	27th	08.45	Work as above. 1 OR attached ASC rejoins Coy. with supply G.S. wagon & 1 double set harness	HH
"	28th	08.45	Work as before. 156 Fd. COY. R.E. billet with this Company in FACTORY.	HH
"	29th	08.45	" " " 2 OR attached CRE for work.	HH
"	30th	10.00	Sunday. Kit inspection. 3 OR dispatched to TOURNAI for demobilization.	HH
"	31st	08.45	Coy. parade for work as before. Coy. strength now 4 officers & 59 OR including 6 OR on leave to U.K. II Lt P. WORSLEY & II Lt R.A.V.G. MONTIETH struck off strength of this Company & transferred to 157 Field Coy. RE. Auty. 1st Corps No A 19/779 & 16 DIV. No. A 1025/27 24/3/19 and 1st Army No 1125/5189 A & 16 Div. No. A 906/185 of 14-3-19.	HH

31-3-19.

H Hollerow Major R.E.
O.C. 155th FIELD COY. R.E.

155th FIELD COY. R.E.
No.
Date

D. D. & L., London, E.C. (A8001) Wt. W1771/M2031 750,000 5/17 Sch. 52 Forms C2118/14

Original 12

War Diary

of

153 Field Coy RE

from 1-4-19 to 30-4-19.

(Volume 4)

16

Army Form C. 2118.

Instructions regarding War Diaries and Intelligence Summaries are contained in F. S. Regs., Part II. and the Staff Manual respectively. Title pages will be prepared in manuscript.

WAR DIARY
or
~~INTELLIGENCE SUMMARY.~~
(Erase heading not required.)

APRIL 1919 — VOL. 4 — PAGE 1 — 41

Place	Date	Hour	Summary of Events and Information	Remarks and references to Appendices
			Ref. Sheet 36 1/40,000 FRANCE	
COY. H.Q. IN BILLETS FACTORY X28 b5-9 FRETIN TRANSPORT PARKED AT TEMPLEUVE	1st	08.45	Company parade for work at TEMPLEUVE STN. repairs etc.	HH
	2nd	"	" " " " " " " " completed.	HH
	3rd	"	" " " " 2/Lt BOWES detailed to be DIV. SALES Officer & reports to CRE at AVELIN at 11-00hrs. 1 OR returned from leave to U.K.	HH
	4th	08.45 / 17.30	Coy. parade for work at TEMPLEUVE. 1 OR proceeded on 14 days leave to U.K. " " " Pay.	HH
	5th	08.45	Coy. parade for work " " work completed & damage to Ramp at STN. repaired.	
"	"	14.30	Football match.	HH
"	6th	10.00	Sunday Check parade & billet cleaning.	HH
"	7th	08.45	Company parade for work in Camp.	
"	8th	08.30	" " " " " " . The 6% of OR allowed for Sick	
"	9th		on Cadre now cancelled & to be included as available for demobilization.	
"	10th	8.30	Company Parade for work in Camp. 1 OR proceeded on leave to U.K.	HH
"	11th		" " " " "	HH
	12th		" " " " "	HH
	13th	10.00	Sunday Check Parade	HH

D. D. & L. London, E.C. (A8001) Wt. W1771/M2031 750,000 5/17 Sch. 52 Forms C2118/14

Army Form C. 2118.

WAR DIARY
or
~~INTELLIGENCE SUMMARY.~~
(Erase heading not required.)

Instructions regarding War Diaries and Intelligence Summaries are contained in F. S. Regs., Part II. and the Staff Manual respectively. Title pages will be prepared in manuscript.

APRIL 1919 Vol. 4 PAGE 2.

Place	Date	Hour	Summary of Events and Information	Remarks and references to Appendices
			Ref. Sheet 36, FRANCE 1/40,000	
COY. H.Q.	14th	09.00	Company Parade for linewashing billets etc.	HH
IN BILLETS AT FACTORY	15th	09.00	" " " work at TEMPLEUVE STN. repairs to siding.	HH
X28b5-9	16th	09.00	" " " work in Camp	
FRETIN	17th	09.00	" " " " "	HH
TRANSPORT LESS ANIMALS	18th	09.00	3 Officers + 9 OR sent to BRUSSELS on three days leave in lorry provided by CRE.	HH
PARKED AT	19th	09.00	Parade for work. Saturday half holiday for Recreation.	HH
TEMPLEUVE	20th	10.00	Church parade, no work	
		19.30	Party returning from BRUSSELS	HH
	21st	08.00	1 OR demobilized. OC + 9 OR proceeded to BRUSSELS on 3 days leave. II LT BOWES remains i/c of Cadre.	HH
	22nd	09.00	Parade for work at TEMPLEUVE repairs to hut. 1 OR returned from 14 days leave to U.K.	HH
	23rd	09.00	work as above.	HH
	~~24th~~	~~09.00~~	" " " OC + party returned from BRUSSELS via	
		19.00	WATERLOO & MONS.	HH
		20.00	Entertainment + dance in billets.	
	2~~4~~5th	09.00	Parade for work in Camp.	HH
	25th	09.00	10 OR to BRUSSELS in lorry from CRE. for 3 days leave. 1 OR " U.K. on 14 days leave.	HH

D. D. & L., London, E.C. (A8004) Wt. W1771/M2031 750,000 5/17 Sch. 52 Forms C2118/14

Army Form C. 2118.

WAR DIARY

or

~~INTELLIGENCE SUMMARY.~~ Vol. 4 PAGE 3

(Erase heading not required.)

Instructions regarding War Diaries and Intelligence Summaries are contained in F. S. Regs., Part II. and the Staff Manual respectively. Title pages will be prepared in manuscript.

APRIL 1919

Place	Date	Hour	Summary of Events and Information	Remarks and references to Appendices
			Ref. Sheet 36 / FRANCE 40,000	
COY. HQ IN BILLETS	26th	09.00	Parade for work. Half holiday.	HH
AT FACTORY	27th	09.00	Sunday no work. 1 OR returned from Hospital.	HH
X28 b5-9 FRETIN	28th	09.00	Parade for work. 1 OR demobilized (Repatriation).	HH
TRANSPORT	29th	09.00	" " "	
PARKED AT TEMPLEUVE.	30th	09.00	" " " in Camp repairs to billets.	
			Strength of Coy. now 4 Officers 57 OR. of which 10 OR are detached on Local Guards. 7 OR on leave to U.K.	HH

155th FIELD COY., R.E.
No. ....
Date 30/4/19

A Hollows Major RE
O.C. 155th FIELD COY. R.E.

D. D. & L., London, E.C. (A5001) Wt. W1771/M2031 750,000 5/17 Sch. 52 Forms C2118/14

WAR DIARY.

155th FIELD COY. R.E.

MAY. 1919.

Instructions regarding War Diaries and Intelligence Summaries are contained in F. S. Regs., Part II, and the Staff Manual respectively. Title pages will be prepared in manuscript.

CADRE

WAR DIARY
~~or~~
~~INTELLIGENCE SUMMARY.~~
(Erase heading not required.)

Army Form C. 2118.

MAY 1919

Vol. 5. PAGE I.

Place	Date	Hour	Summary of Events and Information	Remarks and references to Appendices
			REF. SHEET 36 FRANCE 1/40,000	
FRETIN BILLETS IN FACTORY X28b5-9	1st	09.00	Capt. H.E. McKEEN, R.E. and II Lt N.W. GALLAGHER R.E. to Concentration Camp SOMMAIN for Demobilization Authority 16 Div. Group wire 700 A.	HH
			2 OR do do do do do	
			Parade for work at TEMPLEUVE & in Camp.	HH
TRANSPORT PARKED AT TEMPLEUVE	2nd	09.00	" " " in Camp.	HH
	3rd		" " " 1 OR to U.K. 14 days leave.	
	4th		" " " 2 " " " " "	HH
	5th		" " " 1 " " " " " Cadre to be reduced to 2 Offrs. & 40 OR Authority 16 Div. Group NO A 1026/32 5/5/19.	HH
	6th	09.00	" " " 2 OR to U.K. 14 days leave	HH
	7th	09.00	Work as usual. 1 OR to U.K. 14 days leave.	HH
	8th	09.00	" " " 2 OR to U.K. " " "	HH
	9th	09.00	" " " 1 OR to U.K. 14 days leave.	HH
	10th		" " " 2 OR " U.K. " " " 2 OR dispatched for Demobilization SOMMAIN.	HH
	11th	09.00	1 OR to U.K. on 14 days leave	
	12th	09.00	2 OR to U.K on 14 " " 5 OR to SOMMAIN for demobilization	HH
	13th	09.00	1 OR to U.K. " 14 " " Escort for prisoner sent to 157th Bde on the Rhine returned.	HH
				HH

D. D. & L., London, E.C. (A8001) Wt. W1771/M2031 750,000 5/17 Sch. 52 Forms C2118/14

Instructions regarding War Diaries and Intelligence Summaries are contained in F. S. Regs., Part II. and the Staff Manual respectively. Title pages will be prepared in manuscript.

WAR DIARY

or

~~INTELLIGENCE SUMMARY.~~

(Erase heading not required.)

Army Form C. 2118.

MAY 1919 PAGE II Vol. 5.

Place	Date	Hour	Sheet 36 1/40,000 Summary of Events and Information	Remarks and references to Appendices
FACTORY FRETIN	14th	09.00	2 OR to U.K. on 14 days leave.	HH
COY. HQ & BILLETS	15th	09.00	1 OR returned from 14 days leave to U.K.	HH
CADRE	16th	09.00		HH
X28 b 5-9	17th	09.00	OC visits Base Cashier LILLE & draws 5000 fr for Imprest.	HH
TRANSPORT	18th	09.00	Major HUGHES, M.C. R.E returns from leave to U.K. & takes over 156 Field Coy. Cadre.	HH
AT	19th	09.00		HH
TEMPLEUVE	20th	09.00	1 OR returned from 14 days leave to U.K.	HH
	21st		Receive orders from 16 Div Bde Group to take over 156 Field Coy. R.E. & appoint II Lt T S Bowes i/c. Major Hughes to be demobilized at once. 1 OR returned from 14 days leave to U.K.	HH HH
"	22		3 OR returned from 14 days leave to U.K. Major A.E. HUGHES MCRE demobilized.	HH
"	23		2 " " " " " " "	HH
"	24		1 " " " " " " "	HH
			2 " proceeded on leave to U.K.	
"	25th		1 " " " " " " 2 OR returned from leave to U.K.	HH
"	26th		1 " " " " " "	

D. D. & L., London, E.C. (A8001) Wt. W1771/M2031 750,000 5/17 Sch. 52 Forms C2118/14

Army Form C. 2118.

Instructions regarding War Diaries and Intelligence Summaries are contained in F. S. Regs., Part II. and the Staff Manual respectively. Title pages will be prepared in manuscript.

WAR DIARY

or

~~INTELLIGENCE SUMMARY.~~ PAGE 3 Vol. 5.

(Erase heading not required.)

MAY 1919

Place	Date	Hour	Summary of Events and Information	Remarks and references to Appendices
			Ref. sheet 36, FRANCE 1/40,000	
COY. H.Q. IN FACTORY X28 b 5-9 FRETIN TRANSPORT PARKED AT TEMPLEUVE	27th		Imprest a/c No C.M.1151 Closed.	
			2 OR proceeded on leave to U.K.	HH
			2 OR returned from " " "	HH
	28th		1 OR proceeded on leave to U.K.	
	29th		2 OR returned from leave	HH
	30th		1 OR proceeded on leave to U.K.	HH
			2 OR returned from leave to U.K.	
	31st		1 OR granted 14 days leave to PARIS.	
			1 OR returned from leave to U.K.	HH
			Received orders for Cadre to be reduced by 75% of original strength.	
			Strength of Coy. 2 officers 40 - OR.	
			On leave 10. OR	
			detached 1. OR. PONT A MARCQ. included in 40 above.	

155th FIELD COY., R.E.
No.
Date 31/5/19.

H Hollbrow
Major R.E.
O.C. 155th FIELD COY. R.E.

D. D. & L., London, E.C. (A8001) Wt. W1771/M2031 750,000 5/17 Sch. 52 Forms/C2118/14